주한미군지위협정(SOFA)

서명 및 발효 13

주한미군지위협정(SOFA)

서명 및 발효 13

한국외교정보

| 머리말

　미국은 오래전부터 우리나라 외교에 있어서 가장 긴밀하고 실질적인 우호 · 협력관계를 맺어 온 나라다. 6 · 25전쟁 정전 협정이 체결된 후 북한의 재침을 막기 위한 대책으로서 1953년 11월 한미 상호방위조약이 체결되었다. 이는 미군이 한국에 주둔하는 법적 근거였고, 그렇게 주둔하게 된 미군의 시설, 구역, 사업, 용역, 출입국, 통관과 관세, 재판권 등 포괄적인 법적 지위를 규정하는 것이 바로 주한미군지위협정(SOFA)이다. 그러나 이와 관련한 협상은 계속된 난항을 겪으며 한미 상호방위조약이 체결로부터 10년이 훌쩍 넘은 1967년이 돼서야 정식 발효에 이를 수 있었다. 그럼에도 당시 미군 범죄에 대한 한국의 재판권은 심한 제약을 받았으며, 1980년대 후반 민주화 운동과 함께 미군 범죄 문제가 사회적 이슈로 떠오르자 협정을 개정해야 한다는 목소리가 커지게 되었다. 이에 1991년 2월 주한미군지위협정 1차 개정이 진행되었고, 이후에도 여러 사건이 발생하며 2001년 4월 2차 개정이 진행되어 현재에 이르고 있다.

　본 총서는 외교부에서 작성하여 최근 공개한 주한미군지위협정(SOFA) 관련 자료를 담고 있다. 1953년 한미 상호방위조약 체결 이후부터 1967년 발효가 이뤄지기까지의 자료와 더불어, 이후 한미 합동위원회을 비롯해 민 · 형사재판권, 시설, 노무, 교통 등 각 분과위원회의 회의록과 운영 자료, 한국인 고용인 문제와 관련한 자료, 기타 관련 분쟁 자료 등을 포함해 총 42권으로 구성되었다. 전체 분량은 약 2만 2천여 쪽에 이른다.

2024년 3월
한국학술정보(주)

| 일러두기

· 본 총서에 실린 자료는 2022년 4월과 2023년 4월에 각각 공개한 외교문서 4,827권, 76만 여 쪽 가운데 일부를 발췌한 것이다.

· 각 권의 제목과 순서는 공개된 원본을 최대한 반영하였으나, 주제에 따라 일부는 적절히 변경하였다.

· 원본 자료는 A4 판형에 맞게 축소하거나 원본 비율을 유지한 채 A4 페이지 안에 삽입 하였다. 또한 현재 시점에선 공개되지 않아 '공란'이란 표기만 있는 페이지 역시 그대로 실었다.

· 외교부가 공개한 문서 각 권의 첫 페이지에는 '정리 보존 문서 목록'이란 이름으로 기록물 종류, 일자, 명칭, 간단한 내용 등의 정보가 수록되어 있으며, 이를 기준으로 0001번부터 번호가 매겨져 있다. 이는 삭제하지 않고 총서에 그대로 수록하였다.

· 보고서 내용에 관한 더 자세한 정보가 필요하다면, 외교부가 온라인상에 제공하는 『대한 민국 외교사료요약집』 1991년과 1992년 자료를 참조할 수 있다.

| 차례

정/리/보/존/문/서/목/록

기록물종류	문서-일반공문서철	등록번호	931 9604		등록일자	2006-07-27
분류번호	741.12	국가코드	US		주제	
문서철명	한.미국 간의 상호방위조약 제4조에 의한 시설과 구역 및 한국에서의 미국군대의 지위에 관한 협정 (SOFA) 전59권. 1966.7.9 서울에서 서명 : 1967.2.9 발효 (조약 232호) *원본					
생산과	미주과/조약과	생산년도	1952 - 1967		보존기간	영구
담당과(그룹)	조약	조약		서가번호	--	
참조분류						
권차명	V.33 실무교섭회의, 제81차, 1965.6.7					

내용목차	* 일지 :
	1953.8.7 이승만 대통령-Dulles 미국 국무장관 공동성명 - 상호방위조약 발효 후 군대지위협정 교섭 약속 1954.12.2 정부, 주한 UN군의 관세업무협정 체결 제의 1955.1월, 5월 미국, 제의 거절 1955.4.28 정부, 군대지위협정 제의 (한국측 초안 제시) 1957.9.10 Hurter 미국 국무차관 방한 시 각서 수교 (한국측 제의 수락 요구) 1957.11.13, 26 정부, 개별 협정의 단계적 체결 제의 1958.9.18 Dawling 주한미국대사, 형사재판관할권 협정 제외 조건으로 행정협정 체결 의사 전달 1960.3.10 정부, 토지, 시설협정의 우선적 체결 강력 요구 1961.4.10 장면 국무총리-McConaughy 주한미국대사 공동성명으로 교섭 개시 합의 1961.4.15, 4.25 제1, 2차 한.미국 교섭회의 (서울) 1962.3.12 정부, 교섭 재개 촉구 공한 송부 1962.5.14 Burger 주한미국대사, 최규하 장관 면담 시 형사재판관할권 문제 제기 않는 조건으로 교섭 재개 통고 1962.9.6 한.미국 간 공동성명 발표 (9월 중 교섭 재개 합의) 1962.9.20~ 제1-81차 실무 교섭회의 (서울) 1965.6.7 1966.7.8 제82차 실무 교섭회의 (서울) 1966.7.9 서명 1967.2.9 발효 (조약 232호)

마/이/크/로/필/름/사/항

촬영연도	*롤 번호	화일 번호	후레임 번호	보관함 번호
2006-11-23	I-06-0070	01	1-228	

0001

한·미국 간의 상호방위조약 제4조에 의한 시설과 구역 및 한국에서의 미국군대의 지위에 관한 협정(SOFA) 전59권. 1966.7.9 서울에서 서명 : 1967.2.9 발효(조약 232호) (V.33 실무교섭회의, 제81차, 1965.6.7)

7

FACILITIES AND AREAS
(Article IV)

(To be presented at 81st session)

Agreed Minute #2

All removable facilities, equipment and material or portions thereof provided by the Republic of Korea under this Agreement and located within the areas and facilities referred to in this Article shall be returned to the Republic of Korea whenever they are no longer needed for the purpose of this Agreement.

0002

AREAS AND FACILITIES - RETURN OF FACILITIES
ARTICLE (IV)·

1. The United States is not obliged, when it returns facilities and areas to the Republic of Korea on the expiration of this Agreement or at an earlier date, to restore the facilities and areas to the condition in which they were at the time they became available to the United States armed forces, or to compensate the Republic of Korea in lieu of such restoration.

2. The Government of the Republic of Korea is not obliged to make any compensation to the Government of the United States for any improvements made in facilities and areas or for the buildings and structures left thereon on the expiration of this Agreement or the earlier return of the facilities and areas.

3. The foregoing provisions shall not apply to any construction which the Government of the United States may undertake under special arrangements with the Government of the Republic of Korea.

AGREED MINUTE

All removable facilities erected or constructed by or on behalf of the United States at its expense and all equipment, material and supplies brought into or procured in the Republic of Korea by or on behalf of the United States in connection with the construction, development, operation, maintenance, safeguarding and control of the facilities and areas will remain the property of the United States Government and may be removed from the Republic of Korea.

8-3

0003

한·미국 간의 상호방위조약 제4조에 의한 시설과 구역 및 한국에서의 미국군대의 지위에 관한 협정(SOFA)
전59권. 1966.7.9 서울에서 서명 : 1967.2.9 발효(조약 232호) (V.33 실무교섭회의, 제81차, 1965.6.7)

9

81st session

15 Thanking Mr. Fleck for his explanation, Mr. Chang
stated that the Korean negotiators accepted the U.S.
draft of the article ~~taking Mr. Fleck's explanation as~~ *under such* *wid*
an <u>understanding</u> that the term "maintenance of the U.S.
armed forces includes maintenance of the facilities
and areas used by the U.S. armed forces. Additionally,
Mr. Chang clarified that the desire expressed by Korean
side to obtain languages of other SOFAs was always based
on its own merit and validity on their presentation, but
was not intended to obtain those indentical languages
solely by reason of being appeared in other SOFAs.

not presented

0004

<u>FACILITIES AND AREAS</u>

(To be presented at 81st session)

1. The discussion on this Article relating to facilities and areas has been deferred since the 42nd session held on February 14 last year. It is recalled that there had been difference in their positions over the question of compensation to private property. The Korean side is now prepared to withdraw our previous ~~position maintained~~ *contention with* ~~in~~ respect ~~of~~ *to* compensation ~~toward~~ private-owned property *extremely unworkable by the use of additional State* and accept three paragraphs and Agreed Minute #1 provided *U.S. armed forces* for in Article IV. However, the Korean side propose ~~newly tabled~~ Agreed Minute #2 which reads:

"All removal facilities, equipment and material or portions thereof *and located* within the areas and facilities *referred to in this* ~~provided by the Republic of Korea under this Agree-~~ *Article* ~~ment~~ shall be returned to the Republic of Korea whenever they are no longer needed for the purpose of this Agreement."

This *additional Agreed Minute* ~~new proposal~~ is made in the same intent of Agreed Minute of Article IV of the U.S. draft. Korean side consider it logical that all removable properties ~~which~~ *and located in any area or facilities used* provided by our government should be returned to the *by U.S. armed forces* owners whenever they are no longer needed for the U.S. Armed Forces. ~~Therefore, we hope that our proposal is~~ *we propose this minute in our* ~~acceptable to the U.S. side.~~ *belief that this would prevent us difficulty on the part of U.S.* This provision is also ~~essential in spite of the~~ provisions/provided for in *side* paragraph 2 and 3 of Article II~~4~~, because those are merely related with the return of the facilities and areas as a whole or in part which are no longer needed *located within* and, therefore do no refer the removable property ~~while~~ they ~~are used by the US armed forces.~~

an area ~ facilities.

intended to supplement

0005

3. Turning to Article V relating to cost and maintenance, the Korean side now withdraws ~~again~~ our ~~draft.~~ ^prepared to ~~standing position~~ with regard to the compensation to the private-owned property and accepts the U.S. draft ~~Article as a whole without change, with a view to concluding~~ ~~this Agreement as early as possible.~~

~~With certain understanding and clarification to be made by U.S. side.~~

~~certain modification of wording~~

~~with certain understanding depending upon clarification to be made by~~ U.S. side. on certain Wordings. ~~as much as~~

Last discussion on this point of the present Article was ~~been centered~~ on principle of compensation. both sides have ~~failed~~ had no opportunity of discussing the contents of U.S draft. the ~~~~

~~Question Answer~~
~~following~~

~~① Modification~~
정리으로   ① ~~Modification~~
공부   ② Understanding

0006

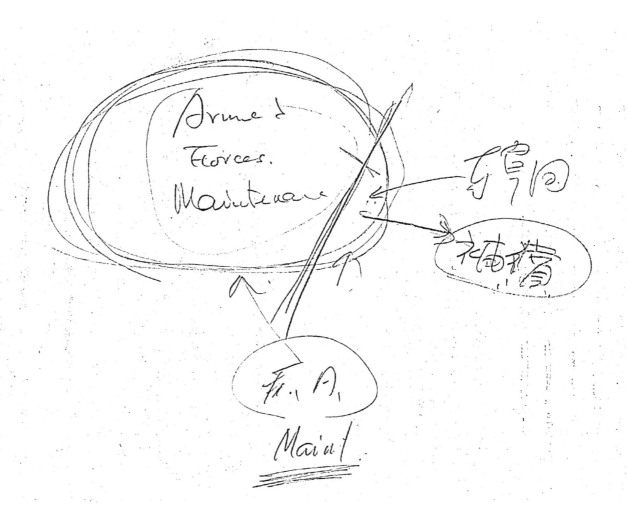

AREAS AND FACILITIES - RETURN OF FACILITIES
ARTICLE (VI)

AGREED MINUTE

2. In case of private property used by the United States under this Agreement, the Government of the United States shall return all facilities, furnishings, equipment, material and supplies or portions thereof, wherever removable, to the owners of such property, whenever they are no longer needed for the purpose of this Agreement with a view to all eviating their losses.

AREAS AND FACILITIES - COST AND MAINTENANCE
ARTICLE (V)

1. It is agreed that the United States will bear for the duration of the Agreement without cost to the Republic of Korea all expenditures incident to the maintenance of the United States armed forces in the Republic of Korea, <u>Including that of the facilities and areas granted under this Agreement.</u>

2. It is agreed that the Republic of Korea will furnish for the duration of this Agreement without cost to the United States all facilities and areas and rights of way, including facilities and areas jointly used such as those at airfields and ports as provided in Articles II and III. The Government of the Republic of Korea

assures the use of such facilities and areas to the
United States Government and will hold the United States
Government as well as its agencies and employees
harmless from any third party claims which may be
advanced in connection with such use.

0009

4. "Witnin the scope of this Agreement, Paragraph 13 of Article III of the Agreement on Economic Coordination between the Republic of Korea and the Unified Command of May 24, 1952 shall not apply to members of the United States armed forces, civilian component, invited contractors or dependents thereof."

(Proposed to the U.S. side on June 8, 1965, withdrawing paragraph 4 tabled at 81st session, June 7, 1965.)

3-1   0010

RATIFICATION OF AGREEMENT

1. This Agreement shall enter into force thirty days after
    the date of a written notification from the Government
    of the Republic of Korea to the Government of the United
    States that it has approved the Agreement in accordance
    with its legal procedures.

2. The Government of the Republic of Korea shall undertake
    to seek from its legislature all legislative and
    budgetary action necessary to give effect to its provi-
    sions of this Agreement.

3. Subject to the provisions of Article XXII, Paragraph 12,
    this Agreement shall, upon its entry into force, supersede
    and replace the agreement between the Government of the
    United States and the Government of the Republic of Korea
    on jurisdictional matters, effected by an exchange of
    notes at Taejon on July 12, 1950.

4. The provisions of the present Agreement shall apply to
    the United States armed forces, their members, civilian
    component, invited contractors or dependents thereof,

- 1 -

0011

8-2

while in the Republic of Korea pursuant to the resolution of the United Nations Security Council or pursuant to the Mutual Defense Treaty. Such provisions will not, however, apply to members of the United States armed forces for whom status is provided in the Agreement for the Establishment of the United States Military Advisory Group to the Republic of Korea signed on January 26, 1950 and personnel of the United States armed forces attached to the Embassy of the United States.

서명일 (1966. 12. 31.)

- 2 -

RATIFICATION OF AGREEMENT

ARTICLE (XXX)

1. This agreement shall enter into force four months after the date
of a written notification from the Government of the Republic of Korea
to the Government of the United States that it has approved the agreement
and has taken all legislative and budgetary action necessary to give
effect to its provisions.

2. Subject to the provisions of Article XXII, Paragraph 12, this
agreement shall, upon its entry into force, supersede and replace the
agreement between the Government of the United States and the Government
of the Republic of Korea on jurisdictional matters, effected by an
exchange of notes at Taejon on July 12, 1950.

재분류(1966.12.31.

1967.1.6
의거 일반문서로 재분류

0013

(一/

RATIFICATION OF AGREEMENT

1. This Agreement shall enter into force ~~thirty~~ *ninety* days
   after the date of a written notification from the
   Government of the Republic of Korea to the Government of the United States that it has approved
   the Agreement <u>in accordance with its legal proce-</u>
   <u>dures.</u>

2. The Government of the Republic of Korea shall undertake to seek from its legislature all legislative and budgetary action necessary to give effect
   to its provisions of this Agreement.

3. Subject to the provisions of Article XXII, Paragraph 12, this agreement shall, upon its entry
   into force, supersede and replace the agreement
   between the Government of the United States and
   the Government of the Republic of Korea on
   jurisdictional matters, effected by an exchange
   of notes at Taejon on July 12, 1950.

5-1

0014

4. "Within the scope of this Agreement, Paragraph 13 of Article III of the Agreement on Economic Coordination between the Republic of Korea and the Unified Command of May.24, 1952 shall not apply to members of the United States armed forces, civilian component, invited contractors or dependents thereof."

5-2

0015

RATIFICATION OF AGREEMENT

4. "Within the scope of this Agreement, Paragraph 13
of Article III of the Agreement on Economic Coordination
between the Republic of Korea and the Unified Command
of May 24, 1952 shall not apply to members of the United
States armed forces, civilian component, invited
contractors or dependents thereof."

    (Proposed to the U.S. side on June 8, 1965,
    withdrawing paragraph 4 tabled at 81st session,
    June 7, 1965.)

5-3

0016

RATIFICATION OF AGREEMENT

(handwritten: 80)

(handwritten signature)

1. This Agreement shall enter into force thirty days after
   the date of a written notification from the Government
   of the Republic of Korea to the Government of the United
   States that it has approved the Agreement in accordance
   with its legal procedures.

2. The Government of the Republic of Korea shall undertake
   to seek from its legislature all legislative and
   budgetary action necessary to give effect to its provisions of this agreement.

3. Subject to the provisions of Article XXII, Paragraph 12,
   this agreement shall, upon its entry into force, supersede
   and replace the agreement between the Government of the
   United States and the Government of the Republic of Korea
   on jurisdictional matters, effected by an exchange of
   notes at Taejon on July 12, 1950.

   (handwritten: modified)

4. The provisions of the present Agreement shall apply to
   the United States armed forces, their members, civilian
   component, invited contractors or dependents thereof,

- 1 -

(handwritten: 5-4)   0017

while in the Republic of Korea pursuant to the resolution of the United Nations Security Council or pursuant to the Mutual Defense Treaty. Such provisions will not, however, apply to members of the United States armed forces for whom status is provided in the Agreement for the Establishment of the United States Military Advisory Group to the Republic of Korea, signed on January 26, 1950 and personnel of the United States armed forces attached to the Embassy of the United States.

보통문서로 재분류(1966. 12. 31)

- 2 -

5 - 5

0018

FACILITIES AND AREAS AND RATIFICATION
OF THE ARTICLE

1. The Korean negotiators would like to appreciate the U.S. side for their accpetance of our newly proposed Agreed Minute #2 which is the corollary to Agreed Minute #1 in Article IV, thereby we have reached full agreement on Return of Facilities and Areas.

2. Turning to last Article on Ratification of the Agreement, the Korean negotiators thank to the U.S. negotiators for their concurrance of our revised Ratification Article and accept the two modifications proposed by the U.S. side in Paras. 1 and 2, thereby we have also reached full agreement on this Article.

3. Similarly, the Korean side has no objection to exchange, on a continuing basis, copies of pertinent documents and regulations issued by both authorities to give effect to the provisions of the Agreement and any other information on our progress in carrying out the Agreement, in order to insure the maximum possible efficiency and effectiveness in the implementation of the present Status of Force Agreement between the Republic of Korea and the United States.

4. It is gratifying that we have now reached the full agreement on all Articles after the 82 successive negotiating sessions. It is recalled that both sides had embarked on the negotiations of this Agreement with wide differences in their positions on September 20, 1962 and since then, we have made our utmost to narrow the differences and to reach the agreement, overcoming the hardships.

4 - 1

0019

Furthermore, I would like to pay our tribute for
their patience and friendly cooperations to those
who have tirelessly participated in one of the most
lengthy and controverital negotiations between our
two countries.

0020

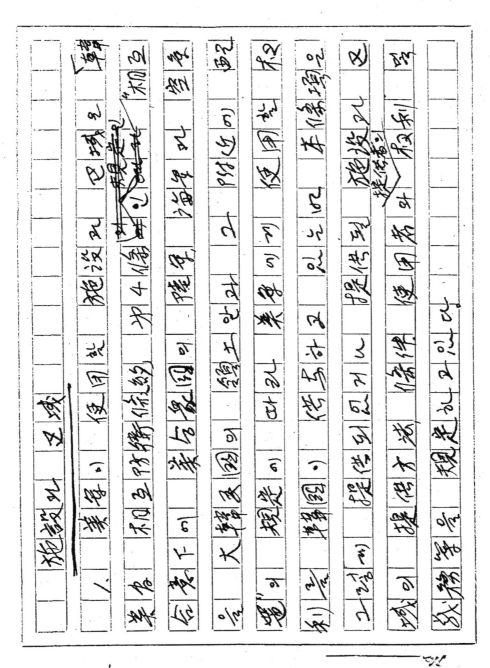

한·미국 간의 상호방위조약 제4조에 의한 시설과 구역 및 한국에서의 미국군대의 지위에 관한 협정(SOFA)
전59권. 1966.7.9 서울에서 서명 : 1967.2.9 발효(조약 232호) (V.33 실무교섭회의, 제81차, 1965.6.7)

29

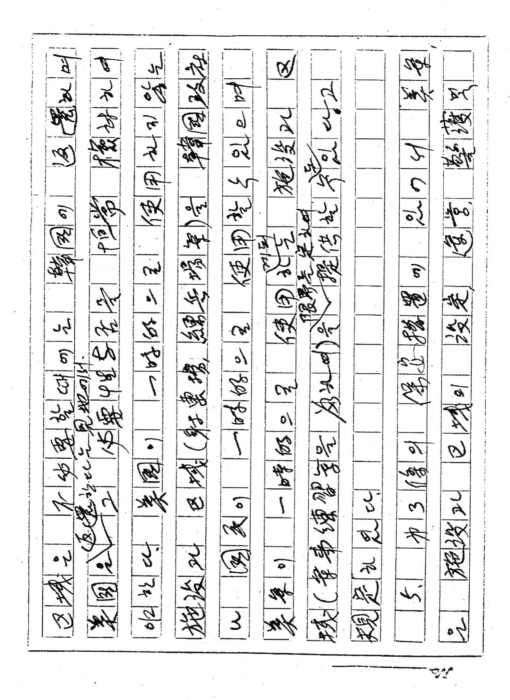

한·미국 간의 상호방위조약 제4조에 의한 시설과 구역 및 한국에서의 미국군대의 지위에 관한 협정(SOFA)
전59권. 1966.7.9 서울에서 서명 : 1967.2.9 발효(조약 232호) (V.33 실무교섭회의, 제81차, 1965.6.7)

31

한·미국 간의 상호방위조약 제4조에 의한 시설과 구역 및 한국에서의 미국군대의 지위에 관한 협정(SOFA)
전59권. 1966.7.9 서울에서 서명 : 1967.2.9 발효(조약 232호) (V.33 실무교섭회의, 제81차, 1965.6.7)

35

기 안 지

<table>
<tr><td rowspan="2">기 안 자</td><td>미 주 과
함 명 재</td><td>전 화
번 호</td><td></td><td>공 보</td><td>필 요</td><td>불필요</td></tr>
<tr><td colspan="2">과 장　　국 장　　차 관　　장 관</td><td></td><td></td></tr>
</table>

<table>
<tr><td colspan="3">과 장</td><td>국 장</td><td>차 관</td><td>장 관</td><td></td><td></td></tr>
<tr><td colspan="3"></td><td>2년</td><td></td><td></td><td></td><td></td></tr>
<tr><td>협 조
서</td><td>자 명</td><td></td><td></td><td></td><td></td><td>보 존
년 한</td><td></td></tr>
<tr><td>기 안
년 월 일</td><td></td><td colspan="2">1965. 6. 1.</td><td>시 행
년월일</td><td>통
제
관</td><td>정 서　기 장</td><td></td></tr>
<tr><td>분 류 기 호
문 서 번 호</td><td></td><td colspan="3">외구미 722.2</td><td></td><td></td><td></td></tr>
<tr><td>경 유
수 신
참 조</td><td></td><td colspan="2">건　　의</td><td>발 신</td><td></td><td></td><td></td></tr>
<tr><td>제　　목</td><td colspan="7">주한미군의 안전 및 보호조치 조항에 관한 우미측 입장</td></tr>
</table>

　　　　주둔군지위협정 체결교섭에 있어 주한미군의 안전 및 보호조치

조항에 관한 우미측 입장을 별첨과 같이 수립하여 미국측에 제안코저

하오니 재가하여 주시기 바랍니다.

유첨: 주한미군의 안전 및 보호조치 조항에 대한 우미측 입장. 끝

주한미군의 안전 및 보호조치 조항에 대한 우리측 입장

현재 미해결중에 있는 주한미군의 안전 및 보호 조치 조항에 대하여 아래와 같이 우리측의 입장을 수립한다.

1. 양측의 입장

한국안

The Republic of Korea and the United States will cooperate in taking such steps as may from time to time be necessary to ensure the security of the United States armed forces, the members thereof, the civilian component, (the persons who are present in the Republic of Korea pursuant to Article _____,)* their dependents, and their property. The Government of the Republic of Korea agrees to seek such legislation and to take such other action as may be necessary to ensure the adequate security and protection within its territory of installations, equipment, property, records and official information of the United States, and, (consistent with Article _____)*for the punishment of offenders under the applicable laws of the Republic of Korea.

* 한국측은 미국안중의

"of the persons referred ...."

를 삭제할것에 동의 한다면 ※표를한 두문장을 수락하겠다고 제안함.

미국안

The United Stats and the Republic of Korea will cooperate in taking such steps as may from time to time be necessary to ensure the security of the United States armed forces, the members thereof, the civilian component, the persons who are present in the Republic of Korea pursuant to Article _____, and their dependents and their property. The Government of the Republic of Korea agrees to seek such legislation and to take such other action as may be necessary to ensure the adequate security and protection within its territory of installations, equipment, property, records, and official information of the United States, (of the persons referred to in this paragraph, and their property)*and, consistent with Article _____ to ensure the punishment of offenders under the applicable laws of the Republic of Korea

* 미국측은 아래와 같은 양해 사항을 수락할것을 조건으로 미국안중의 "of the persons referred to in this paragraph, and their property"

를 삭제 하겠다고 제안함.

양해사항

"In cooperating with each other under this Article the two governments agree that each will take such measures as may be necessary to ensure the security and protection of the U.S. Armed Forces, the members thereof, the civilian component, the persons who are present in the Republic of Korea pursuant to the article dealing with Invited Contractors, their dependents and their property."

0031

2. 문제점

　가. 미국측은 양해사항으로 군인, 군속, 군계약자, 가족
　　　및 그들의 재산에 대한 입법조치를 포합한 필요한
　　　조치 (Such measures as may be necessary) 를 각당사국이
　　　취할것에 합의할 것을 요구하고 있음.

　나. 한국안의 " ... for the punishment of ..." 를 " ....
　　　to ensure the punishment of ...." 로 제안하고 있음.

3. 해결방안 : 미국안을 수락

　가. 미국측 양해사항중 "필요한 조치"는 한국정부가
　　　필요하다고 생각되는 조치로 해석할수 있으므로
　　　여하한 입법조치도 한국정부가 필요하다고 생각될때에
　　　한하여 입법조치를 하게될 것임.

　나. 한국안의 "for the punishment of ..." 나 미국안의
　　　" to ensure the punishment of ..." 나 모두 한국법규에
　　　입각한 처벌을 보장하는 것이므로 사실상 효력상의
　　　차이는 없을것임.

　다. 따라서 미국안을 수락하여도 무방할 것으로 사료
　　　되는 것임.

0032

Agreed Minute Re Paragraph 1(b)

1.   In the event that martial law is declared by the Republic of Korea, the provisions of this Article shall be immediately suspended in the part of the Republic of Korea under martial law, and the military authorities of the United States shall have the right to exercise exclusive jurisdiction over members of the United States armed forces or civilian component, and their dependents, in such part until martial law is ended.

0033

US DRAFT
SAFETY AND SECURITY MEASURES ~~OF~~ FOR US FORCES

The United Ststes and the Republic of Korea will cooperate in taking such steps as may from time to time be necessary to ensure the security of the United States armed forces, the members thereof, the civilian component, the persons who are present in the Republic of Korea pursuant to Article_____ (Invited Contractors), and their dependents and their property. The Government of the Republic of Korea agrees to seek such legislation and to take such other action as may be necessary to ensure the adequate security and protection within its territory of installations, equipment, property, records and official information of the United States, and, consistent with Article___ (Criminal Jurisdiction) to ensure the punishment of offenders under the applicable laws of the Republic of Korea.

0034

ARTICLE _____

SAFETY AND SECURITY MEASURES FOR U.S. FORCES

The Republic of Korea and the United States will cooperate in taking such steps as may from time to time be necessary to ensure the security of the United States armed forces, the members thereof, the civilian component, (the persons who are present in the Republic of Korea pursuant to Article ____,)* their dependents, and their property. The Government of the Republic of Korea agrees to seek such legislation and to take such other action as may be necessary to ensure the adequate security and protection within its territory of installations, equipment, property, records and official information of the United States, and, (consistent with Article ____)*for the punishment of offenders under the applicable laws of the Republic of Korea.

- - - - - - - - - - - - - -

*...At 46th Session, Korean negotiators stated that they would agree to the inclusion of those phrases in the Korean draft if the U.S. negotiators would agree to delete the phrase "...of the persons referred to in this paragraph, and their property".

The United States and the Republic of Korea will cooperate in taking such steps as may from time to time be necessary to ensure the security of the United States armed forces, the members thereof, the civilian component, the persons who are present in the Republic of Korea pursuant to Article____, and their dependents and their property. The Government of the Republic of Korea agrees to seek such legislation and to take such other action as may be necessary to ensure the adequate security and protection within its territory of installations, equipment, property, records, and official information of the United States, (ofthe persons referred to in this paragraph, and their property)*and, consistent with Article____ to ensure the punishment of offenders under the applicable laws of the Republic of Korea.

- - - - - - - - - - - - - -

*...At 55th Session, the U.S. negotiators stated that they were prepared to agree to adoption of the original U.S. draft of the article, with the deletion of the phrase "of the persons........", provided the Korean negotiators would agree to the inclusion in the negotiating record of the following understanding:

"In cooperating with each other under this Article the two governments agree that each will take such measures as may be necessary to ensure the security and protection of the U.S. Armed Forces, the members thereof, the civilian component, the persons who are present in the Republic of Korea pursuant to the article dealing with Invited Contractors, their dependents and their property."

한·미국 간의 상호방위조약 제4조에 의한 시설과 구역 및 한국에서의 미국군대의 지위에 관한 협정(SOFA)
전59권. 1966.7.9 서울에서 서명 : 1967.2.9 발효(조약 232호) (V.33 실무교섭회의, 제81차, 1965.6.7)   41

In cooperating with each other under this Article the two governments agree that each will take such measures as may be necessary to ensure the security and protection of the U. S. Armed Forces, the members thereof, the civilian component, the persons who are present in the Republic of Korea pursuant to the article dealing with Invited Contractors, their dependents and their property.

0036

Proposed Security measures Article (informal)
—M.S

(at dinner)

The Republic of Korea will take such actions as
may be necessary, with the cooperation of the United
States where appropriate, to ensure the adequate security
and protection of the United States Armed Forces, the
members thereof, the civilian component, the persons
present in the Republic of Korea pursuant to Article XVIII,
their dependents and their property, and the installations,
equipment, property, records and official information of
the United States, and, consistent with Article XXII, to
for the punishment
ensure the punishment of offenders under the applicable
laws of the Republic of Korea.

한·미국 간의 상호방위조약 제4조에 의한 시설과 구역 및 한국에서의 미국군대의 지위에 관한 협정(SOFA)
전59권. 1966.7.9 서울에서 서명 : 1967.2.9 발효(조약 232호) (V.33 실무교섭회의, 제81차, 1965.6.7)

43

The Republic of Korea and the United States will cooperate in taking such steps as may from time to time be necessary to ensure the security of the United States armed forces, the members thereof, the civilian component, *the persons who are present in ROK* their dependents, and their property. The Government of the Republic of Korea agrees to seek such legislation and to take such other action as may be necessary to ensure the adequate security and protection within its territory of installations, equipment, property, records and official information of the United States, *consistent with Art* and for the punishment of offenders under the applicable law of the Republic of Korea.

The United States and the Republic of Korea will cooperate in taking such steps as may from time to time be necessary to ensure the security of the United States armed forces, the members thereof, the civilian component, the persons who are present in the Republic of Korea pursuant to Article , their dependents and their property. The Government of the Republic of Korea agrees to seek such legislation and to take such other action as may be necessary to ensure the adequate security and protection within its territory of installations, equipment, property, records, and official information of the United States, of the persons referred to in this paragraph, and their property, and, consistent with Article , to ensure the punishment of offenders under the applicable laws of the Republic of Korea.

0038

기 안 지

기 안 자	미주과 황영재		전화 번호		공 보		필 요	불필요
	과장	국장	차관	장관				
협 조 자 서 명	법무부: 법무과장	법무국장	법무차관	법무장관		보존 년한		
기 안 년 월 일	65.6.1.		시행 년월일		통제 관		정 서	기 장
분류기호 문서번호	외구미 722.2							
경 유 수 신 참 조	건 의			발 신				
제 목	민사청구권 조항에 대한 우리측 입장							

주둔군지위협정 체결교섭에 있어 민사청구권

조항에 관한 제80차 실무자회의에서 미국측이 제안한

수정안에 대하여 별첨과 같이 우리측의 입장을 수립

하여 차기 회의에서 미국측에 제안코저 하오니 재가하여

주시기 바랍니다.

유첨 - 민사청구권 조항에 대한 우리측 입장 1부. 끝

민사청구권 조항에 대한 우리측입장

제80차 회의에서 미국측이 제안한 민사청구권 조항에 관한 수정안에 대하여 아래와 같이 우리측의 입장을 수립하여 미국측에 제안한다.

1. 공무집행중 정부재산 및 제3자에 대하여 손해를 가한 경우로서 그손해의 책임이 미국측에만 있을 때의 양국정부의 배상금 분담비율 (5(c)(i) 항) :

   가. 한국안   한국 15 퍼센트, 미국 85퍼센트
   나. 미국안   한국 25 " , 미국 75 "
   다. 문제점   현재민사청구권 조항에 있어 Formula Concept 를 채택하고 있는 협정 (미.일 " 나토 " 및 미.호주) 은 미국안과 같이 모두 25퍼센트 - 75퍼센트의 비율로 접수국과 파견국이 배상금을 분담하게 되어 있음.
   라. 해결방안   미국안 수락

2. 공무집행중 제3자에 대한 손해에 있어 손해배상 책임과 배상금액의 합의문제 (5 (c) (iii) 항) :

   가. 한국안
   1) 한국정부 당국에 의하여 해결하게되는 사건에 관하여는 사전에 손해배상 책임과 배상금액에 대하여 미국당국과 상호합의하나, 재판의 판결은 양당사국을 구속하며,
   2) 이를 아래와 같은 합의의사록으로 규정하여야 한다 :
   " 본조제5항에 해당되는 청구에 관하여는 대한민국당국이 해결하기 전에 손해배상의 책임과 그손해에 사정할 배상금에 관하여 대한민국과 합중국의 당국이 상호합의하여야 한다 . 그러나 청구권자가 제기할수 있는

0040

소의 결과로 대한민국의 권한있는 재판소에
의한 그사건에 대한 어떠한 판결도 본협정의
당사국에 대하여 구속력을 가지며 또한 최종적인
것이다 . "

나. 미국안

1) 한국정부 당국에 의하여 해결하게되는 사건에
   관하여는 사전에 손해배상 책임과 배상금에
   대하여 미국당국이 인정한 것에 한하여 미국정부
   가 책임을 지며, 재판의 판결은 양당사국을
   구속한다 .

2) 이를 위하여 본문 5(e)(iii)항을 아래와 같이 수정
   한다 :
   "손해배상책임, 배상금액 및 비율에 의한 분담안
   에 대하여 합중국이 인정한 각사건에 관하여
   대한민국이 6개월기간에 지불한 금액의 명세서는,
   지불청구서와 더불어, 매6개월마다 적합한 합중국
   당국에 송부한다 . 그러한 지불은 가능한한
   빠른시일내에 "원"화로 하여야 한다 . "

3) 한국안의 " .... 상호 합의하여야 한다 . "
   (shall seek mutual agreement) 로서는 불충분하며,
   한국법정의 판결은 5(c) 항에 의하여 당사국을
   구속하게 되어 있으므로 이를 합의의사록으로
   재차 규정할 필요는 없다 .

다. 문제점

1) 미국측은 재판의 판결은 양당사국을 구속하며,
   한국정부가 해결하는 사건에 관하여는 배상책임과
   배상금액에 대하여 사전에 상호합의할것을 주장
   하고 있어, 실제에 있어서는 한국측 입장과 동일한
   것임.

2) 그러나 이를 위하여 미국측이 제안하는 바와 같이
   5(e)(iii)항을 수정하게 되면, 아래와 같이 본문
   해석상 모순이 일어나게 될것임 :

0041

한·미국 간의 상호방위조약 제4조에 의한 시설과 구역 및 한국에서의 미국군대의 지위에 관한 협정(SOFA)
전59권. 1966.7.9 서울에서 서명 : 1967.2.9 발효(조약 232호) (V.33 실무교섭회의, 제81차, 1965.6.7)

47

(가) 이미 합의된 5 (c) 항에 의하여 한국정부
당국의 해결에 의하거나 재판의 판결에
의하거나를 불문하고 한국정부가 지불한
배상금은 양당사국을 구속 하게 되어 있으나,

(나) 미국측의 5 (e) (iii) 항에 의하면 손해배상의
책임과 배상금액에 대하여 미국정부가 인정한
사건에 한하여 미국정부가 한국정부에 대한
만상책임을 갖게되어 있어,

(다) 미국안은 그들의 주장과는 달리, 5 (c) 항에
의거 한국정부가 지불한 모든 배상금에 대하여
미국은 구속을 받게되는 동시에 또한 5 (e) (iii)
항에 의거 한국정부가 지불한 모든 배상금에
대하여 미국은 구속을 받지 않는다고 해석될수
밖에 없는바,

(라) 미국측의 주장과 같이 5 (c) 항중의 재판의
판결에만 미국이 구속된다고 해석할수 없을
뿐만 아니라, 한국정부가 해결하는 사건에
대하여만 양국정부가 배상책임과 배상금액에
합의한다고 해석할수도 없는 것임.

(마) 또한 미국안은 " ....미국정부가 인정한
(approved) "   으로 되어 있어, 그들의
주장과 같이 상호 합의 (mutual agreement)
한다고는 말할수 없는 것임.

라. 해결방안: 한국측의 합의 의사록을 철회하고 미국측의 5(e)(iii)항을 아래와 같이 수정 제안 한다:

1) 상기 미국안의 모순을 시정하기 위하여는 한국안과
같이 합의 의사록으로 예외규정을 만들어,
5 (c) 항에 의거 한국정부가 지불한 모든 배상금은
원칙적으로 양당사국을 구속하나 합의 의사록에
의거 한국정부가 해결할때에는 배상책임과 배상금에
대하여 사전에 미국당국과 상호합의하게 합이
타당할 것임.

0042

2) 따라서 미국안은 수락할수 없으며 그대신 한국 측이 제안한 합의의사록을 계속 주장하되, 우리측이 제안한 합의의사록중 재판의 판결은 양당사국을 구속한다는 구절은 삭제하고, "본조제5항에 해당되는 청구에 관하여는 대한민국당국이 해결하기 전에 손해배상의 책임과 그 손해에 사정할 배상금에 관하여 대한민국과 합중국의 당국이 상호합의 하여야 한다."로 수정하여 주장한다.

3. KSC 문제 (12 항)

가. 한국안 KSC 는 청구권조항을위하여 미군의 고용원 으로 간주한다.

나. 미국안 KSC 는 청구권조항에 언급하지 않고, 다음과 같은 양해사항을 채택한다 :
"본조는 KSC 인원에 의하여 발생된 청구에 적용하지 않는다. KSC 인원의 지위는 대한 민국과 합중국간의 별도의 교섭에 의거 결정한다. "

다. 문제점 KSC 가 별도 협정에서 해결되기 전에 "KSC 인원에 의하여 발생된 청구에 대하여 는 본조를 적용하지 않는다 " 라는 양해사항을 수락할수는 없음.

라. 해결방안 KSC 를 청구권조항에서 삭제하는데 동의 하고, 미국측이 제안한 양해사항을 아래와 같이 수정제안한다 :
"KSC 인원의 지위는 대한민국과 합중국간의 별도의 교섭에 의거 결정한다. "

4. 서울지역을 제외한 기타 지역에 있어서의 주요조항의 적용시기 (합의의사록 △2)

가. 한국안 협정발효 12개월후 부터 적용하되, 한국정부가 근각관내에 (그때까지) 본조의 규정에 의한 임무를 수행

0043

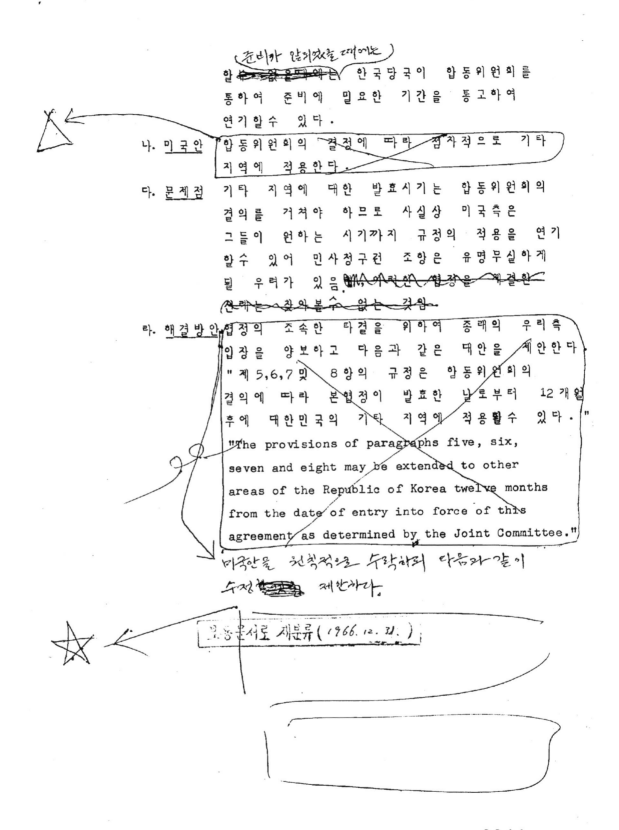

（준비가 않되었을 때에는）

합~~~~에는 한국당국이 합동위원회를
통하여 준비에 필요한 기간을 통고하여
연기할수 있다.

나. 미국안 합동위원회의 결정에 따라 점차적으로 기타
지역에 적용한다.

다. 문제점 기타 지역에 대한 발효시기는 합동위원회의
결의를 거쳐야 하므로 사실상 미국측은
그들이 원하는 시기까지 규정의 적용을 연기
할수 있어 민사청구권 조항은 유명무실하게
될 우려가 있음, ~~이러한 협정을 체결한~~
~~~~는 찾아볼수 없는 것임.~~

라. 해결방안 협정의 조속한 타결을 위하여 종래의 우리측
입장을 양보하고 다음과 같은 대안을 제안한다
" 제 5,6,7 및 8항의 규정은 합동위원회의
결의에 따라 본협정이 발효한 날로부터 12개월
후에 대한민국의 기타 지역에 적용될수 있다. "

"The provisions of paragraphs five, six,
seven and eight may be extended to other
areas of the Republic of Korea twelve months
from the date of entry into force of this
agreement as determined by the Joint Committee."

미국안을 원칙적으로 수락하되 다음과 같이
수정~~~~ 제안하다.

보통문서로 재분류(1966. 12. 31.)

0044

Regarding the claims falling under the provisions of paragraph

"Every half year, a statement of the sums paid by the Republic of Korea in the course of the half-yearly period in respect of every case regarding which the liability, amount, and proposed distribution on a percentage basis has been approved by <u>both governments</u> shall be sent to the appropriate authorities of the United States, together with a request for reimbursement. Such reimbursement shall be made in won within the shortest possible time. <u>The preceding approval by both governments shall not prejudice any decision taken by the arbitrator or adjudication by a competent tribuanl of the Republic of Korea as set forth in paragraphs 2(c) and 5(c) respectively.</u>"

"손해배상책임, 배상금액 및 비율에 의한 분담안에 대하여 <u>양국정부가 인정한</u> 각사건에 관하여 대한민국이 6개월기간에 지불한 금액의 명세서는, 지불청구서와 더불어, 매 6개월마다 적합한 합중국당국에 송부한다. 그러한 지불은 가능한한 빠른시일내에 "원"화로 하여야 한다. <u>상기 양국정부에 의한 인정은, 2(c) 및 5(c)항에 각각 규정되어 있는 중재인에 의한 어떠한 결정이나 혹은 대한민국의 권한있는 재판소에 의한 판결을 침해하지 못한다.</u>

0045

"The provisions of paragraphs five, six, seven and eight will
be extended, at the earliest date practicable, to other areas
of the Republic of Korea as determined by the Joint Committee."

"제5, 6, 7 및 8항의 규정은 ~~가능한한~~ ~~빠른시일에~~
합동위원회의 결정에 따라 가능한한 빠른시일에
대한민국의 기타지역에 적용된다."

(영문)

"The provisions of paragraphs five, six, seven and eight will
be progressively extended to other areas of Korea as determined
and defined by the Joint Committee."

"제5, 6, 7 및 8항의 규정은 합동위원회에 ~~의하여~~
바에 따라
결정하고 규정하는 한국의 기타지역에 점차적으로
정한
적용된다."

(영문)

0046

기 안 지

기 안 자	미주과 황영재		전 화 번 호		공 보		필 요	불필요
	과장	국장	차관	장관				

참조	자명	법무부: 법무과장	법무국장	법무차관	법무장관	보존한
기 안	년 월 일	65.6.	시행 년월일		통제관	정서 기장
분류기호 문서번호		외구미 722.2				
경 수 참 조	유신	건 의		발 신		

제 목   민사청구권 조항에 대한 우리측 입장

주둔군지위협정 체결 교섭에 있어 민사청구권

조항에 관한 제80차 실무자회의에서 미국측이 제안한

수정안에 대하여 별첨과 같이 우리측의 입장을 수립

하여 차기 회의에서 미국측에 제안코저 하오니 재가

하여 주시기 바랍니다.

유첨-민사청구권 조항에 대한 우리측 입장 1부.끝

1969. 1. 8

공통서식 1-2 (갑)   (16절지)

0047

0048

민사청구권 조항에 대한 우리측입장

제 80차 회의에서 미국측이 제안한 민사청구권 조항에 관한 수정안에 대하여 아래와 같이 우리측의 입장을 수립하여 미국측에 제안한다.

1. 공무집행중 정부재산 및 제3자에 대하여 손해를 가한 경우로서 그손해의 책임이 미국측에만 있을 때의 양국정부의 배상금 분담비율 (5(c) (i) 항)

    가. 한국안 한국 15 퍼센트 , 미국 85 퍼센트

    나. 미국안 한국 25   "   , 미국 75   "

    다. 문제점 현재민사청구권 조항에 있어 Formula Concept 를 채택하고 있는 협정 (미 · 일 " 나토 " 및 미 · 호주) 은 미국 안과 같이 모두 25퍼센트 – 75퍼센트의 비율로 접수국과 파견국이 배상금을 분담하게 되어 있음.

    라. 해결방안 : 미국안 수락.

2. 공무집행중 제3자에 대한 손해에 있어 손해배상 책임과 배상금액의 합의문제 (5(c) (iii) 항) :

    가. 한국안

    1) 한국정부 당국에 의하여 해결하게 되는 사건에 관하여는 사전에 손해배상 책임과 배상금액에 대하여 미국당국과 상호 합의 하나 , 재판의 판결은 양당사국을 구속하며 ,

    2) 이를 아래와 같은 합의의사록으로 규정 하여야 한다 :

    " 본조제5항에 해당되는 청구에 관하여는 대한민국당국이 해결하기 전에 손해배상의 책임과 그손해에 사정할 배상금에 관하여 대한민국과 합중국의 당국이 상호합의하여야 한다 . 그러나 청구권자가 제기할수 있는

0049

소의 결과로 대한민국의 권한있는 재판소에
의한 그사건에 대한 어떠한 판결도 본협정의
당사국에 대하여 구속력을 가지며 또한 최종적
인 것이다."

나. 미국안

1) 한국정부 당국에 의하여 해결하게되는 사건에
   관하여는 사전에 손해배상 책임과 배상금에
   대하여 미국당국이 인정한 것에 한하여 미국정부
   가 책임을 지며, 재판의 판결은 양당사국을
   구속한다.

2) 이를 위하여 본문 5(e)(iii)항을 아래와 같이
   수정한다 :

   "손해배상책임, 배상금액 및 비율에 의한 분담안
   에 대하여 합중국이 인정한 각사건에 관하여
   대한민국이 6개월기간에 지불한 금액의 명세서는,
   지불청구서와 더불어, 매6개월마다 적합한 합중국
   당국에 송부한다. 그러한 지불은 가능한한
   빠른시일내에 "원"화로 하여야 한다."

다. 문제점

1) 미국측은 재판의 판결은 양당사국을 구속하며,
   한국정부가 해결하는 사건에 관하여는 배상책임과
   배상금액에 대하여 사전에 상호합의할 것을 주장
   하고 있어, 실제에 있어서는 한국측 입장과
   동일한 것임.

2) 그러나 이를 위하여 미국측이 제안하는 바와
   같이 5(e)(iii) 항을 수정하게 되면, 아래와 같이
   조문해석상 모순이 일어나게 될것임:

   (가) 이미 합의된 5(c)항에 의하여 한국정부
       당국의 해결에 의하거나 재판의 판결에
       의하거나를 불문하고 한국정부가 지불한
       배상금은 양당사국을 구속하게 되어 있으나,

0051

(나) 미국측의 5(e)(iii)항에 의하면 손해배상의
책임과 배상금액에 대하여 미국정부가 인정한
사건에 한하여 미국정부가 한국정부에 대한
만상책임을 갖게되어 있어,

(다) 미국안은 그들의 주장과는 달리, 5(c)항에
의거 한국정부가 지불한 모든 배상금에
대하여 미국은 구속을 받게되는 동시에
또한 5(e)(iii)항에 의거 한국정부가 지불한
모든 배상금에 대하여 미국은 구속을 받지
않는다고 해석될수 밖에 없는바,

(라) 미국측의 주장과 같이 5(c)항중의 재판의
판결에만 미국이 구속된다고 해석할수 없을
뿐만 아니라, 한국정부가 해결하는 사건에
대하여만 양국정부가 배상책임과 배상금액에
합의한다고 해석할수도 없는 것임.

(마) 또한 미국안은 " .... 미국정부가 인정한
(approved)" 으로 되어 있어, 그들의
주장과 같이 상호합의 (mutual agreement)
한다고는 말할수 없는 것임.

라. 해결방안

한국측의 합의의사록을 철회하고 미국측의 5(e)(iii)
항을 아래와 같이 수정제안한다 :

"손해배상책임, 배상금액 및 비율에 의한 본담안에
대하여 양국정부가 인정한 각사건에 관하여 대한
민국이 6개월기간에 지불한 금액의 명세서는,
지불청구서와 더불어, 매6개월마다 적합한 합중국
당국에 송부한다. 그러한 지불은 가능한한 빠른
시일내에 "원"화로 하여야 한다. 상기 양국정부에
의한 인정은, 2(c) 및 5(c)항에 각각 규정되어
있는 중재인에 의한 어떠한 결정이나 혹은 대한
민국의 권한있는 재판소에 의한 판결을 침해하지
못한다."

0053

0054

"Every half year, a statement of the sums paid by the
Republic of Korea in the course of the half-yearly period
in respect of every case regarding which the liability,
amount, and proposed distribution on a percentage basis
has been approved by <u>both governments</u> shall be sent to
the appropriate authorities of the United States,
together with a request for reimbursement. Such
reimbursement shall be made in won within the shortest
possible time. <u>The preceding approval by both governments
shall not prejudice any decision taken by the arbitrator
or adjudication by a competent tribunal of the Republic
of Korea as set forth in paragraphs 2(c) and 5(c)
respectively.</u>"

3. <u>KSC 문제 (12 항)</u>

　　가. <u>한국안</u>　KSC 는 청구권조항을 위하여 미군의
　　　　　　　　　　고용원으로 간주한다.

　　나. <u>미국안</u>　KSC 는 청구권조항에 언급하지 않고,
　　　　　　　　　　다음과 같은 양해사항을 채택한다:
　　　　　　　　　　"본조는 KSC 인원에 의하여 발생된 청구에
　　　　　　　　　　적용하지 않는다. KSC 인원의 지위는 대한
　　　　　　　　　　민국과 합중국간의 별도의 교섭에 의거
　　　　　　　　　　결정한다."

　　다. <u>문제점</u>　KSC 가 별도 협정에서 해결되기 전에
　　　　　　　　　　"KSC 인원에 의하여 발생된 청구에
　　　　　　　　　　대하여는 본조를 적용하지 않는다" 라는
　　　　　　　　　　양해사항을 수락할수는 없음.

　　라. <u>해결방안</u>　KSC 를 청구권조항에서 삭제하는데 동의
　　　　　　　　　　하고, 미국측이 제안한 양해사항을 아래와
　　　　　　　　　　같이 수정제안한다:
　　　　　　　　　　" KSC 인원의 지위는 대한민국과 합중국
　　　　　　　　　　간의 별도의 교섭에 의거 결정한다."

0055

0056.-

4. 서울지역을 제외한 기타 지역에 있어서의 주요조항의
   적용시기 (합의의사록 A 2)
   가. <u>한국안</u> 협정발효 12 개월후 부터 적용하되 , 한국
                  정부가 그때까지 본조의 규정에 의한
                  임무를 수행할 준비가 안되었을 때에는
                  한국당국이 합동위원회를 통하여 준비에
                  필요한 기간을 통고하여 연기할수 있다 .
   나. <u>미국안</u> " 제 5,6,7 및 8 항의 규정은 합동위원회에
                  의하여 결정하고 규정하는바에 따라 한국의
                  기타 지역에 점차적으로 적용된다 . "
                  "The provisions of paragraphs five, six,
                  seven and eight will be progressively extended
                  to other areas of Korea as determined and
                  defined by the Joint Committee."
   다. <u>문제점</u> 기타 지역에 대한 발효시기는 합동위원회의
                  결의를 거쳐야 하므로 사실상 미국측은
                  그들이 원하는 시기까지 규정의 적용을
                  연기할수 있어 민사청구권 조항은 유명
                  무실하게 될우려가 있음 .
   라. <u>해결방안</u> 미국안을 원칙적으로 수락하되 다음과 같이
                  수정제안한다 .
                  " 제 5,6,7 및 8 항의 규정은 합동위원회의
                  결정에 따라 가능한한 바른시일에 대한
                  민국의 기타 지역에 적용된다 . "
                  "The provisions of paragraphs five, six,
                  seven and eight will be extended, at the
                  earliest date practicable, to other areas
                  of the Republic of Korea as determined by
                  the Joint Committee."

보통문서로 재분류 (1966. 12. 31.)

0057

5-5

기　안　지

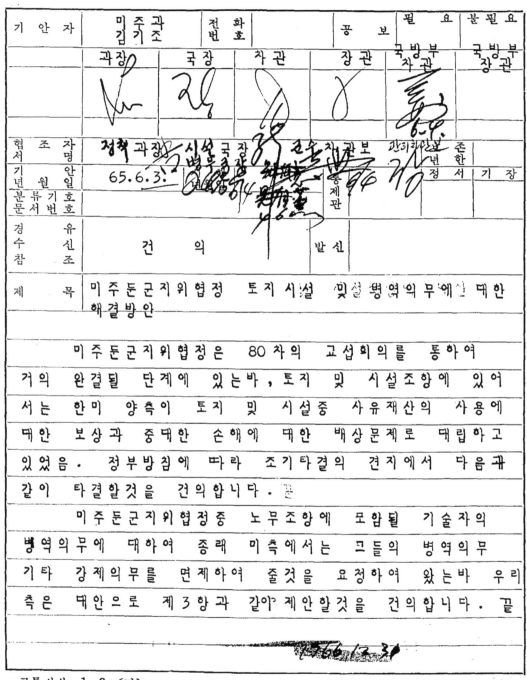

기 안 자	미주과 김기조	전화번호		공보	필요 불필요
	과장	국장	차관	장관	국방부 차관	국방부 장관
협조 서명	정책과장 시설국장 노무과 관리과 존한
기안년월일	65.6.3.	정서기장
분류기호 문서번호		통제판
경수 유신		
참조	건　의	발신
제　목	미주둔군지위협정 토지시설 및설병역의무에 대한 해결방안

　　　미주둔군지위협정은 80차의 고섭회의를 통하여

거의 완결될 단계에 있는바, 토지 및 시설조항에 있어

서는 한미 양측이 토지및 시설중 사유재산의 사용에

대한 보상과 중대한 손해에 대한 배상문제로 대립하고

있었음. 정부방침에 따라 조기타결의 견지에서 다음과

같이 타결할것을 건의합니다.

　　　미주둔군지위협정중 노무조항에 포함될 기술자의

병역의무에 대하여 종래 미측에서는 그들의 병역의무

기타 강제의무를 면제하여 줄것을 요청하여 왔는바 우리

측은 대안으로 제3항과 같이 제안할것을 건의합니다. 끝

1966.12.31

공통서식 1-2 (갑)　　　　　　　　　　　　　　　　　　(16절지)

0058

한·미국 간의 상호방위조약 제4조에 의한 시설과 구역 및 한국에서의 미국군대의 지위에 관한 협정(SOFA)
전59권. 1966.7.9 서울에서 서명 : 1967.2.9 발효(조약 232호) (V.33 실무교섭회의, 제81차, 1965.6.7)　65

1. 토지 및 시설의 사용에 대한 보상

    종래 우리측은 미군이 사용한, 혹은 사용중인
토지 및 시설중 사유재산에 속하는 것에 대하여
정당한 액의 보상(사용료)을 주장하여 왔으나
미국측에서는 그러한 보상은 미국군역사상 선례가
없으며 토지, 시설을 미군에게 제공한 본래의 취지에
위배된다는 견지에서 한국정부가 직접 해결하도록
주장하고 있음. 따라서 타국의 예에 비추어 한국정부
가 대내적으로 보상문제를 해결하기로 하고 미측제안
을 수락한다.

2. 토지 시설의 반환

    가. 미국은 토지시설을 한국정부에 반환시
그것이 미국에 제공될 당시의 형태로 복구하거나
복구를 위한 보상책임을 지지아니한다.(미국안)

    나. 한국정부는 미군이 토지, 시설을 개선한데
대한 보상책임을 지지아니한다.(한국안)

    다. 미군의 토지 시설내에 있는 가동시설,
장비, 자재 및 공급품을 미국재산으로 하며 미국은
그것을 반출할수 있다.(미국안)

    라. 상기 조항은 미국이 한국정부와의 특별
조치하에 취하여진 것에는 적용되치 아니한다.(미국안)

    이상은 한미 양측의 안으로 타결하기로 하고
종래한국측이 주장하든 "미군의 사용으로 극심하게
손상된 사유재산의 경우 미국은 한국정부의 요청에

0060

따라 복구, 혹은 복구를 위한 보상에 대한 적절한
고려를 한다"를 철회하고 합의의사록이나 양해사항
으로 "미군에게 제공된 재산에 속하는 토지 및
시설내에 있는 설비, 비품 및 정착물중 가동품으로서
미군에게 불필요할 경우에는 그러한 재산을 소유권
자에게 반환하도록 한다"를 삽입시키도록 가능한한
추진한다.

3. "전시등. 비상시 미군업무수행에 긴요한 기술을
   습득한자는 미군이 사전에 요청하고 한국정부와의
   협의하에 병역의무 혹은 기타 강제동원으로 부터
   연기되어야 한다. 이경우 미군은 그와같이 긴요한
   기술자의 명단을 사전에 한국정부에 제출하여야
   한다. "끝

0062

and Return of
Article A Grant of/Facilities and Areas

1. (a) The United States is granted, under Article IV of the Mutual Defense Treaty, the use of facilities and area in the Republic of Korea. Agreements as to specific facilities and areas shall be concluded by the two Governments through the Joint Committee provided for in Article ___ of this Agreement. "Facilities and Areas" include existing furnishings, equipment and fixtures, wherever located, used in the operation of such facilities and areas.

(b) The facilities and areas of which the United States armed forces have the use at the effective date of this Agreement together with those areas and facilities which the United States armed forces have returned to the Republic of Korea with the reserved right of re-entry, when these facilities and areas have been re-entered by U.S. forces, shall be considered as the facilities and areas agreed upon between the two Governments in accordance with sub-paragraph (a) above. Records of facilities and areas of which the United States armed forces have the use or right of re-entry shall be maintained through the Joint Committee after this Agreement comes into force.

2. At the request of either Government, the Governments of the United States and the Republic of Korea shall review such agreements and may agree that such facilities and areas or portions thereof shall be returned to the Republic of Korea or that additional facilities and areas may be provided.

3. The facilities and areas used by the United States shall be returned to the Republic of Korea under such conditions as may be agreed through the Joint Committee whenever they are no longer needed for the purposes of this Agreement and the United States agrees to keep the needs for facilities and areas under continual observation with a view toward such return.

4. (a) When facilities and areas are temporarily not being used and the Government of the Republic of Korea is so advised, the

0063

Government of the Republic of Korea may make, or permit Korean
nationals to make, interim use of such facilities and areas provided that it is agreed between the two Governments through the
Joint Committee that such use would not be harmful to the purposes
for which the facilities and areas are normally used by the United
States armed forces.

(b) With respect to facilities and areas which are to be used
by United States armed forces for limited periods of time, the
Joint Committee shall specify in the agreements covering such
facilities and areas the extent to which the provisions of this
Agreement shall not apply.

Article B   Measures Which May Be Taken in Facilities and Areas

1. Within the facilities and areas, the United States may take
all the measures necessary for their establishment, operation,
safeguarding and control. In order to provide access for the United
States armed forces to the facilities and areas for their support,
safeguarding and control, the Government of the Republic of Korea
shall, at the request of the United States armed forces and consultation between the two Governments through the Joint Committee,
take necessary measures within the scope of applicable laws and
regulations over land, territory waters and airspace adjacent to,
or in the vicinities of the facilities and areas. The United States
may also take necessary measures for such purposes upon consultation between the two Governments through the Joint Committee.

2. (a) The Government of the United States agrees not to take
the measures referred to in paragraph 1 in such a manner as to
interfere unnecessarily with navigation, aviation, communication,
or land travel to or from or within the territories of the Republic
of Korea.

(b) All questions relating to telecommunications including
radio frequencies for electromagnetic radiating devices, or like
matters, shall continue to be resolved expeditiously in the utmost
spirit of coordination and cooperation by arrangement between the
designated communications authorities of the two Governments.

(c) The Government of the Republic of Korea shall, within the

0064

scope of applicable laws, regulations and agreements, take all
reasonable measures to avoid or eliminate interference with electromagnetic radiation sensitive devices, telecommunications devices,
or other appratus required by the United States armed forces.

3. Operations in the facilities and areas in use by the United
States armed forces shall be carried on with due regard for the
public safety.

<u>Article C   Return of Facilities and Areas</u>

1. The United States is not obliged, when it returns facilities
and areas to the Republic of Korea on the expiration of this
Agreement or at an earlier date, to restore the facilities and
areas to the condition in which they were at the time they became
available to the United States armed forces, or to compensate the
Republic of Korea in lieu of such restoration.

However, in case of private
property extremely demolished by
the use of the United States, the
Government of the United States
shall, upon the request of the
Government of the Republic of
Korea, pay due consideration to
its restoration or compensation
in lieu thereof.

2. The Government of the Republic of Korea is not obliged to make
any compensation to the Government of the United States for any
improvements made in the facilities and areas or for the buildings or
structures left thereon on the expiration of this Agreement or the
earlier return of the facilities and areas.

3. All removable facilities erected or constructed by or on
behalf of the United States at its expense and all equipment, materials and supplies brought into or procured in the Republic of
Korea by or on behalf of the United States in connection with the
construction, development, operation, maintenance, safeguading
and control of the facilities and areas will remain the property
of the United States Government and may be removed from the Republic
of Korea.

0065

4. The foregoing provisions shall not apply to any construction which the Government of the United States may undertake under special arrangements with the Government of the Republic of Korea.

Article D   Compensation for the Use of Facilities and Areas

4. With regard to the private property used as facilities and areas by the United States armed forces under this Agreement, the United States shall make reasonable compensation through the Government of the Republic of Korea to the owners of such facilities and areas with a view to alleviating their losses. Detailed arrangements, including the amounts of compensation, shall be made between the two Governments through the Joint Committee.

5. The Government of the United States bears without cost to the Republic of Korea all expenditures incident to the maintenance of the facilities and areas granted under this Agreement.

1. It is agreed that the United States will bear for the duration of the Agreement without cost to the Republic of Korea all expenditures incident to the maintenance of the United States armed forces in the Republic of Korea, except those to be borne by the Republic of Korea as provided in paragraph 2.

2. It is agreed that the Republic of Korea will furnish for the duration of this Agreement without cost to the United States and make compensation where appropriate to

0066

the owners and suppliers thereof
all facilities and areas and rights
of way, including facilities and
areas jointly used such as those
at airfields and ports as provided
in Article II and III. The Government of the Republic of Korea
assures the use of such facilities
and areas to the United States
and will hold the United States Government,
Government as well as its agencies
and employees harmless from any
third party claims which may be
advanced in connection with such
use.

AGREED MINUTE

It is agreed that in the event of an emergency, the United
States armed forces shall be authorized to take such measures in
the vicinity of the areas and facilities as may be necessary to
provide for their safeguarding and control.

0067

FACILITIES AND AREAS

Article A Grant of and Return of Facilities
and Areas

1. (a) The United States is granted, under Article IV of
the Mutual Defense Treaty, the use of facilities and area in
the Republic of Korea. Agreements as to specific facilities
and areas shall be concluded by the two Governments through the
Joint Committee provided for in Article _____ of this Agreement.
"Facilities and Areas" include existing furnishings, equipment
and fixtures, wherever located, used in the operation of such
facilities and areas.

(b) The facilities and areas of which the United States
armed forces have the use at the effective date of this Agreement
together with those areas and facilities which the United States
armed forces have returned to the Republic of Korea with the
reserved right of re-entry, when these facilities and areas have
been re-entered by U.S. forces, shall be considered as the facilities
and areas agreed upon between the two Governments in accordance
with sub-paragraph (a) above. Records of facilities and areas
of which the United States armed forces have the use or right of
re-entry shall be maintained through the Joint Committee after
this Agreement comes into force.

2. At the request of either Government, the Governments of
the United States and the Republic of Korea shall review such agreements and may agree that such facilities and areas or portions
thereof shall be returned to the Republic of Korea or that additional
facilities and areas may be provided.

3. The facilities and areas used by the United States shall be
returned to the Republic of Korea under such conditions as may be
agreed through the Joint Committee whenever they are no longer
needed for the purposes of this Agreement and the United States

0068

agrees to keep the needs for facilities and areas under continual observation with a view toward such return.

4. (a) When facilities and areas are temporarily not being used and the Government of the Republic of Korea is so advised, the Government of the Republic of Korea may make, or permit Korean nationals to make, interim use of such facilities and areas provided that it is agreed between the two Governments through the Joint Committee that such use would not be harmful to the purposes for which the facilities and areas are normally used by the United States armed forces.

(b) With respect to facilities and areas which are to be used by United States armed forces for limited periods of time, the Joint Committee shall specify in the agreements covering such facilities and areas the extent to which the provisions of this Agreement shall not apply.

Article B   Measures Which May Be Taken in
                 Facilities and Areas

1. Within the facilities and areas, the United States may take all the measures necessary for their establishment, operation, safeguarding and control. In order to provide access for the United States armed forces to the facilities and areas for their support, safeguarding and control, the Government of the Republic of Korea shall, at the request of the United States armed forces and consultation between the two Governments through the Joint Committee, take necessary measures within the scope of applicable laws and regulations over land, territory waters and airspace adjacent to, or in the vicinities of the facilities and areas. The United States may also take necessary measures for such purposes upon consultation between the two Governments through the Joint Committee.

0069

2. (a) The Government of the United States agrees not to take the measures referred to in paragraph 1 in such a manner as to interfere unnecessarily with navigation, aviation, communication, or land travel to or from or within the territories of the Republic of Korea.

(b) All questions relating to telecommunications including radio frequencies for electromagnetic radiating devices, or like matters, shall continue to be resolved expeditiously in the utmost spirit of coordination and cooperation by arrangement between the designated communications authorities of the two Governments.

(c) The Government of the Republic of Korea shall, within the scope of applicable laws, regulations and agreements, take all reasonable measures to avoid or eliminate interference with electromagnetic radiation sensitive devices, telecommunications devices, or other apparatus required by the United States armed forces.

3. Operations in the facilities and areas in use by the United States armed forces shall be carried on with due regard for the public safety.

Article C   Return of Facilities and Areas

1. The United States is not obliged, when it returns facilities and areas to the Republic of Korea on the expiration of this Agreement or at an earlier date, to restore the facilities and areas to the condition in which they were at the time they became available to the United States armed forces, or to compensate the Republic of Korea in lieu of such restoration.

However, in case of private property extremely demolished by the use of the United States, the Government of the United States

0070

shall, upon the request of the
Government of the Republic of
Korea, pay due consideration to
its restoration or compensation
in lieu thereof.

2. The Government of the Republic of Korea is not obliged to
make any compensation to the Government of the United States for any
improvements made in the facilities and areas or for the buildings
or structures left thereon on the expiration of this Agreement or
the earlier return of the facilities and areas.

3. All removable facilities erected or constructed by or on
behalf of the United States at its expense and all equipment, materials
and supplies brought into or procured in the Republic of Korea by
or on behalf of the United States in connection with the construction,
development, operation, maintenance, safeguarding and control of
the facilities and areas will remain the property of the United
States Government and may be removed from the Republic of Korea.

4. The foregoing provisions shall not apply to any construction
which the Government of the United States may undertake under
special arrangements with the Government of the Republic of Korea.

Article D   Compensation for the Use of
             Facilities and Areas

4. With regard to the private
property used as facilities and
areas by the United States armed
forces under this Agreement, the
United States shall make reasonable compensation through the
Government of the Republic of Korea
to the owners of such facilities
and areas with a view to alleviating
their losses. Detailed arrangements,

0071

including the amounts of compensation, shall be made between the
two Governments through the Joint
Committee.

5. The Government of the
United States bears without cost to
the Republic of Korea all expenditures incident to the maintenance of
the facilities and areas granted
under this Agreement.

1. It is agreed that the United
States will bear for the duration
of the Agreement without cost to
the Republic of Korea all expenditures
incident to the maintenance of the
United States armed forces in the
Republic of Korea, except those to
be borne by the Republic of Korea
as provided in paragraph 2.

2. It is agreed that the Republic
of Korea will furnish for the duration
of this Agreement without cost to
the United States and make compensation where appropriate to the owners
and suppliers thereof all facilities
and areas and rights of way, including
facilities and areas jointly used
such as those at airfields and ports
as provided in Article II and III.
The Government of the Republic of
Korea assures the use of such
facilities and areas to the United
States Government and will hold the
United States Government as well as
its agencies and employees harmless
from any third party claims which
may be advanced in connection with
such use.

0072

<u>AGREED MINUTE</u>

It is ageed that in the event of an emergency, the United
States armed forces shall be authorized to take such measures in
the vicinity of the areas and facilities as may be necessary to
provide for their safeguarding and control.

0073

기 안 지

관리
번호 3/04

기 안 자	미주과 김기조	전 화 번 호	74-3073	공 보	필 요	불 필 요

미주과장	구미국장	외무부차관	외무부장관	노동청장	보사부차관	보사부장관
	3/6					

협 조 서 명	자 명	노정과장 3/2	노정국장	노동청차장	보 존 년 한	
기 안 년 월 일		1965. 6. 3.	시 행 년 월 일 (통신과 경유)	통제관	정 서	기 장
분 류 기 호 문 서 번 호		외구미 722.2-				

意見書

1. 「나」(고용인) 을 다음과 같이 함.

勤勞者라 함은 使用主에 依하여 雇傭된 韓國國籍을 가진 모-든 民間人을 말한다

理由. K.S.C 를 一般勤勞者와 區別取扱할 理由가 없고 家事使用人은 韓國勞勞基準法 適用을 받지 않을 것이나 其他에 雇傭關係은 他勤勞者와 同等히 保護되어야 할 것임.

2. 「다」(분쟁 해결 절차)(2)

同項中 "承認된 雇傭人團體" 는 團體交涉의 對象으로 承認된 雇傭人團體 로 변경할것.

理由. 勤勞者의 團結權은 法에서 保護된 것이며 "承認된 雇傭人團體" 라 하면 마치 그團體의 設立이 使用主에 依하여 承認되는 듯한 感이 있어 美國 外國의 例에 따라 團體交涉乃至 爭議의 保護對象으로서의 承認根據로 하여 規定하는 것이 可한 할 것임.

3. 「자」(合意議事録 第5項)의 末尾를 다음과 같이 고칠것.

----- 遂行되지 않는限 團體交涉 의 對象으로 承認되어야 함

理由. 前項理由에 依함.

보건사회부

"6월 7일 次官과 保社長官 및 電話協調로 撤回함. [서명]

0074

공통서식 1-2 (갑)   3-1   (16절지)

개획하고 있는

제안을 참작하

합니다.

공동으로 재심

전에 한미양

을 제의함 (미군

에서 그 지위를

교섭에서 근

을 저해하는

0075

접 수 참	신 조	건 의	발 신

제 목 | 미주둔군지위협정 노무조항의 일부개정안 제안

정부에서는 연안중인 미주둔군지위협정의 조기 타결을 계획하고 있는
바, 노무조항에 있어서는 금번 제80차회의에서의 미국측 신제안을 참작하
여 최종적으로 아래와 같이 타결하도록 제안할것을 건의합니다.

1. 고용주와 고용인의 정의 (제 1 항)

가. 고용주: 미군(비세출기관포함) 및 군초청계약자.

　　(군초청계약자는 현존하는 회사는 한미공동으로 재심
　　하여 결정하고 앞으로 들어올 회사는 사전에 한미양
　　측이 협의하여 결정한다.)

나. 고용인: 한국노무근로단(KSC)와 가사사용인을 제외한 (미군
　　군속이 아닌) 한국국적을 가진 민간인.

　　(한국노무근로단은 한미간에 별도의 교섭에서 그 지위를
　　결정하되 본조항에서의 재의는 앞으로의 교섭에서 근
　　로단의 노무자가 향유할 권익와 피보호권을 저해하는

공통서식 1-2 (갑)　　　　　3-1　　　　　(16절지)

0075

한·미국 간의 상호방위조약 제4조에 의한 시설과 구역 및 한국에서의 미국군대의 지위에 관한 협정(SOFA)
전59권. 1966.7.9 서울에서 서명 : 1967.2.9 발효(조약 232호) (V.33 실무교섭회의, 제81차, 1965.6.7)　81

할수 있는 것으로 해석되여서는 아니된다.)

√ 2. 노동조건의 적용범위 (제3항)

　　본조의 규정에 상반하지 않거나 별도로 합의되지 않는한 고용조건, 보상 및 노사관계는 대한민국 노동법령의 제규정과 일치하여야한다.

　3. 분쟁해결절차 (제4항 (a))

　　고용주와 고용인 혹은 승인된 고용인단체간의 분쟁은 노동청, 합동위원회(합동위원회가 지정하는 특별분과위원회에 회부할 수 있음)에 회부하여 조정한다. 고용인 혹은 고용인 단체는 분쟁이 합동위원회(분과위원회에 회부여부를 불문하고)에 회부되여 70일이 경과하여도 해결되지 않을 경우에는 정상업무 방해행위를 할수있다. 고용인 혹은 고용인단체가 합동위원회의 결정에 불복하거나 상기 냉각기간 70일이 경과하기 이전에 정상업무 방해행위를 할 경우에는 고용인단체를 승인하지 않거나 고용인을 해고할수 있는 원인으로 간주한다. (전기 승인된 고용인단체란 합의의사록 제5항에 규정된바 한미 공동이익에 반하여 해체될 단체를 제의한 모든 단체를 말한다.)

　4. 단체행동권의 행사 (제4항 (b))

　　합동위원회는 전기 절차에 의하여 분쟁이 해결되지 않을 경우 단체행동권을 행사하지 못할 긴요한 고용인의 범위를 결정한다. 이 문제에 대하여 합동위원회에서 합의에 도달하지 못할 경우에는 한국정부와 미국의 교사절간에 토의할수 있다.

　5. 비상시의 조치 (제 4 항(c))

　　전시등 비상시에는 본조의 적용은 한국정부가 취하는 비상조치에 따라, 미국군사당국과 협의하여 제한한다.

√ 6. 고용인 해고권(합의의사록 제2항)

　　미국정부는 군사상 필요시 해고권을 가진다. (한국노동법령의 제규정

3-2

0076

에 의한 합법적인 해고를 제외한 소위 군사상 필요에 의한 해고는
합의의사록제4항에 따라 합동위원회에서 사전에 합의하여야한다.)

  7. 노동조합 혹은 기타 고용인단체 (합의의사록 제5항)

  노동조합과 기타 고용인단체는 그 목적이 한미 공동이익에
위배되지 않는 한 승인되여야한다.   끝

┌─────────────────────────────────┐
│ 보통문서로 재분류 (1966. 12. 31.) │
└─────────────────────────────────┘

※ "별도합의 되지않는한"을 "미군의 군사상필요"로
   변경제안함. (1965. 6. 8.) 에 동의함

┌────────────────────────┐
│ 196 . .   에 예고문에 │
│ 의거 일반문서로 재분류됨 │
└────────────────────────┘

한·미국 간의 상호방위조약 제4조에 의한 시설과 구역 및 한국에서의 미국군대의 지위에 관한 협정(SOFA) 83
전59권. 1966.7.9 서울에서 서명 : 1967.2.9 발효(조약 232호) (V.33 실무교섭회의, 제81차, 1965.6.7)

LABOR ARTICLE

(Underlining indicates modifications from
the U.S. draft tabled at 8th session)

1. (b) ... Such civilian personnel shall be nationals of
the Republic of Korea.

3. To the extent not inconsistent with the provisions of
this Article or ~~except as may~~ *the military requirements of the United States Armed Forces,* otherwise be mutually agreed,
the conditions of employment, compensation, and labor-manage-
ment (relations) established by the United States Armed Forces
for their employees shall conform with provisions of labor
legislation of the Republic of Korea.

4. (a)(5) .... to the Joint Committee, as stipulated in
subparagraph (2) above.

5. (b)....... ~~United States Armed Forces and~~ *be deferred* through mutual
consultation, ~~upon~~ *from Republic of Korea*---

Agreed Minutes

4. When employers cannot conform with provisions of labor
legislation of the Republic of Korea applicable under
Paragraph 3 on account of the military requirements of the
United States Armed Forces, the matter shall be referred, in

- 1 -

9-6.

0078

advance whenever possible, to the Joint Committee for mutual agreement.

5. A union or other employee group shall be recognized unless its objectives are inimical to the common interests of the United States and the Republic of Korea. Membership or non-membership in such group shall not be a factor in employment or other actions affecting employees.

- 2 -

9-7

LABOR ARTICLE

(Underlining indicates modifications from
the U.S. draft tabled at 80th session)

1. (b) ... <u>Such civilian personnel shall be nationals</u>
<u>of the Republic of</u> ^Korea.

3. To the extent not inconsistent with the provisions
of this Article or the military requirements of the
United States Armed Forces, the conditions of employment,
compensation, and labor-management <u>relations</u> established
by the United States Armed Forces for their employees
<u>shall conform with provisions of labor legislation</u>
of the Republic of Korea.

4. (a)(5) ..... to the Joint Committee, as stipulated
in subparagraph <u>(2)</u> above.

5. (b) ...... be deferred, <u>through mutual consultation,</u>
from Republic of Korea ....

<u>Agreed Minutes</u>

4. When employers cannot conform with provisions of
labor legislation <u>of the Republic of Korea</u> applicable
under <u>Paragraph 3</u> on account of the military requirements
of the United States Armed Forces, the matter shall be
<u>referred</u>, in advance whenever possible, to the Joint
Committee <u>for mutual agreement</u>.

9-4

0080

5. A union or other employee group shall be recognized
unless its objectives are inimical to the <u>common</u> interests
of the United States <u>and the Republic of Korea</u>.
Membership or non-membership in such group shall not be
a facter in employment or other actions affecting
employees.

9-5

0081

Labor Article

Re Para. 1(b)

With regard to Paragraph 1(b), local residents, who are third-country nationals and are also local-hire employees of the United States armed forces or of invited contractors, paid in won, on the effective date of this Agreement, shall be excluded from the application of this provision.

Re Para 1(b)

The provisions of Paragraph 1(b) do not preclude the United States armed forces from bringing into Korea, without privileges, third-country contractor employees possessing special skills not available from the Korean labor force.

Re AM. #4

With regard to Agreed Minute #4, it is understood that the deviation from Korean labor legislation need not be referred to the Joint Committee in cases when such referral would seriously hamper military operations.

proposed by U.S. side

8 - 1

0082

意見書

第25條　勞務

1. 本條第12項 나號中 KSC 및 家事使用人問題에 對하여는 貴部에서 數次 合意要請한 快裁公文書에 當部의 意見을 提示한 바 있으니 이를 參照하시기 바랍니다

2. 第3項에 있어서는 "聚合衆國軍隊의 軍事上 必要에 依하여 相互合意하는 限度內에서" 로 訂正하는것이 追後解釋上 明白을 期할수 있을것으로 思料합니다

3. 會議事錄 第4項 前段에 있어서는 "雇傭하는 本條 第3項에 依한 合衆國軍隊의 軍事上必要로 때문에 大韓民國勞動協會을 따를수 없다고 生覺될때에는 ‥‥‥" 로 하는것이 좋겠읍니다

　　　　65. 7. 2.

勞動廳 勞政局長　許成俊

0083

9-2

목 차

비고 : 1. 형사 재판권 조항 중에서 미 합의사항 부분은 괄호
또는 하선으로 해당 조항에서 이를 표시하였음.
2. 노무 조항은 비 공식적으로 합의 된 것을 기초로
한 것임.

0084

9-2

기 안 지

기 안 자	미주과 이근팔	전화 번호		공 보	필 요	불필요
	과장	국장	차관	장관		
협조 자서명 서	법무부 검찰과장 해	검찰국장 시행 년월일	차관	장관 ㉺ 통제 관	보존 한	
기안 년월일 분류기호 문서번호	65.6.3. 외구미 722.2				정서	기장
경수 수 신조 참 조	유신 건 의			발 신		
제 목	주둔군지위협정 체결 교섭에 임할 우리측입장					

　　　당부에서는 박대통령 방미시 형사재판관할건의
도기문제에 관하여 미측이 제안한 서독보충협정의 형태를
원칙적으로 수락하게 되었음을 계기로 현안인 교섭을
일괄타결하기 위하여 형사재판관할건 조항 선반에 걸친
해결방안을 별첨과 같이 수립코저 하오니 재가하여
주시기 바랍니다.

　　유첨－형사재판관할건에 관한 우리측 입장 1부. 끝

공통서식 1－2 (갑) 　　　　　　　　　　　　　　(16절지)

0085

0086

형사재판 관할권에 관한 우리측입장

1. 제 1 차 관할권의 모기 (합의의사록제 3 (b) 항)

　금번 박대통령 방미를 계기로 한 한·미양국간의
합의에 따라 한국당국에 부여된 제 1 차관할권의
모기를 규정한 미측제안을 수락하고 다음과 같은
우리측 입장을 제안한다 :

(1) 한국당국의 제 1 차 관할권을 미측에 모기할 것을
　　규정한 미측합의의사록 제 1 항은 미측안을 수락하되
　　미측안 서두에 "미국의 요청에 따라" (At the
　　request of the United States) 라는 문구를
　　삽입하기 위하여 다음과 같은 규정을 제 8 항으로
　　신설할것을 제안한다.

　　　　"미국은 본합의의사록 제 1 항에 규정된 대한
　　민국의 제 1 차관할권의 모기를 위한 요청을 본
　　협정발효시에 하여야 한다." (제2안: 미측안 수락)

(2) 우리측이 제 78 차회의에서 미측 모기 조항 제 4 항
　　말미에 "모기의 철회는 본합의의사록 제 3 항에
　　규정된 철회를 위한 통고가 그러한 통고 발행후
　　21 일내에 대한민국 정부에 의하여 취소되지 않는
　　한 최종적이며 확정적이어야 한다"는 규정을 추가
　　삽입할 것을 제안하였던바, 미측은 제 80 차 회의시
　　일정한 기한을 설정하는 것은 수락할수 없으며
　　또한 한국측 제안은 중복되는 규정임으로 합의
　　의사록에 규정하는데는 반대이지만 "모기의 철회는
　　본합의의사록 제 3 항에 규정된 모기의 철회를 위한
　　통고가 대한민국 정부에 의하여 취소되지 않는한
　　최종적이며 확정적이다"라고 양해사항으로 기록에
　　남길것을 제안하여 온바 이를 미측 제안대로 수락
　　한다.

　　　　　　　　　　11 - 1

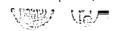

(3) 한국당국이 포기하는 사건의 재판과 공무집행중
　　범죄로서 대한민국 또는 대한민국 국민에 대한
　　사건의 재판장소 및 대한민국대표의 그러한 재판
　　에의 참석에 관한 우리측 제안에 관하여는 미측이
　　제80차 회의에서 이를 수락할수 없다고 답변한바
　　있음에 감하여 미측제6항의 규정을 수락한다.

2. 공무집행중 범죄 (합의의사록 제3 (a) 항)
　공무집행중 범죄본제에 관하여는 제80차회의 때의
　미측입장을 다음과 같이 수락함으로서 이문제에 대하여
　완전 합의를 본다.

　(1) 공무집행증명서의 발행건자를 미측 주장대로 "미국
　　　군대의 건한있는 당국"으로 하되 다음과 같은
　　　양해사항을 기록에 남기는데 동의한다.
　　　　"증명서는 반드시 미군법무관의 의견을 들은
　　　후에 발행되어야 하며 미군당국의 증명서 발행
　　　기관은 장성급 또는 그가 지정하는 자이어야 한다."

　(2) 우리측이 제77차 회의시 제안한 다음과 같은 공무
　　　집행의 정의는 미측 주장을 참작하여 합의의사록
　　　또는 양해사항으로 수락한다.
　　　　"공무라 함은 미군대 구성원 및 군속이
　　　공무중 행한 모든 행위를 포함하는 것을 의미하는
　　　것이 아니며 개인이 집행하는 공무의 기능으로서
　　　행하여질 것이 요구되는 행위에만 적용되는 것을
　　　의미한다. 그러므로 어떤자가 특정공무에 있어서
　　　행할것이 요구되는 행위로부터 실질적으로 이탈한
　　　행위는 통상 그의 공무밖의 행위이다."

3. 재판관할건 행사기관 및 관할건에 복하는 자의 범위
　(제1항)
　(1) 미군당국의 관할건에 복하는 자 (제1 (a) 항)
　　(가) 양측입장
　　　(ㄱ) 한국측 : 미군법에 복하는 모든자.
　　　(ㄴ) 미국측 : 미군대 구성원, 군속 및 그들의 가족.

11 - 2　　　　　　　　　　0089

0030

(나) 해결방안 : 미측안 수락 .

(2) 한국측 관할건 행사기관 (제 1 (b) 항)

　　(가) 양측입장

　　　(ㄱ) 한국측 : 대한민국 당국

　　　(ㄴ) 미국측 : 대한민국 민사당국 .

　　(나) 해결방안 :

　　　제 1안 : 한국당국의 관할건행사기관을 " 대한
　　　　　　　민국당국 " 으로 하고 " 미군인 , 군속
　　　　　　　및 그들의 가족을 대한민국군법회의에
　　　　　　　회부하지 아니한다 " 라는 미측제안을
　　　　　　　합의의사록으로 수락한다 . (미측도
　　　　　　　우리측이 미측합의의사록을 수락하는
　　　　　　　것을 조건으로 우리측안을 수락할수
　　　　　　　있을것이라고 시사하였음 .)

4. 관할건의 적용지역 (합의의사록 제 1 (b) 항)

　①계엄령 선포지역의 관할건 행사 (합의의사록제 1(b) 1 항)

　　(가) 양측입장

　　　(ㄱ) 한국측 : 삭제주장   第一次 ~~ 을 포기, 철회 ~~
　　　　　　　　　　　　　　　　　　~~ 東屬管轄權~~ ~~ 統制 ~~ 의 要請에
　　　　　　　　　　　　　　　　　　~~ 美軍側 ~~ 유려 ~~ 求함 ~~
　　　(ㄴ) 미국측 : 계엄령 선포지역에서는   ~~ 統制權 ~~ 을
　　　　　　　　　　전속적 관할건을 행사한다 .   함

　　(나) 해결방안 :   수락한다.
　　　미측안을 원칙적으로 ~~ 수락하여 " 대한민국이 ~~
　　　~~ 계엄령을 선포할 경우에는 계엄령선포지역에서 ~~
　　　~~ 계엄령이 해제될때까지 본조항의 효력이 주시 ~~
　　　~~ 정지된다 " 는 것을 합의의사록으로 수락한다 . ~~

(2) 한국영역외 범죄 (합의의사록 제 1 (b) (2) 항)

　　(가) 양측입장

　　　(ㄱ) 한국측 : 삭제주장 .

　　　(ㄴ) 미국측 : 대한민국당국의 관할건은 미군인 ,
　　　　　　　　　　군속 및 그들의 가족이 대한민국
　　　　　　　　　　영역외에서 행한범죄에 미치지 아니한다 .

　　(나) 해결방안 :

11 - 3   0091

0092

미측안을 수정하여 "미국이 전속적 관할권의
포기를 요청하면 대한민국은 호의적인 고려를
하며 경합적관할권의 경우에는 한국당국은
포기의 철회를 삼가한다 " 는 것을 합의의사록
으로 수락한다. (제 2 안: 미측안 수락)

5. 전속적 관할권의 포기 (합의의사록 제 2 항)
   (가) 양측입장
       (ㄱ) 한국측 : 삭제주장.
       (ㄴ) 미국측 : 미군당국으로부터의 전속적 관할권 포기
                    요청에 대하여 대한민국 당국은 호의적
                    고려를 하여야 한다.
   (나) 해결방안 : 미측안 수락.

6. 2중 국적자에 대한 관할권 (합의의사록 제 4 항)
   (가) 양측입장
       (ㄱ) 한국측 : 한·미 양국의 2중국적자인 미군인,
                    군속은 미국시민으로 간주한다.
       (ㄴ) 미국측 : 규정없음.   (나) 해결방안 : 우리측안 삭제.

7. 수사상의 협조 (합의의사록 제 6 항)
   (가) 양측입장
       (ㄱ) 한국측 : 1) 미군인 또는 군속이 증인으로 소환
                       되었을 때에는 한국당국에 출두
                       하여야 한다.
                    2) 만약에 증인으로 소환된 자가 출두
                       하지 않을때에는 한국당국은 관계
                       법령에 따라 필요한 조치를 취한다.
       (ㄴ) 미국측 : 1) 한·미 양국당국은 증인의 출두를
                       위하여 상호협력한다.
                    2) 미군인이 증인 또는 피고인으로
                       한국법원에 소환되었을때에는 미군
                       당국은 군사상의 긴급사태로 달리
                       요구되지 않을때에는 그러한 출두가

11 - 4

0093

0094

한국법에 의거 강제적인 것을 조건
으로 그를 출두케 한다.

3) 한국당국의 영장은 영문으로 송달
되어야 한다.

4) 미군인, 군속 또는 가족이 관련된
형사소송에 있어서 모든 소송 서류
사본이 미군당국이 지정하는 대리인
에게 송달되어야 한다.

5) 한국국민이 증인 또는 감정인으로
미군당국에 의하여 소환되었을 때에는
한국당국이나 법원은 한국법에 따라
그러한 자를 출두시켜야 한다.

6) 증인을 위한 수수료 기타 보수는
합동위원회가 결정한다.

7) 증인의 특권과 면제는 그러한 증인이
출두하는 법원 또는 당국의 법령에
의하여 부여된다. 증인은 자기가
소추당할지도 모르는 증언을 강요
당하지 아니한다.

8) 소송진행상 국가의 공적 기밀을 발표
또는 어떤국가의 안전을 침해할 우려
가 있는때에는 그국가관계당국의 허가
를 얻어야 한다.

(나) 해결방안 : 미측안을 수락한다. (서도보충협정 제 37 조
와 동일함)

8. 한국당국이 언도한 형의 집행 (제 7 (b) 항)

(가) 양측입장

(ㄱ) 한국측 : 삭제주장

(ㄴ) 미국측 : 미군당국이 신병 인도를 요청하면
한국당국이 호의적 고려를 하여야 한다.
신병구금이 미군당국에 인도되었을 경우
에는 미군당국은 미국구금시설내에서
구금을 계속한다.

0095

0096

(나) 해결방안 : 미측제안을 수락하되 복영상황에 관한
　　　　　　 정보제공과 한국정부대표의 시찰건의 부여
　　　　　　 를 요구한다. (제2안: 미측안 수락)

9. 미의자의 권리 (합의의사록 제9항)

미측이 제80차회의에서 다음과 같은 미의자의 권리에
관한 우리측 입장을 수락할수 없다고 주장한데 감하여
우리측은 이를 전부수락한다.

(가) 한국의 군법재판을 받지 않는권리 (합의의사록
　　 제 9 (a) 항)

　　 (1) 양측입장

　　　　 (ㄱ) 한국측 : 삭제주장

　　　　 (ㄴ) 미국측 : 미군인, 군속 및 가족을 대한민국
　　　　　　　　　　　 군법회의에 회부하지 아니한다.

(나) 미국정부 대표와 접견하는 권리 (합의의사록 제 9 (b) 항)

　　 (1) 양측입장

　　　　 (ㄱ) 한국측 : 삭제주장

　　　　 (ㄴ) 미국측 : 미국정부 대표의 겁석시의 미의자의
　　　　　　　　　　　 진술은 유죄의 증거로할수 없다.

　　 미측안을 수락하되 "한국법원 규칙이나, 한국의
　　 안전과 상반될시는 미국정부대표는 참석할수 없다"는
　　 것을 추가삽입할 것을 제안한다. (제2안: 미측안 수락)

(다) 미고의 상소권 (합의의사록 제9항의 제2 (a) 세항)

　　 미측은 제80차 회의에서 미고인의 상소권에 관하여
　　 다음과 같은 양해사항을 신설할 것을 요구한바,
　　 이를 수락한다 :

　　　　 "대한민국 법원의 상소제도에 의거 미고는
　　 상급법원에의한 새로운 발견의 근거로서의 새로운
　　 증거 또는 증인을 포함한 증거의 재검증을 요청
　　 할수 있다."

11 - 6

0097

(라) 불리의 변경의 금지에 관한 권리(합의의사록 제9항의 제2 (d) 세항)

  (1) 양측입장

    (ㄱ) 한국측 : 피고인이 상소한 사건과 피고인을 위하여 상소한 사건에 있어서는 원심판결보다 중한형을 선고받지 아니하는 권리.

    (ㄴ) 미국측 : 원심판결의 형보다 중한 형을 선고받지 아니하는 권리.

(마) 검사의 상소권의 제한 (합의의사록 제9항의 제4세항)

  (1) 양측입장

    (ㄱ) 한국측 : 삭제주장

    (ㄴ) 미국측 : 법률의 착오의 경우를 제외하고 검찰로부터 상소당하지 아니하는 권리.

(바) 심판불출두 권리 (합의의사록제9항의제2 (j) 세항)

  (1) 양측입장

    (ㄱ) 한국측 : 피고인이 심판에 출두하거나 자기의 방어에 참여하기에 신체상 또는 정신상 부적당한 때에는 출두연기를 신청할수 있는 권리.

    (ㄴ) 미국측 : 육체적 또는 정신적으로 부적당한 경우의 심판 불출두 권리.

(사) 위법부당한방법으로 수집된 증거의 능력 (합의의사록 제9항의 제3세항)

  (1) 양측입장

    (ㄱ) 한국측 : 고문, 폭행, 협박, 기망 또는 신체구속의 부당한 장기화, 기타의 방법으로 임의로 진술한 것이 아니라고 의심할만한 이유가 있는 자백, 자인, 기타 진술은 유죄의 증거로 할수없다.

11 - 7

0100

106 주한미군지위협정(SOFA) 서명 및 발효 13

(ㄴ) 미국측 : 고문, 폭행, 협박, 기망 또는
신체구속의 부당한 장기화, 기타의
방법으로 임의로 진술한 것이
아니라고 의심할 만한 이유가 있는
자백, 자인, 기타진술과, 고문, 폭행,
협박, 기망 또는 영장없는 불합리한
수사 및 압수의 결과로 수집된
물적증거는 유죄의 증거로할수없다.

10. 토지시설내외 경찰권 (합의의사록 제 10 (a) 항 및
동 10 (b) 항)

(가) 토지시설내

(1) 양측입장

(ㄱ) 한국측 : 1) 미군당국은 미군인, 군속만 체포
할수 있다.

2) 한국당국은 미군당국이 동의하는
경우 및 현행법을 추적하는 경우
모든자를 체포할수 있다.

3) 한국당국은 미국군대 및 군인의
재산에 대하여 압수, 수색 또는
검증을 행하지 않는다. 단, 한국
당국의 요청이 있으면 미군당국
이 이를 행하고 한국당국도 미군
당국의 동의를 얻어행할수 있다.

(ㄴ) 미국측 : 1) 미군당국은 통상 모든 자를 체포
할수 있다.

2) 한국당국은 통상 미국군대 및
군인의 재산에 대하여 압수, 수색
또는 검증을 할수 없다.
단, 미군당국이 동의할때에는 이를
행할수 있다.

11 - 8

0101

0102

(2) 해결방안 : 미측안을 수락하되 다음과 같은 규정을 추가 삽입할것을 제안한다.

"이 규정은 미군당국이 동의한 경우 또는 중대한 죄를 범한 현행법인을 추적하고 있을 경우에 대한민국 당국이 전기토지 및 시설내에서 체포를 행함을 방해하는 것은 아니다. 대한민국 당국이 체포할것을 희망하는 자로서 미군당국의 관할건에 복하지 아니하는 자가 미군이 사용하는 토지 및 시설내에 있을경우에는 미군당국은 대한민국 당국의 요청에 의하여 그러한 자를 체포할것을 약속한다. 미군당국에 의하여 체포된 자로서 한국당국이 신병을 구금할자와 미군대 구성원, 군속 또는 가족이 아닌자는 즉시 대한민국당국에 인도되어야 한다."
(제 2 안 : 미측안 수락)

(나) 토지시설주변
(1) 양측입장
(ㄱ) 한국측 : 1) 미군당국은 정당한 법절차에 따라 시설의 안전에 관한 현행법을 체포할수 있다.
2) 미군당국의 관할건에 복하지 않는자는 즉시 대한민국당국에 인도한다.

(ㄴ) 미국측 : 1) 미군당국은 기수 또는 미수 현행범을 체포할수 있다.
2) 미군인, 군속 또는 가족이 아닌자는 즉시 대한민국당국에 인도한다.

(2) 해결방안 : "한국당국이 신병을 구금할자와 미군인, 군속 또는 가족이 아닌자는 즉시 대한민국당국에 인도한다" 는 것을 삽입할것을 주장한다. (제 2 안 : 미측안 수락)

0103

0104

11. 전쟁발발시의 본조항의 효력 (제 11 항)

    (가) 양측입장

        (ㄱ) 한국측 : 삭제주장

        (ㄴ) 미국측 : 한미상호방위조약 제 2 조가 적용될 전쟁상태의 경우는 형사재판관할건 조항은 즉시 효력이 정지되고 미군당국 은 미군인, 군속 및 그들의 가족에 대하여 전속적 관할건을 행사한다.

    (나) 해결방안 : 미측안 수락.

12. 본협정발효 이전의 범죄(제 12 항)

    (가) 양측입장

        (ㄱ) 한국측 : 규정없음.

        (ㄴ) 미국측 : 본조항의 규정은 협정발효이전에 발생한 범죄의 적용되지 아니하며 그러한 범죄 는 대전협정의 규정이 적용된다.

    (나) 해결방안 : 미측안 수락.

13. 미군을 제외한 유엔군인에 대한 효력 (합의의사록 서문)

    (가) 양측입장

        (ㄱ) 한국측 : 규정없음.

        (ㄴ) 미국측 : 본 조항의 규정은 미군대 이외의 유엔 군인에 대한 관할건 행사에 관한 기존 협정, 약정 또는 관행에는 미치지 아니 한다.

    (나) 해결방안 : 미측안 수락.

14. 군계약자에 대한 형사재판관할건 (군계약자 조항제 8 항)

    (가) 양측입장

        (ㄱ) 한국측 : 1) 한국당국은 한국내에서 행한 범죄로서 한국법에 의하여 처벌될수 있는 범죄 에 관하여 군계약자 및 그들의 가족 에 대한 제 1 차관할건을 갖는다.

11 - 10

0106

2) 만약 한국당국이 그의관할권을 행사
않기로 결정하는 경우에는 미군당국에
통고하여야 하며 미군당국은 통고접수후
미국법에 따라 부여된 관할권을 행사한다.

(ㄴ) 미국측 : 군계약자 및 그들의 가족은 미군속 및
그들의 가족에 관한 형사재판관할권
조항의 관계 규정에 복하여야 한다.

(나) 해결방안 : 우리측안 계속주장. (~~우의측안 미측안 수락~~)

15. 미군표 관계 범법자의 처벌 (군표조항 1 (b) 항)

(가) 양측입장

(ㄱ) 한국측 : 미국당국은 허가되지 아니한 자에게
미군표를 제공한 미군인, 군속 및
그들의 가족을 체모 처벌한다.

(ㄴ) 미국측 : 미국당국은 허가되지 아니한 자에게
미군표를 제공한 미군인, 군속 및
그들의 가족을 미국법이 규정하는
바에 따라 체모 처벌한다.

(나) 해결방안 : 미측안 수락.

한·미국 간의 상호방위조약 제4조에 의한 시설과 구역 및 한국에서의 미국군대의 지위에 관한 협정(SOFA) 113
전59권. 1966.7.9 서울에서 서명 : 1967.2.9 발효(조약 232호) (V.33 실무교섭회의, 제81차, 1965.6.7)

8121 (handwritten)

RATIFICATION OF AGREEMENT

1. This Agreement shall enter into force thirty days after
   the date of a written notification from the Government
   of the Republic of Korea to the Government of the United
   States that it has approved the Agreement in accordance
   with its legal procedures.

2. The Government of the Republic of Korea shall undertake
   to seek from its legislature all legislative and
   budgetary action necessary to give effect to its provisions of this agreement.

3. Subject to the provisions of Article XII, Paragraph 12,
   this agreement shall, upon its entry into force, supersede
   and replace the agreement between the Government of the
   United States and the Government of the Republic of Korea
   on jurisdictional matters, effected by an exchange of
   notes at Taejon on July 12, 1950. 大田協定에서 關係

4. The provisions of the present Agreement shall apply to
   the United States armed forces, their members, civilian
   component, invited contractors or dependents thereof,

- 1 -

0108

while in the Republic of Korea pursuant to the resolution of the United Nations Security Council or pursuant to the Mutual Defense Treaty. Such provisions will not, however, apply to members of the United States armed forces for whom status is provided in the Agreement for the Establishment of the United States Military Advisory Group to the Republic of Korea, signed on January 26, 1950 and personnel of the United States armed forces attached to the Embassy of the United States.

LABOR ARTICLE

(Underlining indicates modifications from
the U.S. draft tabled at 80th session.)

1. (b) ... Such civilian personnel shall be nationals of the Republic of Korea.

3. To the extent not inconsistent with the provisions of this Article or except as may otherwise be mutually agreed, the conditions of employment, compensation, and labor-management relations established by the United States Armed Forces for their employees shall conform with provisions of labor legislation of the Republic of Korea.

4. (a)(5) ...... to the Joint Committee, as stipulated in subparagraph (2) above.

5. (b)....... United States Armed Forces and through mutual consultation, upon

Agreed Minutes

4. When employers cannot conform with provisions of labor legislation of the Republic of Korea applicable under Paragraph 3 on account of the military requirements of the United States Armed Forces, the matter shall be referred, in

- 1 -

0110

advance whenever possible, to the Joint Committee for mutual agreement.

5. A union or other employee group shall be recognized unless its objectives are inimical to the common interests of the United States and the Republic of Korea. Membership or non-membership in such group shall not be a factor in employment or other actions affecting employees.

- 2 -

0111

CLAIMS ARTICLE

Para. 5(e)(iii)

Every half year, a statement of the sums paid by the Republic of Korea in the course of the half-yearly period in respect of every case regarding which the liability, amount, and proposed distribution on a percentage basis has been approved by both governments shall be sent to the appropriate authorities of the United States, together with a request for reimbursement. Such reimbursement shall be made in won within the shortest possible time. <u>The approval by both governments as referred to in this subparagraph shall not prejudice any decision taken by the arbitrator or adjudication by a competent tribunal of the Republic of Korea as set forth in paragraphs 2(c) and 5(c) respectively.</u>

Para. 12

(UNDERSTANDING)

The status of the KSC members will be determined by other negotiations between the Republic of Korea and the United States.

Para. A2 of the Agreed Minute

The provisions of paragraphs five, six, seven and eight will be extended, at the earliest date practicable, to other areas of the Republic of Korea as determined by the Joint Committee.

0112

181번

FACILITIES AND AREAS
(ARTICLE IV)

(To be presented at 81st session)

Agreed Minute #2

All removable facilities, equipment and material
or portions thereof provided by the Republic of Korea
under this Agreement and located within the areas and
facilities referred to in this Article shall be returned
to the Republic of Korea whenever they are no longer
needed for the purpose of this Agreement.

0113

Agreed Minute Re Paragraph 3(b)

Revised Paragraph 1

1. At the request of the United States, the Government of the Republic of Korea waives in favor of the United States the primary right granted to the Korean authorities under sub-paragraph (b) of Paragraph 3 of this Article in cases of concurrent jurisdiction, in accordance with Paragraphs 2,3,4,5,6 and 7 of this Minute.

Revised Paragraph 4

4. If, pursuant to Paragraph 3 of this Minute, the competent Korean authorities have recalled the waiver in a specific case and in such case an understanding cannot be reached in discussions between the authorities concerned, the Government of the United States may make representations to the Government of the Republic of Korea through diplomatic channels. The Government of the Republic of Korea, giving due consideration to the interests of Korean administration of justice and to the interests of the Government of the United States, shall resolve the disagreement in the exercise of its authority in the field of foreign affairs. The recall of waiver shall be final and conclusive unless the statement for recall referred to in Paragraph 3 of this

- 1 -

0114

<u>Minute is withdrawn by the Government of the Republic</u>
<u>of Korea through consultation between both Governments.</u>

<u>Paragraph 6</u>

6. Trials of cases in which the authorities of
the Republic of Korea waive the primary right to
exercise jurisdiction, and trials of cases involving
offenses described in paragraph 3(a) (ii) committed
against the State or nationals of the Republic of Korea
<u>shall</u> be held <u>promptly in the Republic of Korea</u> within
a reasonable distance from the place where the offenses
are alleged to have taken place unless other arrangements are mutually agreed upon. Representatives of the
Republic of Korea may be present at such trials.
(U.S. draft proposed at the 67th meeting)

- 2 -

한·미국 간의 상호방위조약 제4조에 의한 시설과 구역 및 한국에서의 미국군대의 지위에 관한 협정(SOFA)
전59권. 1966.7.9 서울에서 서명 : 1967.2.9 발효(조약 232호) (V.33 실무교섭회의, 제81차, 1965.6.7) 121

proceedings and until custody is requested by the authorities of the Republic of Korea. If he is in the hands of the Republic of Korea, he shall be promptly handed over to the authorities of the United States and remain in their custody pending completion of all judicial proceedings and until custody is requested by the authorities of the Republic of Korea. When an accused has been in the custody of the military authorities of the United States, they shall give sympathetic consideration to any request for the transfer of custody which may be made by the authorities of the Republic of Korea in specific cases. The United States authorities will make any such accused available to the authorities of the Republic of Korea upon their request for purposes of investigation and trial. The authorities of the Republic of Korea shall give sympathetic consideration to a request from the authorities of the United States for assistance in maintaining custody of an accused member of the United States armed forces, the civilian component, or a dependent.

(d) In respect of offenses solely against the security of the Republic of Korea provided in Paragraph 2(c), an accused shall be in the custody of the authorities of the Republic of Korea. (Subject US-ROK agreement on two understandings.)

~17~

0116

Paragraph 5(d)

An accused member of the United States Armed Forces
or civilian component over whom the Republic of Korea is
to exercise jurisdiction will, if he is in the hand of the
United States, be under the custody of the United States
during all judicial proceedings and until custody is requested
by the authorities of the Republic of Korea.

The military authorities of the United States may
transfer custody to the Korean authorities at any time and shall
give sympathetic consideration to any request for the transfer
of custody which may be made by the Korean authorities in
specific cases.

Paragraph 5(e)

In respect of offenses solely against the security
of the Republic of Korea provided in Paragraph 2(c), custody
shall remain with the authorities of the Republic of Korea.

0117

Agreed Minute

Re Paragraph 3(a) (ii)

Where a member of the United States armed forces or civilian component is charged with an offense, a certificate issued by a staff judge advocate on behalf of his commanding officer stating that the alleged offense, if committed by him, arose out of an act or omission done in the performance of official duty, shall be sufficient evidence of the fact for the purpose of determining primary jurisdiction, unless the contrary is proved.

If the chief prosecutor of the Republic of Korea considers that there is proof contrary to the certificate of official duty, he will refer the matter to the Joint Committee for decision.

The above statements shall not be interpreted to prejudice in any way Article 308 of the Korean Code of Criminal Procedure.

0118

Agreed Minute

Re Paragraph 3(c)

The authorities of the Republic of Korea will, upon the notification of individual cases falling under the waiver provided in Article ____ paragraph 3(c) from the military authorities of the United States, waive its primary right to exercise jurisdiction under Article ____ except where they determine that it is of particular importance that jurisdiction be exercised by the authorities of the Republic of Korea.

0119

5. (a) The <u>military</u> authorities of the United States and the authorities of the Republic of Korea shall assist each other in the arrest of members of the United States armed forces, the civilian component, or their dependents in the territory of the Republic of Korea and in handing them over to the authority which is to have custody in accordance with the following provisions.

(b) The authorities of the Republic of Korea shall notify promptly the <u>military</u> authorities of the United States of the arrest of any member of the United States armed forces, or civilian component, or a dependent. The military authorities of the United States shall promptly notify the authorities of the Republic of Korea of the arrest of a member of the United States armed forces, the civilian component, or a dependent in any case in which the Republic of Korea has the primary right to exercise jurisdiction.

(c) The custody of an accused member of the United States armed forces or civilian component, or of a dependent, over whom the Republic of Korea is to exercise jurisdiction shall, if he is in the hands of the <u>military authorities</u> of the United States, remain with the <u>military authorities</u>

- 1 -

0120 .

of the United States pending the conclusion of all judicial proceedings and until custody is requested by the authorities of the Republic of Korea. If he is in the hands of the Republic of Korea, he shall, on request, be handed over to the military authorities of the United States and remain in their custody pending completion of all judicial proceedings and until custody is requested by the authorities of the Republic of Korea. When an accused has been in the custody of the military authorities of the United States, the military authorities of the United States may transfer custody to the authorities of the Republic of Korea at any time, and shall give sympathetic consideration to any request for the transfer of custody which may be made by the authorities of the Republic of Korea in specific cases. The military authorities of the United States shall promptly make any such accused available to the authorities of the Republic of Korea upon their request for purposes of investigation and trial, and shall take all appropriate measures to that end and to prevent any prejudice to the course of justice. They shall take full account of any special request regarding custody made by the authorities of the the Republic of Korea. The authorities of the Republic of Korea shall give sympathetic consideration

- 2 -

0121

to a request from the military authorities of the United
States for assistance in maintaining custody of an accused
member of the United States armed forces, the civilian
component, or a dependent.

(d) In respect of offenses solely against the secur
of the Republic of Korea provided in Paragraph 2(c),
an accused shall be in the custody of the authorities
of the Republic of Korea.

- 3 -

0122

LABOR ARTICLE

(Underlining indicates modifications from
the U.S. draft tabled at 80th session)

1. (b) ... Such civilian personnel shall be nationals
of the Republic of Korea.

3. To the extent not inconsistent with the provisions
of this Article or the military requirements of the
United States Armed Forces, the conditions of employment,
compensation, and labor-management relations established
by the United States Armed Forces for their employees
shall conform with provisions of labor legislation
of the Republic of Korea.

4. (a)(5) ..... to the Joint Committee, as stipulated
in subparagraph (2) above.

5. (b) .... be deferred through mutual consultation,
from Republic of Korea ....

Agreed Minutes

4. When employers cannot conform with provisions of
labor legislation of the Republic of Korea applicable
under Paragraph 3 on account of the military requirements
of the United States Armed Forces, the matter shall be
referred, in advance whenever possible, to the Joint
Committee for mutual agreement.

0123

17-16

5. A union or other employee group shall be recognized unless its objectives are inimical to the common interests of the United States and the Republic of Korea. Membership or non-membership in such group shall not be a factor in employment or other actions affecting employees.

17-17

0124

LABOR ARTICLE

(Underlining indicates modifications from the U.S.
draft tabled at 80th session)

1. (b) .... <u>Such civilian personnel shall be nationals
of the Republic of Korea</u>.

3. To the extent not inconsistent with the provisions
of this Article or <u>except as may otherwise be mutually
agreed</u>, the conditions of employment, compensation, and
labor-management <u>relations</u> established by the United
States Armed Forces for their employees <u>shall conform
with provisions of labor legislation</u> of the Republic of
Korea.

4. (a) .... employees or <u>any employee organization</u> ....

(4) Failure of <u>any employee organization</u> ...... for the
withdrawal of <u>consultation right</u> of that organization .....

(5) .... to the Joint Committee, as stipulated in
subparagraph (<u>2</u>) above.

5. (b) .... hostilities <u>is</u> imminent, or ....
United States Armed Forces and <u>through mutual consultation</u>,
~~....~~ ....

5. (c) .... hostilities <u>is</u> imminent ....

<u>Agreed Minutes</u>

4. When employers cannot conform with provisions of labor
legislation <u>of the Republic of Korea</u> applicable under
<u>Paragraph 3</u> on account of the military requirements of
the United States Armed Forces, the matter shall be
<u>referred, in advance whenever possible</u>, to the Joint
Committee <u>for mutual agreement</u>.

34-1

0125

5. A union or other employee group shall be disorganized unless its objectives are inimical to the common interests of the United States and the Republic of Korea. Membership or non-membership in such group shall not a factor in employment or other actions affecting employees.

0126

1. The Korean negotiators have carefully considered the U.S. draft tabled at the previous session with a view to early conclusion of this Agreement. Now, we are going to make most significant concessions to meet satisfaction of the U.S. side to the maximum extent possible taking into account of the principles agreed upon at Washington between the leaders of both sides.

2. The Korean negotiators are now happy to state that the Korean side accepts most of the U.S. proposals with minor changes of wordings and with certain understandings, which are at least essential on the part of Korean side. Accepted portions of U.S. draft are to cover Paragraphs 1 (a) and (b), 2, 4 (a), (b), and (c), and 5 (b) and Agreed Minutes 2 and 5. Putting aside the already agreed paragraphs 5 (a) and 6 and Agreed Minutes #1 and #3, there remains only one paragraph 3 together with its related Agreed Minute #4, to which the Korean side maintains it imperative to be adopted along the lines of Korean formula. Now, we turn back to discuss the Article on paragraph by paragraph basis.

3. <u>Paragraph 1</u>

The Korean side accepts the U.S. version as appeared in (a) and (b) with certain understandings. As for the invited contractors, "this provisions shall apply to those invited contractors who are operating in Korea under the provisions of paragraph 2 of contractors article." With regard to the Korean Service Corps, "our acceptance to exclude them from this Article does not imply in any way that the Korean Government has conceded to affecting their rights and protection which are normally accorded to Korean laborers under the relevant provisions of Korean labor legislation." The insertion of the second sentence is still maintained in conformity with an agreed understanding made in respect of the contractors article.

0127

4. Paragraph 2

We accept the U.S. vision without change.

5. Paragraph 3 and Agreed Minute #4

This is the only one paragraph the Korean side strongly asks the U.S. side to accept the Korean formula under which deviation from our law shall be referred to Joint Committee for mutual agreement. As an evidence of concession we incorporated the U.S. phrase "ehenever possible" in Agreed Minute #4, by which the Korean version meets all but substantial requirements of U.S. side. We deleted the word "Government" after the labor legislation, because it is not proper. We inserted the phrase "under para. 3" in place of "under this article," because the latter implies, dual deviations from already agreed provisions which are unnecessary.

6. Paragraph 4(a)

We have already stated our acceptance of paragraph 4(b) and (c). As is shown in our draft, we accept in full U.S. version from first sentence down to sub-paragraph 5, except a phrase "sub-para (2)" in place of sub-para. (3). Our substantial difference is concerned with the starting date of cooling-off period. Our draft provides that the cooling-off period shall be for 70 days after the dispute is referred to the Joint Committee mentioned in sub-para. (2). Additionally, attention is drawn to the word "recognized" in first sentence and in sub-para. (5). Inclusion of this word stands upon U.S. acceptance of revised Korean version of Agreed Minute #5. We understand accordingly, that the "recognized employee organization" referred to in this paragraph means a labor union or other employee group, except that which is not recognized pursuant to the provisions of Agreed Minute #5 or para. 4(a)(5).

34-4

0128

7. Paragraph 5(b)

Both sides agreed on sub-paragraph (a). As for (b),
we accept the U.S. word "shall" in place of "will." Nevertheless, the Korean side maintains the phrase "through mutual
agreement", to which the U.S. side might have no objection.

8. Agreed Minute #2

We have reiterated the unnecessity of the second
sentence in many occasions in the past. Employers can
terminate legally employment at any time in accordance
with our relevant legislation whenever they have justifiable
reasons. Termination of Employment on account of the military
requirement is a matter of thing which shall be subject to
the paragraph 3 and Agreed Minute #4. However, taking into
consideration of the U.S. insistence on insertion of this
sentence, we now accept it with an understanding that "the
termination of employment on account of the U.S. military
requirements referred to in the second sentence of Agreed
Minute #2 shall be referred to the Joint Committee for
mutual agreement, as in the case of Agreed Minute #4, but
except in such cases of the termination as may be legally
made in accordance with the relevant provisions of labor
legislation of the Republic of Korea."

9. Agreed Minute #5

The Korean side believes that the provision of the
phrase "inimical to the interests of the United States"
in the U.S. draft is not intended to imply them in terms of
economic nature--wages, compensations or such other payments
and treatment of employees in relation to their rights and
protection, but rather in terms of political nature--
leadership of the labor groups dominated or influenced by

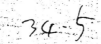

한·미국 간의 상호방위조약 제4조에 의한 시설과 구역 및 한국에서의 미국군대의 지위에 관한 협정(SOFA)
전59권. 1966.7.9 서울에서 서명 : 1967.2.9 발효(조약 232호) (V.33 실무교섭회의, 제81차, 1965.6.7)   135

communists elements. That is also inimical to the interests of the Republic of Korea. Therefore, our draft provides "common interests," to which, we convince, the U.S. side has no objection and which would meet with what the U.S. side intended to.

10. In conclusion, our draft shows itself our earnest evidence of concession to the maximum extent possible. We have tried our best to make least modifications over the U.S. draft. Therefore, the Korean side hopes that the U.S. side will find it possible to accept our new proposals with a view to early conclusion of the long-pending Agreement.

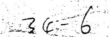

0130

(Underlining indicates modifications from the U.S.
draft tabled at 80th session)

1. (b) .... <u>Such civilian personnel shall be nationals</u>
<u>of the Republic of Korea</u>.

3. To the extent not inconsistent with the provisions
of this Article or <u>except as may otherwise be mutually</u>
<u>agreed</u>, the conditions of employment, compensation, and
labor-management <u>relations</u> established by the United
States Armed Forces for their employees <u>shall conform</u>
<u>with provisions of labor legislation</u> of the Republic
of Korea.

4. (a) (5) ..... to the Joint Committee, as stipulated
in <u>sub-paragraph (2) above</u>.

5. (b) In the event of a national emergency, such as
war or hostilities, or situations where war or hostilities
may be imminent, employees who have acquired skills
essential to the mission of the United States Armed
Forces shall, upon request of the United States Armed
Forces <u>and through mutual agreement</u>, be deferred from
Republic of Korea military service or other compulsory
service.

<u>Agreed Minutes</u>

4. When employers cannot conform with provisions of
labor legislation <u>of the Republic of Korea</u> applicable
under <u>Paragraph 3</u> on account of the military requirements
of the United States Armed Forces, the matter shall be
<u>referred</u>, in advance whenever possible, to the Joint
Committee <u>for mutual agreement</u>.

34-7

0131

5. A union or other employee group shall be recognized
unless its objectives are inimical to the common
interests of the United States and the Republic of Korea.
Membership or non-membership in such group shall not a
factor in employment or other actions affecting employees.

34-8

0132

(To be presented at the 81st session)

1. The Korean negotiators have carefully considered the U.S. draft
tabled at the previous session with a view to early conclusion of the
Agreement. Now, we are going to make greater concessions to meet
the U.S. satisfaction to the maximum extent possible taking into account
of the principles agreed at Washington between the leaders of both sides.

2. The Korean negotiators are now happy to announce that the Korean
side accepts most of the U.S. proposals with minor changes of wordings
or with certain understandings which are at least essential on the part
of Korean side. Accepted portions of U.S. draft cover the paragraphs
1(a) and (b), 2, 4(a),(b) and (c), and 5(b) and the Agreed Minutes 2 and
5. Putting aside the already agreed paragraphs 5(a) and 6 and Agreed
Minutes #1 and 3, there remains only one paragraph 3 together with
the Agreed Minute #4, to which the Korean side maintains them imperative
to be adopted along the lines of Korean version. Now, we turn back
to discuss the Article on paragraph by paragraph basis.

3. Paragraph 1

The Korean side accepts the U.S. versions as appeared in (a) and
(b) with certain understandings. As for the invited contractors, "this
provisions shall apply to those invited contractors who are operating
in Korea under contracts with the United States Armed Forces at the
time of coming into force of this Agreement and such others who thereafter
come into Korea as may be determined by the Joint Committee." With
regard to the Korean Service Corps, "our acceptance to exclude them
from this Article does not imply in any way that the Korean Government
has conceded to affecting their rights and protection which are normally
accorded to Korean laborers under the relevant provisions of Korean
labor legislation." The insertion of the second sentence is still
necessary on our part and we believe the U.S. side has no objection to this.

4. Paragraph 2

We accept the U.S. phrase "insofar as is practicable", while we maintain the word "shall" has to be replaced in lieu of "will".

5. Paragraph 3 and Agreed Minute #4

This is the only one paragraph the Korean side strongly asks the U.S. side to accept the Korean version. In asserting the Korean version, we incorporated, as a concession, the U.S. phrase "whenever possible" in Agreed Minute #4, by which the Korean version meets all but substantial requirements of U.S. side. We do not think it necessary to repeat our reasoning on this paragraph, since we have done so in full length in the past.

6. Paragraph 4

As we have already stated our acceptance of paragraph 4 (b) and (c), we would like to concentrate our deliberation on paragraph 4(a) regarding the dispute settlement procedures. As is shown in our draft, we accept in full U.S. version from first sentence down to sub-paragraph 3. Our substantial difference is concerned with the starting date of cooling-off period. Our draft provides that the cooling-off period shall be for 70 days after the dispute is referred to the Joint Committee mentioned in sub-para. (2). Additionally, attention is drawn to the word "recognized" in first sentence and in sub-para. (5). Inclusion of this word stands upon U.S. acceptance of revised Korean version of Agreed Minute #5. We understand accordingly, that the "recognized employee organization" referred to in the paragraph (a) means a labor union or other employee group, except that which is not recognized pursuant to the provisions of Agreed Minute #5 or paragraph 4 (a)(5).

7. Paragraph 5(b)

Both sides agreed on sub-paragraph (a). As for (b), we accept the U.S. word "shall" in place of "will". Nevertheless, the Korean side maintains the phrase "through mutual agreement", to which the U.S. side might have no objection.

34-10

0134

8. Agreed Minute #2

   Now, we accept the second sentence of U.S. draft with an understanding
that "the termination of employment on account of the U.S. military
requirements referr d to in the second sentence of Agreed Minute #2
shall be referred to the Joint Committee for mutual agreement, as in
the case of Agreed Minute #4, but except in such cases of the termination
as may be legally made in accordance with the relevant provisions of
labor legislation of the Republic of Korea."

9. Agreed Minute #5

   The Korean side believes that the provision of the phrase "inimical
to the interests of the United States" in the U.S. draft is not intended
to imply them in terms of economic nature—wages, compensations or
such other payments and treatment of employees in relation to their
rights and protection, but rather in terms of political nature—
leadership of the labor groups dominated or influenced by communists
elements. That is also inimical to the interests of the Republic of
Korea. Therefore, our draft provides "common interests," to which we
convince the U.S. side has no objection and which would meet with what
the U.S. side intended to.

10. In conclusion, our draft shows itself earnest evidence of
concession to the maximum extent possible. We have tried our best to make
least modifications over the U.S. draft. Therefore, the Korean side hopes
that the U.S. side will find it possible to accept our new proposals with
a view to early conclusion of the long-pending Agreement.

36-11

0135

기 안 지

기 안 자	미주과 이근팔	전 화 번 호		공 보	필 요	불필요
	과장	국장	차관	장관		
협 조 서 명	자				보 존 년 한	
기 안 년 월 일	1965. 6. 9.	시 행 년월일		통 제관	정 서	기 장
분류기호 문서번호	의구미 722. 2 —			69		
경 수 참 조	유 신 대 통 령 비 서 실 장		발 신		장 관	
제 목	제 81 차 한·미간 주둔군지위협정 체결 교섭실무자회의 특별보고.					

1965 년 6 월 7일 하오 4시 부터 동 7시 까지 외무부
제 1 회의실에서 개최된 제 81 차 한·미간 주둔군지위협정 체결
교섭실무자회의에서 토의된 문제중 형사재판관할권, 군개약자,
노무조달, 협정의 발효 등 중요문제에 대한 내용을 별첨과 같이
보고합니다.

유 첩: 제 81 차 한·미간 주둔군지위협정 체결교섭실무자회의
특별보고서 1 부.   끝.

공통서식 1—2 (갑)   (16절지)

0136

0137

제 81차 한미간 주둔군지위협정
체결교섭 실무자회의 특별보고

1. 일시   1965년 6월 7일 오후 4시부터 동 7시까지
2. 장소   외무부 제 1 회의실
3. 중요토의사항
    가. 형사재판관할건
        1) 미측제안에 대하여 우리측이 중요수정안을
           제출한 항목
           (1) 제 1 차 관할건의 포기
               한국당국이 행사할 제 1 차 관할건을 일괄적
               으로 미군당국에 협정발효와 동시에 포기하고
               특정한 경우에 포기를 철회하는 것을
               내용으로한 미측의 포기조항을 원칙적으로
               수락하고 실지운영상 불필요한 분쟁을 미연
               에 방지하기 위하여 다음과 같은 규정을
               제 4 항끝에 신설할것을 제안하였음.
               " 대한민국 정부가 상기규정에 의하여
               의견차이를 해결함에 있어서 대한민국이
               관할건을 행사함이 불가피하다고 결정하는
               경우에는 포기의 철회는 확종적이며 확정적이다. "
           (2) 계엄령 선포와 형사재판관할건 조항의 효력.
               미측은 " 대한민국이 계엄령을 선포한 경우
               에는 본조의 규정이 즉시 효력을 정지하고
               미국당국은 계엄령이 해제될때까지 미군인,
               군속 및 가족에 대하여 전속적인 관할건을
               행사한다 " 라고 주장하고 있는바 우리측은
               제 1 차관할건의 포기는 물론 한국의 전속적
               관할건까지도 미국당국이 포기를 요청하면
               호의적 고려를 할것을 수락하였으며 또한

0138

0139

"미군인, 군속 및 가족은 한국의 군법회의
에 회부되지 아니한다"는 미측제안을
수락하였음으로 미측주장이 불필요한 것임을
지적하고 미측제안을 철회할 것을 요구하였음.

(3)공무의 정의

미측은 공무의 정의를 양해사항으로 회의록
에 기록할것을 주장하고 있는바 우리측은
공무의 정의는 실지운영상의 중요한 지침임
으로 합의의사록에 명백히 규정하여야 한다고
주장하였음.

2) 미측원안대로 수락하는 항목

(1) 미군당국의 관할권에 복하는 자의 태도 범위

(2) 한국당국의 전속적 관할권의 포기를 요청
하면 한국당국은 호의적 고려.

(3) 전쟁발발시의 형사재판관할권의 효력 정시.

(4) 협정발효이전의 법죄처벌.

(5) 미군과 유엔군과의 기존약정의 존속.

(6) 증인 또는 미고의 법정 소환

(7) 외국인의 국외범에 대하여 한국당국은
관할권 불행사.

(8) 미군인, 군속 및 가족은 한국군법회의에
회부되지 아니함.

(9) 미의자의 권리

3) 약간의 기술적인 수정을 조건으로 미측안을
수락한 항목

(1) 한국의 관할권 행사당국

(2) 한국당국이 언도한 형의 복역중인 사에 대한
미측의 인도요청에 한국당국은 포희적 고려

(3) 미군사용 토지 및 시설내외 경찰권

나. 군계약자에 대한 형사재판관할권 조항의 적용

1) 미측은 군계약자와 그들의 가족도 미군속과
그들의 가족과 동등하게 형사재판관할권 조항의
규정이 적용되어야 한다고 주장하고 있는바
우리측은 군계약자들 관계계약은 수행

0140

0141

하는 일반민간인이며 따라서 미국정부의
고용인인 미군속과는 구별하여야 한다는
입장에서 그들에 대하여서는 우리당국이 제1차
관할권을 행사하여야 한다고 주장하였음.

다. 노동조건의 적용범위

1) 미측은 고용조건에 있어 한국법령은 준수치
   못할 경우 가능한한 사전에 합동위원회에
   보고하여 심의한다는 등에 대하여 우리측은
   가능한한 사전에 상호합의를 위하여 합동위원회
   에 회부되어야 한다고 제의하였음.

2) 미측은 노동조합이 미국의 이익에 배반되는
   경우에는 노동조합을 결정하지 않는다는
   제안에 대하여 우리측은 노동조합은 그목적
   이 미국과 한국의 공동이익에 배반되지 않는한
   승인되어야 한다고 수정제안하였음.

라. 협정의 발효

1) 미측은 한국정부가 국회의 비준동의와 본
   협정시행에 필요한 입법 및 예산조치를 취
   하였음을 미국정부에 통고하고 4개월후 발효
   한다고 제의하였음.
   이에 대하여 우리측은 다음과 같은 개정안을
   제의하였음.
   "본협정은 한국정부가 비준을 미국정부에
   통고하고 30일 이후에 발효한다.
   한국정부는 본협정시행에 필요한 입법 및
   예산조치를 취하도록 한다.
   1952년경제조정에 관한 협정 제5조 13항은
   본협정의 범위내에서 미군인, 군속, 군계약자
   또는 그가족에게는 적용되지 아니한다"

0142

65 5 16

마무 113-5

0143

4. 당부의견

　가. 우리측은 교섭을 단시일내에 타결하기 위하여
　　　다소 문제점이 있음에도 불구하고 미측제안을
　　　대목 수락하였으며 다만 실지운영상 또는 협정의
　　　체제상 중요하다고 착토하는 점에 관하여서는
　　　상기 수정안을 제시한바 있으며 미측교섭자들도
　　　우리측입장의 타당성을 충분히 이해하고 있음.
　　　그러나 우리측제안의 수락여부는 어디까지나 본국
　　　정부의 결정에 달려있다 함.

　나. 우리측은 수정안에 대한 미측회답이 빠르면 금주에
　　　늦으면 내주초에 있을것으로 보며 만약 미측이
　　　우리측 수정안을 수락하는 경우에는 오는 17일에
　　　조인이 가능할 것으로 봄.

0144

0145

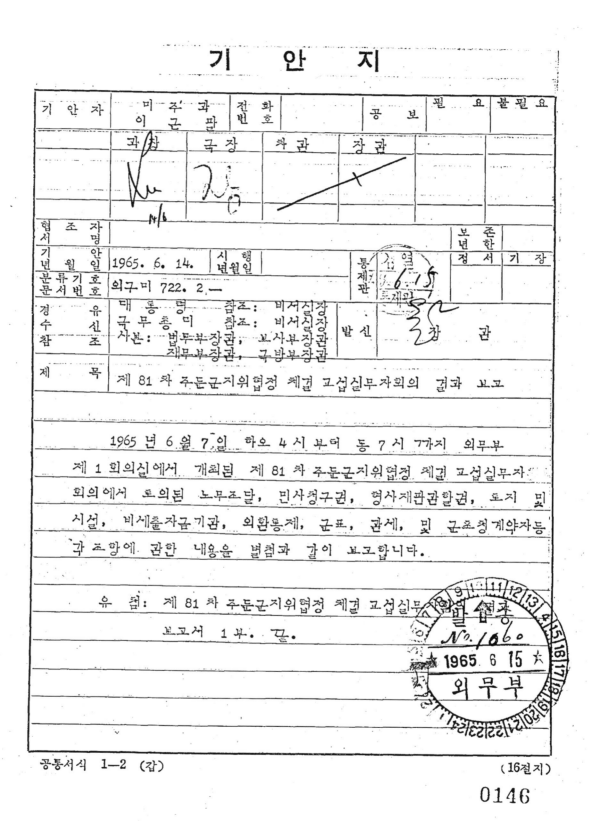

기 안 지

기 안 자	미주과 이근판		전화 번호			공 보		필 요	불필요
	과장	국장	차관	장관					

협 조 자 서 명				보 존 년 한	
기 안 년 월 일	1965. 6. 14.	시 행 년월일	통 제 관	정 서	기 장
분 류 기 호 문 서 번 호	의구미 722. 2 —				
경 유 수 신 참 조	대통령 참조: 비서실장 국무총리 참조: 비서실장 사본: 법무부장관, 보사부장관, 재무부장관, 국방부장관		발신	장 관	
제 목	제 81 차 주둔군지위협정 체결 교섭실무자회의 결과 보고				

1965 년 6 월 7 일 하오 4 시 부터 동 7 시 까지 외무부
제 1 회의실에서 개최된 제 81 차 주둔군지위협정 체결 교섭실무자
회의에서 토의된 노무조달, 민사청구권, 형사재판관할권, 도지 및
시설, 비세출자금기관, 외환통제, 군표, 관세, 및 군조청계약자등
각 조항에 관한 내용을 별첨과 같이 보고합니다.

유 첨: 제 81 차 주둔군지위협정 체결 교섭실무자
보고서 1 부. 끝.

발 합 총
No. 1060
1965. 6. 15
외무부

공통서식 1-2 (갑)   (16절지)

0146

기 안 지

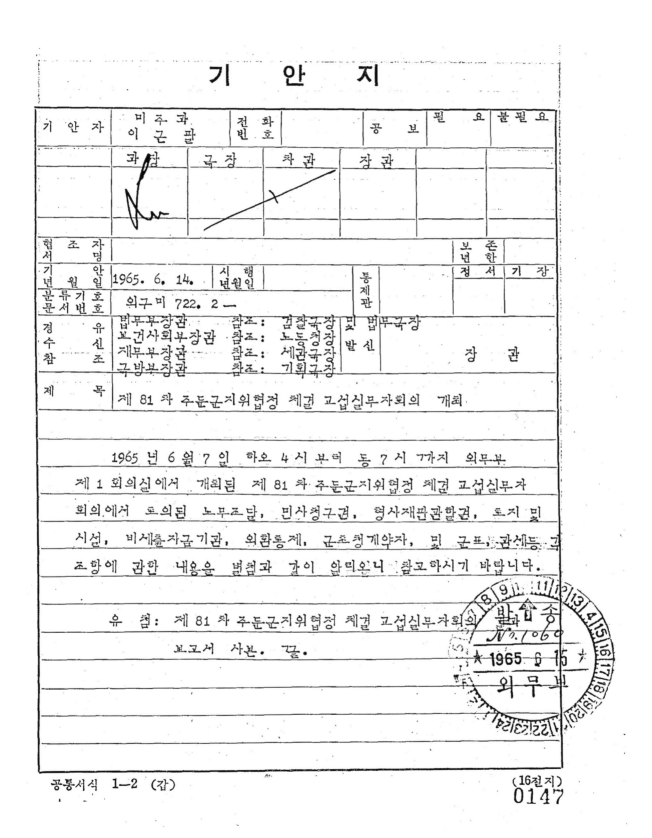

기 안 자	미주과 이근팔	전화번호		공 보		필 요	불필요

	과장	국장	차관	장관			

협조자명서				보존년한	

기안 년월일	1965. 6. 14.	시행년월일		통제관		정서	기장
분류기호 문서번호	외구미 722. 2 —						

경유 수신 참조
법무부장관 　　참조: 검찰국장 및 법무국장
보건사회부장관 　참조: 노동청장　　　발신
재무부장관 　　참조: 세관국장
국방부장관 　　참조: 기획국장 　　　　　　장관

제　목　제 81 차 주둔군지위협정 체결 교섭실무자회의 개최

　　　　1965 년 6 월 7 일 하오 4 시부터 동 7 시 까지 외무부
제 1 회의실에서 개최된 제 81 차 주둔군지위협정 체결 교섭실무자
회의에서 토의된 노무조달, 민사청구권, 형사재판관할권, 토지 및
시설, 비세출자금기관, 외환통제, 군초청계약자, 및 군표, 관세등 각
조항에 관한 내용을 별첨과 같이 알리오니 참고하시기 바랍니다.

　　　　유 첨:　제 81 차 주둔군지위협정 체결 교섭실무자회의
　　　　　　　　보고서 사본. 끝.

공통서식 1—2 (갑)

(16절지)
0147

제 81 차
한 · 미간 주둔군지위협정 체결 고섭실무자회의
보고서

1. 일시   1965 년 6 월 7 일 하오 4 시부터 동 7 시까지
2. 장소   외무부 제 1 회의실
3. 토의사항

　　우리측은 우리정부가 현안인 한 · 미간 협정이 조속
한 시일내에 완전합의에 도달되기를 희망하여 왔음을
지적하고 또한 최근 양국대통령이 화부회담시 협정의
중요문제에 관하여 원칙적인 합의를 본바에 따라
한국정부는 협정전반에 걸친 우리측 입장을 미측에
제시하는 바이라고 밝혔다.

　　첫째로 우리측은 비세출자금기관, 관세, 군묘, 신체
및 재산에 대한 보호조치, 외환통제, 토지시설, 민사청구건,
협정의 유효기간등 각조항에 관하여서는 약간의 기술적인
수정 또는 양해사항의 재택을 조건으로 미측입장을
수락하였으며, 둘째로 형사재판관할권, 노무조달, 군초청
계약자 및 협정의 발효사항등 각조항에 관하여서는
우리정부가 중요하다고 인정하는 수정안을 제기하게
되었음을 밝히고,

　　셋째로 우리나라 국민이나 국회는 협정의 체결
고섭 결과에 대하여 심심한 관심을 표명하고 있으며
이러한 심각한 관심은 국민이나 언론기관이 양국정부에
대하여 비판적인 논평을 가하고 있는 현실을 보아도
쉽사리 이해할수 있을 것이며 이러한 결과는 결코
양국정부에 이로울수 없는 것이니만큼 미국정부는
우리측이 제시하는 한국정부의 입장을 충분히 검토
하여 수락할 것을 촉구하였다:

10 - 1

0148

가. 비세출자금기관

　　비세출자금 기관조항의 본문에는 이미 합의된바 있으며 또한 합의의사록중 비세출자금기관의 사용자의 범위를 규정한 합의의사록 (a)항부터 (e)항까지는 합의한바 있음으로 다만 미해결문제로 남아있는 (f)항 즉 한국정부의 명시적 동의가 있을 경우 사용할수 있는자의 범위에 관하여 우리측은 다음과 같은 양해사항의 채택을 조건으로 미측 입장을 수락하였다:

　　"현재 비세출자금기관을 사용하고 있는 자중 (a)항부터 (e)항까지에 해당하는 기관 또는 개인을 제외한 자의 비세출자금기관 사용은 협정 발효와 동시에 그사용이 정지되어야 하며 (f)항에서 비세출자금기관의 사용이 허용될 기관 또는 개인의 범위는 양국정부 관계당국간의 장차의 교섭에서 결정된다."

나. 관세

　　비세출자금기관의 사용자의 범위에 관한 합의의사록에 완전합의를 봄에 따라 양측은 관세조항의 미군 "코미사리" 사용자의 범위에 관한 관세조항의 합의의사록 제7항에서도 합의를 보게됨으로서 양측은 관세조항에서 완전합의를 보았다.

다. 외환통제

　　상금 해결을 보지 못하고 있던 미측합의의사록의 "대한민국에서 불법적이 아닌 최고환율"을 미군이 원화를 구입함에 있어서 적용할것을 수락함으로서 외환통제조항에서도 완전 합의에 도달하였다.

라. 미군표

　　우리측은 미측 요구대로 "미국당국은 허가되지 아니한 자에게 미군표를 제공한 미군인, 군속 및 그들의 가족을 미국법이 규정하는 바에 따라 체모 처벌한다"는 규정을 수락하고 또한 현재 한국수정에 있는 군표의 처분이나 또는 보상문제는 양국정부가 적당한 경로를

10 - 2

0150

0151

통하여 언제던지 고섭을 할수 있으며 양국정부의 입장
에 변함이 없음"을 상기시키고 본 조항에 완전합의를
보았다.

마. 미군대, 군인, 군속, 단초청계약자 및 그들의 가족에
    대한 신체 및 재산에 대한 보호조치

미군대재산 또는 군인, 군속, 및 그들의 가족의
재산 또는 신체에 대한 보호조치에 관한 미측 원안을
수락하고 다음과 같은 미측 양해사항을 회의록에 넣을
것을 수락함으로서 본조항에 완전합의를 보았다:

"본 조항하에서 상호 협조함에 있어서 양국정부는
미국군대, 군인, 군속, 군계약자 및 그들의 가족과 재산의
안전과 보호를 위하여 필요한 조치를 치할것에 합의한다."

바. 협정의 유효기한

미측이 80차회의시 제안한 원안대로 "한.미
상호방위조약이 존속하는한 본 협정은 유효하다"는
것을 수락하였다.

사. 토지시설의 반환

(1) 미측은 미국이 토지.시설을 반환함에 있어서
토지시설이 제공될때와 동일한 상태로 복구할 책임이
없고 한국은 미국이 토지시설사용후 개선한 것에 대하여
보상할 책임을 지지하니한다고 주장하여 왔으며 또한
우리측은 그러한 토지시설중 사유재산으로서 극심하게
손실을 입은 경우에는 미국이 보상할 것을 요구하여
왔으나 그주장을 철회하고 미측안을 수락하였다.

(2) 미측은 미국이 토지시설 사용중 반입한 동산은
토지시설 반환시 미국의 재산으로 간주하여 미국이
반출할수 있어야 한다고 주장하고 있는바 우리측은 상기
미측이 주장을 수락하고 그대신 한국이 제공한 토지시설
중에 있는 한국의 동산도 불밀요시에는 한국측에 반환
할것을 규정하는 합의의사록의 삽입을 제의하였다.

10 - 3

0152

0153

(3) 토지시설의 사용료 및 유지비

　　　　미측은 토지시설의 유지비는 미측이 부담하고
사용료는 국유이건 사유이건 한국정부가 부담할 것을
주장하여 왔으며 이에 대하여 우리측은 사유재산만은
사용료의 보상을 미국이 부담할것을 주장하여 상반된
입장에 있었으나 우리측은 미측안을 수락함으로서 미군이
사용하는 사유재산에 대한 모든 보상 요구를 철회하였다.

　아. 민사청구건

　　　　제 80 차회의시의 미측 제안에 대하여 우리측은
다음과 같은 최종안을 제안하고 미국측이 이를 수락할
것을 촉구하였다.

　　　　(1) 공무집행중 정부재산 및 제3자에 대한 손해의
경우 양국정부의 분담비율을 미국안대로 25 퍼센트 -
75 퍼센트로 할것을 수락하였다.

　　　　(2) 미국측이 제안한 5 (e) (iii)항이 미측안 5 (c)
항의 내용과 상충되는 점을 제거하기 위하여 미측
5 (e) (iii)항에 " 중재인의 결정 및 재판의 만결은
양당사국을 구속한다 " 는 규정을 추가삽입할 것을
제의하였다.

　　　　(3) KSC 에 관한 양해사항중 " KSC 는 본조의
규정이 적용되지 않는다 " 라는 부분을 삭제할 것을
제의하였다.

　　　　(4) 제 5,6,7 및 8항의 적용시기에 관한 미국측의
제안을 " 합동위원회의 결의에 따라 가급적 빠른 시일
내에 기타 지역에 적용한다 " 라고 수정할 것을 제안
하였다.

　자. 형사재판관할권

　　　　우리측은 다음과 같이 미측제안을 대체적으로
수락하는 한면 우리가 필요로 하는 몇가지 점에 대하여
수정안을 제출하고 우리측 제안을 조속한 시일내에 수락
할것을 촉구하였다:

10 - 4

0154

65-5-16

0155

(1) 미측안 대로 수락한 항목:

   (가) 미군당국의 관할권에 복하는 자의 범위
      (제 1 (a) 항)

   (나) 한국당국의 전속적 관할권의 포기를 요청
      하면 한국당국은 호의적 고려를 한다
      (합의의사록 제 2 항)

   (다) 전쟁발발시의 형사재판관할권의 효력정지
      (제 11 항)

   (라) 협정발효이전의 형사재판관할권의 효력
      효력 (제 12 항)

   (마) 미군과 유엔군간의 기존약정의 존속
      (합의의사록 서문)

   (바) 증인 또는 피고인의 법정 소환 (합의의사록
      제 6 항)

   (사) 한국영역외 법회 (합의의사록 제 1 (b) (2) 항)

   (아) 미군인, 군속 및 가족은 한국군법회의에
      회부되지 아니한다. (합의의사록 제 9 (a) 항)

   (자) 합의의사록 제 9 (g) 항을 제외한 만의작약권리
      전부 (합의의사록 제 9 항)

(2) 미측안의 삭제 또는 수정을 제안한 항목:

   (가) 제 1 차 관할권의 포기 (합의의사록 제 3 (b) 항)

      (ㄱ) 한국당국이 행사할 제 1 차 관할권을
         일괄적으로 미군당국에 협정발효와 동시
         에 포기하고 특정한 경우에 포기를
         철회하는 것을 내용으로 한 미측의
         포기조항을 수락하고 우리측이 제 77 차
         회의시 미측 제안 제 1 항 서두에
         추가할것을 주장하였던 "미국이 요청
         하면" 이란 어구의 삽입요구를 철회하였다.

10 - 5

0156

0157

(ㄴ) 한국당국이 포기를 철회하는 경우 실지
운영상의 불필요한 분쟁 또는 의견차이
를 미연에 방지하기 위하여 다음과
같은 규정을 제4항 끝에 신설할 것을
제안하였다 :
    "대한민국정부가 상기규정에 의하여
의견차이를 해결함에 있어서 대한민국이
관할권을 행사함이 불가피하다고 결정
하는 경우에는 포기의 철회는 최종적
이며 확정적이다."

(ㄷ) 한국당국이 포기하는 사건의 재판과
공무집행중 범죄로서 대한민국 또는
대한민국국민에 대한 사건의 재판 장소
및 대한민국대표의 그러한 재판에의
참석에 관한 미측합의의사록 제6항은
미측 원안대로 수락하였다.

(나) 공무집행중 범죄 (합의의사록 제3 (a)항)

(ㄱ) 공무집행증명서 발행권자에 관하여 우리측
이 "증명서는 반드시 미군법무관의
의견을 들은 후에 발행되어야 하며
미군당국의 증명서 발행기관은 장성급
이어야 한다"라는 양해사항을 제안한바
있는데 미측은 제80차회의에서 "또는
그가 지정하는 자"를 추가할 것을
제의하여 온데 대하여 우리측은 미측이
75차회의에서 행한 진술과 그간의
고섭경위로 보아 미측제안은 수락할수
없음을 밝히고 미측이 자진하여 미측의
추가적 어구를 철회할 것을 요구하였다.

10 - 6

0158

기밀 113-4

0159

(ㄷ) 미측은 공무의 정의를 양해사항으로
회의록에록‥ 기록할 것을 주장하고
있는바 우리측은 공무의 정의는 실지
운영상의 중요한 지침임으로 합의의사록
에 명백히 규정하여야 한다고 주장하였다.

(다) 계엄령 선포와 형사재판관할건 조항의 효력
정지 (합의의사록 제 1 (b) (1)항)
미측은 "대한민국이 계엄령을 선포한 경우
에는 본조의 규정이 즉시 정지되고 미국당국
은 계엄령이 해제될때 까지 미군인, 군속
및 그들의 가족에 대하여 전속적인 관할건
을 행사한다" 라고 주장하고 있는바 우리측은
이미 제1차관할건의 포기는 물론 한국의
전속적관할건까지도 미국당국이 포기를 요청
하면 호의적 고려를 할것을 수락하였으며
또한 "미군인, 군속 및 그들의 가족은
한국의 군법회의에 회부되지 아니한다"는
미측제안을 수락한바 있음으로 미측 주장이
불필요한 것임을 지적하고 미측제안을 수락
할수 없다고 말하였다.

(라) 한국측 관할건행사기관 (제 1 (b)항)
미측은 제 80 차회의에서 한국의 관할건
행사기관을 "대한민국민사당국"으로 할것을
계속 주장하였는바 우리측은 한국의 관할건
행사기관을 "대한민국당국"으로 하고 그대신
"미군인, 군속 및 그들의 가족은 한국의
군법회의에 회부되지 아니한다"는 것을
합의의사록으로 수락할 것을 제안하였다.

(마) 한국당국이 언도한 형의집행 (제 7 (b)항)
우리측은 미측이 "미군당국이 신병 인도를
요청하면 한국당국이 호의적 고려를 하여야

10 - 7   0160

5-5-18

미로113-4

0161

하며 신병구금이 미군당국에 인도되었을
경우에는 미군당국은 미국구금시설내에서
구금을 계속할것"을 주장하고 있는바 우리
측은 미측주장을 수락하되 "그러한 경우
미국당국은 미국구금시설에서 한국당국이 언도
한 형을 복역중인자에 관한 관계정보를
정규적으로 한국당국에 제공할 것과 또한
한국정부대표는 그러한 자를 시찰할수 있는
권리를 갖는다"는 것을 추가할것을 요구
하고 만약 미측이 우리측 제안을 거절한다면
우리나라 형법 제72조 및 행형법 제49조
부터 동52조에서 규정된 가속방제도의
혜택이 그들로 부터 박탈될 것이라고 지적
하였다.

카) 피의자의 권리 (합의의사록 제9항)

(가) 미측이 제의한 피의자의 권리중 상금
합의를 보지 못하고 있던 권리중 (ㄱ)
한국의 군법재판을 받지 않는권리, (ㄴ)
피고의 상소권, (ㄷ)불리익 변경 금지에
관한 권리, (ㄹ)검사의 상소권의 제한,
심판불출두의 권리, (ㅁ)위법부당한
방법으로 수집된 증거의 능력에 관한
미측 수정안은 이를 전부 미측주장대로
수락하였다.

(ㄴ) 미국정부대표와 접견하는 권리 (합의
의사록 제9(g)항)
미측은 미국정부대표는 모든 소송절차
진행중 피의자와 접견할수 있어야 하며
미국정부대표의 건석시의 피의자의 진술
은 유죄의 증거로 할수 없다라고 주장
하고 있는바 우리측이 미측제안을 원칙
적으로 수락하는 조건으로 미측이 모기
조항 제6항에서 한국정부대표의 재판

0162

마무1134

0163

참석에 관하여 제안한 바와 동일하게
하기 위하여 "단, 한국법원 규칙이나
한국의 안전으로서 미국의 안전과 상반
되는 경우에는 미국정부대표는 참석할수
없다"는 것을 추가 삽입할 것을 제안
하였다.

(사) 토지시설내외 경찰건 (합의의사록 제 10 (a) 항
및 10 (b) 항)

(ㄱ) 미측 초안을 수락하되 미군당국의 동의
를 얻었을 경우와 중죄를 범한 현행범인
을 추적하는 경우에는 한국당국이 시설
내에서 범인을 체포할수 있어야 하며

(ㄴ) 미군당국이 토지시설내외에서 체포한
차로서 미군인, 군속, 또는 가족이 아닌
자는 즉시 대한민국당국에 인도하여야
한다"는 것을 주장하였다.

차. 군초정계약자에 대한 형사재만관할건 (군계약자조항
제 8 항)

미측은 군계약자와 그들의 가족도 미군속과 그들의
가족과 동등하게 형사재만관할건조항의 규정이 적용되어야
한다고 주장하고 있는바 우리측은 군계약자들이 미군관계
계약을 수행하는 일반민간인이며 따라서 미국정부의
고용인인 미군속과는 구별되어야 한다는 입장에서 그들에
대하여서는 우리당국이 제 1 차적 관할건을 행사하여야
한다고 주장하였다.

카. 노무조항

우리측은 미측이 80 차회의에서 제의한 제안을
토대로 미측의 주장하는 안에 대하여 다음과 같은
수정을 가할것을 제안하였다.

(1) 고용인의 범위

고용인은 대한민국국적을 가진 민간인이어야 한다.

(2) 분쟁해결절차

분쟁이 제 2 단계인 분과위원회에 회부된 날로

0164

0165

부터 가산하여 70일이 경과하지 않는한 고용인은 정상 업무방해 행위를 하지 못한다.

(3) 병역의무 : 미군업무수행에 긴요한 고용인에 대하여 전시에 미군이 요구하면 상호협의하에 병역의무를 연기하여 준다.

(4) 고용조건의 적용범위

고용조건은 한국노동법령을 준수한다. 단, 준수치 못할때는 가능한한 합동위원회에 상호합의를 위하여 회부되어야 한다.

(5) 노동조합의 승인

노동조합은 미국과 한국의 고동이익에 배반되지 않는한 승인되어야 한다.

상기 수정안 이외의 문제는 대체로 미국안을 수락하였다.

타. 협정의 비준과 발효

미측안에 의하면 발효지기가 4개월로 너무 길기 때문에 60일로 단축할것을 제안하고 입법 및 예산조치는 발효후 치할것을 제안하였다. "대전협정"의 무효는 수락하고 소위 "마이야"협정"은 미군, 군속, 초청계약자, 그가족등 본협정의 적용을 받는자는 적용을 정지시킬 것을 제안하였다.

미측은 우리측의 제안에 대하여 충분히 검토할 것이며 본국정부의 훈령을 받는대로 답변할 것이라고 말하고 산회하였다. 끝

10 - 10

0166

0167

STATUS OF FORCES NEGOTIATIONS: 81st Meeting

SUBJECTS:
1. DURATION
2. 1. Security Measures
3. 2. Non-Appropriated Fund Organizations
4. 3. Foreign Exchange Controls
5. 4. Military Payment Certificates
6. 5. Facilities & Areas
7. 6. Claims
8. 7. Labor
9. 8. Ratification
10. 9. Criminal Jurisdiction
11. 10. Invited Contractors

PLACE: Ministry of Foreign Affairs

DATE: June 7, 1965

PARTICIPANTS:

Republic of Korea

CHANG Sang-mun
CHU Mun-ki
HO Sung-chung
YI Nam-ki
HO Hyong-ku
Colonel KIM Won-kil, ROKA
Major YI Ke-hun, ROKA
KIM Ki-cho
HWANG Yong-chae
KIM Tong-hui
PAK Won-chol
YI Kun-pal (Interpreter)

United States

Benjamin A. Fleck
Colonel Allan G. Pixton, USA
Captain George Hagerman, USN
Colonel Kenneth C. Crawford, USA
Frank R. LaMacchia
Robert A. Kinney
Goodwin Shapiro
Major Alton Harvey, USA
David Y.C. Lee (Interpreter)

Lt. Col. C.M. Thompson, USA,   Observer
Ogden Reed, Observer
G. W. Flowers, Observer

0168

1. Mr. Chang opened the meeting *by stating* ~~and said~~ that the Korean negotiators wished to articulate their position at this final stage of negotiations. Mr. Chang said that it has been the desire and intent of the Korean negotiators to reach full agreement and to conclude these long-pending negotiations as soon as possible. Taking cognizance of the different opinions between the two sides, they have exerted their utmost effort to accommodate the requirements of the U.S. negotiators as far as possible.

2. As the U.S. negotiators had stated at the 80th meeting, Mr. Chang continued, the leaders of the two governments, at the recent conference in Washington, had reached agreement in principle on the major outstanding issues of this Agreement. Therefore, it is the belief of the Korean negotiators that both sides should exert their utmost efforts to resolve the remaining differences which have been hindering an early conclusion of the Agreement.

3. Mr. Chang said the Korean negotiators were now prepared to propose their final, comprehensive draft of this Agreement. ~~They accepted the U.S. drafts of~~ With appropriate understandings and minor modifications, they accepted the U.S. drafts of the following articles: Non-Appropriated Fund Organizations, Customs, Military Payment Certificates, Security Measures, Foreign Exchange Controls, Duration of the Agreement, Facilities and Areas, and Civil Claims.

4. However, Mr. Chang continued, after having given their most careful consideration to the rest of the articles (Criminal Jurisdiction, Labor, Invited Contractors, and Ratification of the Agreement), *they* were prepared to accept the U.S. drafts only after incorporating modifications of an important nature. These modifications are essential and imperative to the Government of the Republic of Korea. As had been pointed out by the Korean negotiators at the past discussions, the people and the National Assembly are deeply concerned and critical toward the possible outcome of these negotiations. This concern is clearly indicated in recent criticisms directed at both governments in the columns of the newspapers and voiced by some eminent and responsible citizens. Mr. Chang stated that such embarrassing consequences would be in the interests of neither the host

0169

state nor the sending state. Keeping these facts in mind, Mr. Chang said, the Korean negotiators wished to present their final position on each of the as-yet unagreed upon articles of the SOFA.

Security Measures *article*

5. Mr. Chang recalled that at the 55th meeting the U.S. negotiators had proposed deletion of the phrase "of the persons referred to in this paragraph, and their property" if the Korean negotiators would agree to the inclusion in the Agreed Joint Summary of the following understanding:

> "In cooperating with each other under this Article, the two governments agree that each will take such measures as may be necessary to ensure the security and protection of the U.S. armed forces, the members thereof, the civilian component, the persons who are present in the Republic of Korea pursuant to the Article dealing with Invited Contractors, their dependents and their property."

Mr. Chang said the Korean negotiators accepted the U.S. proposal and the U.S. draft of the Article as tabled at the 80th meeting.

Non-Appropriated Fund Organizations *Article*

6. Mr. Chang noted that the only remaining issue in the Non-Appropriated Fund Organizations Article was the question of who should be granted the use of these organizations under item (f) of the Agreed Minute proposed by the U.S. negotiators. To meet the requirements expressed by the U.S. negotiators, the Korean negotiators were now prepared to accept the Agreed Minute. However, in accepting, the Korean negotiators wished to include in the Agreed Joint Summary the following understanding:

> "It is understood that the present use of Non-Appropriated Fund organizations by organizations and persons other than those referred to in items (a), (b), (c), (d), and (e) shall immediately be suspended at the time of the entry into force of this Agreement. The extent of organizations and persons to be granted the use of such organizations under item (f) of this Minute shall be left to further negotiations between the appropriate authorities of the two Governments."

7. Mr. Chang noted that agreement on the Non-Appropriated Funds Organizations

0170

Article meant automatic agreement on Agreed Minute #7 of the Customs Article. The negotiators had thereby reached full agreement on the latter article as well.

Foreign Exchange Controls *Article*

8. Mr. Chang stated that the Korean negotiators accepted the U.S. draft of the Agreed Minute to the Foreign Exchange Controls Article, thereby reaching full agreement on that article.

Military Payment Certificates *Article*

9. Mr. Chang recalled that at the 55th meeting both sides agreed to delete their respective drafts of an Agreed Minute and to include in the Agreed Joint Summary the following understanding:

> "The ROK and U.S. negotiators agree that nothing in the Status of Forces Agreement in any way prevents the appropriate authorities of either the Republic of Korea or the United States from raising any appropriate matter at any time with each other. The U.S. negotiators recognize the desire of the ROK authorities to discuss the disposal of Military Payment Certificates under custody of the ROK Government. However, both the ROK and U.S. negotiators have agreed to remove from the SOFA text any reference to the question of compensation for Military Payment Certificates held by unauthorized persons. This agreement does not prejudice the position of that either party in connection with discussion of this question through other channels."

10. Mr. Chang noted that the remaining issue to be solved was whether to include the phrase "to the extent authorized by United States Law" proposed by the U.S. negotiators or the phrase "subject to the military law of the United States" proposed by the Korean negotiators. The Korean negotiators, he said, accepted the language of the U.S. draft, thereby reaching complete agreement on this article. However, the Korean negotiators wished to stress that their acceptance was made in the belief that the U.S. authorities would take every measure necessary to prevent abusive transactions of Military Payment Certificates by the persons authorized to use such certificates.

0171

Facilities and Areas *Articles*

11. Mr. Chang recalled that discussion of the article relating to facilities and areas (U.S. draft article IV) had been deferred since the 42nd meeting, held on February 14, 1964. He recalled that there had been a difference in the positions of the two sides over the question of compensation to owners of private property. The Korean negotiators were now prepared to withdraw their previous contention with respect to compensation for privately-owned property extremely demolished ~~imperiatusasafosion~~ as a result of use by the U.S. armed forces. The Korean negotiators accepted the three paragraphs and Agreed Minute of the U.S. draft. However, they wished to propose a second Agreed Minute reading as follows:

> "2. All removable facilities, equipment and material or portions thereof provided by the Republic of Korea under this Agreement and located within the areas and facilities referred to in this Article shall be returned to the Republic of Korea whenever they are no longer needed for the purpose of this Agreement."

12. Mr. Chang ~~xxxx~~ said the additional Agreed Minute was proposed with the same intent as the Agreed Minute already contained in the U.S. draft. The Korean negotiators consider it logical that all removable properties provided by their government and located in any area or facilities should be returned to the owners whenever the properties are no longer needed by the U.S. armed forces. This additional Agreed Minute should present no difficulty ~~xx~~ to the U.S. negotiators. Furthermore, it is also intended to supplement the provisions of Paragraphs 2 and 3 of Article II because those provisions are merely related to the return of the facilities and areas, as a whole or in part, which are no longer needed. Those provisions, therefore, do not refer to removable property located within the areas or facilities.

13. Turning to Article V, relating to cost and maintenance, ~~xxxxxxx~~ Mr. Chang stated that the Korean negotiators were now prepared ~~xx~~ to withdraw their draft regarding compensation to ~~xxxx~~ owners of private property and to accept the U.S. draft following clarification of the language by the U.S. negotiators. Mr. Chang said the

0172

Korean negotiators thought the language of Paragraph 1 was too broad. It spoke of "all expenditures incident to the maintenance of the U.S. Armed forces in the Republic of Korea" rather than expenditures incident to the maintenance of facilities and areas. Since this article was intended to deal with facilities and areas only, why should the language not be more restrictive?

14. Mr. Fleck replied that this language was identical with the language of the similar article in the SOFA with Japan. Therefore, the U.S. negotiators did not understand why the Korean negotiators should object to it, inasmuch as the Korean negotiators had frequently expressed the desire to obtain language in other parts of this agreement which would be identical or similar to the language of the SOFA with Japan. Furthermore, since the language was broader, it gave the ROK Government a broader exemption from maintenance costs. The term "maintenance of the U.S. armed forces" included maintenance of the facilities and areas occupied by those forces. The Korean negotiators, therefore, should have no difficulty in agreeing to this language.

15. Mr. Chang thanked Mr. Fleck for this explanation and said that the Korean negotiators accepted the U.S. draft of the article.

Claims Article

16. Mr. Chang stated that the Korean negotiators, with a view to reaching full agreement, were prepared to accept the revised draft of the Claims Article tabled by the U.S. negotiators at the 80th meeting, subject only to minor modifications.

17. With regard to Paragraph 5(e)(i), the Republic of Korea accepts the standard 25% - 75% distribution ration, as proposed by the U.S.

18. With regard to Paragraph 5(e)(iii), Mr. Chang continued, the Korean negotiators are prepared to withdraw their proposed Agreed Minute if the

0173

U.S. negotiators will agree to modify the subparagraph as follows (proposed changes underlined):

"iii. Every half year, a statement of the sums paid by the Republic of Korea in the course of the half-yearly period in respect of every case regarding which the liability, amount, and proposed distribution on a percentage basis has been approved by both governments shall be sent to the appropriate authorities of the United States, together with a request for reimbursement. Such reimbursement shall be made in won within the shortest possible time. The approval by both governments as referred to in this ~~sum~~ subparagraph shall not prejudice any decision taken by the arbitrator or adjudication by a competent tribunal of the Republic of Korea as set forth in paragraphs 2(c) and 5(c) respectively."

19. Mr. Chang said the proposed modifications are necessary to ~~define~~ clarify the contradictory provisions in the U.S. draft. Paragraph 5(c) of that draft provides that all the payments made by the Korean government, whether made pursuant to a settlement or to an adjudication, shall be binding upon the Parties, whereas Paragraph 5(e)(iii) implies that none of ~~all the~~ the payments made by the Korean government, regardless of whether the payment was made pursuant to a settlement or to an adjudication, shall be binding unless the U.S. authorities approve the payment in advance. Therefore, the Korean negotiators propose the above modifications to Paragraph 5(e)(iii) in order to avoid possible misunderstanding.

20. With regard to Paragraph 12, Mr. Chang said the Korean negotiators would accept the U.S. proposal to delete the final clause and to include an understanding in the Agreed Joint Summary, with a minor modification. The Korean negotiators believe that any decision as to whether claims generated by Korean Service Corps members should or should not come under the provisions of this article cannot be made until the status of the KSC personnel is determined. Therefore, the Korean negotiators propose deletion of the first sentence of the understanding, which would then read as follows:

"The ~~status of the KSC members~~ *The liability for claims generated by KSC personnel* will be determined by other negotiations between the Republic of Korea and the United States."

21. With regard to Paragraph A2 of the Agreed Minute, Mr. Chang said the

Korean negotiators accepted the principle that the effective date of the claims provisions in areas other than that of the Seoul Special City shall be determined by the Joint Committee, as proposed by the U.S. negotiators at the previous session. However, to meet the requirements of both sides, the Korean negotiators ~~mxiomxtxxpxxpxxsxx~~ proposed the following modified draft of Paragraph A2:

> "The provisions of paragraphs five, six, seven, and eight will be extended, at the earliest date practicable, to other areas of the Republic of Korea as determined by the Joint Committee."

22. As the U.S. negotiators were well aware, Mr. Chang continued, the Korean Claims Service has recorded an efficient operation since 1962. The State Compensation Committee is manned with qualified commissioners and investigators who have ample experience in legal affairs. For the equitable settlement of claims, proper laws and regulations are provided. At the present time, the Claims Service is processing and settling the claims arising out of various ~~immigxx~~ cases of damage caused by members of the Korean armed forces as well as by government officials, to the satisfaction of the claimants concerned. This effectiveness of the Korean Claims Service had been demonstrated by the Korean negotiators, Mr. Chang stated, in previous formal and informal negotiating meetings. Therefore, the Korean negotiators ~~xxxx~~ are certain that the Korean Claims Service is capable of assuming all of the claims responsibilities from the date the SOFA ~~gxxxxixt~~ enters into force.

23. Mr. Chang recalled that the U.S. negotiators had agreed to adopt the proposed system ~~xxtxxxixxiixxij~~ in the Seoul Special City area automatically six months after the entry into force of this agreement without any decision of the Joint Committee. This acceptance, in the belief of the Korean negotiators, was nothing but an admission on the part of the U.S. negotiators that the Republic of Korea has a working and efficient claims system, applicable to other parts of the Republic. Moreover, the authority of the Korean State Compensation Committee extends to the entire territory of the Republic of Korea, as does that of the U.S. armed forces Claims Service. The Korean negotiators

0175

                                    ⌜insistence⌝
cannot understand the /~~insistency~~ of the United States that the application of the
                             ^
Korean system be limited to a specific area.

       24. However, to expedite the negotiations and reach full agreement on this
              ⌜at⌝
article ~~in~~ the earliest possible date, the Korean negotiators were making an important
            ^
concession regarding this provision, Mr. Chang continued. The Korean negotiators believe ~~it~~
that the ~~that~~ United States would give due consideration, in the J₀int Committee, to the
capability of the Korean Claims Service, so that the provisions of paragraphs five, six,
seven and eight could be extended to other areas of the Republic of Korea at the earliest
date practicable.

Labor Article

       25. Turning to the Labor Article, Mr. Chang said that the Korean negotiators,
with a view to reaching prompt agreement, were prepared to accept the U.S. draft as a
whole, with modifications of the following provisions: Paragraphs 1(b), 3, 4(a), 5(b),
and Agreed Minutes #4 and #5. Most of the proposed modifications, he pointed out, were
technical in nature rather than substantive and the Korean negotiators believed they
would present no difficulty to the U.S. negotiators since they are all valid and
reasonable.

       26. Paragraph 1 (a) and (b)

       Mr. Chang stated that the Korean negotiators were now prepared to agree to
inclusion of the invited contractors in the provisions of this article, ⌜~~provided the U.S.~~
~~negotiators would accept the understanding proposed by the Korean negotiators with regard~~
~~to the Invited Contractors Article.~~⌝ The Korean negotiators were prepared to accept sub-
                                ⌜if the U.S. negotiators would agree to⌝
paragraph (b) of the U.S. draft ~~with~~ the addition of the following sentence:
                                         ^

              "Such civilian personnel shall be nationals of
              the Republic of Korea."

By accepting the U.S. draft of subparagraph (b), Mr.Chang stated, the Korean negotiators
                  ⌜specific ~~again~~ exclusion⌝
were ~~acceding~~ acceding to the ~~inclusion~~ of KSC personnel and domestics from the definition
                                        ^
of employee. In making this most significant concession, the Korean negotiators wished to

the Agreed Joint Summary to clearly indicate that exclusion of KSC personnel from the definition of employee shall not be construed as a change in the position taken by the Korean negotiators with regard to the status of KSC personnel. ~~Moreover,~~ Moreover, the addition of the second sentence, proposed by the Korean negotiators, with regard to the nationality of employees is considered necessary by the Korean negotiators to minimize the employment of third-country nationals in Korea.

27. Paragraph 2 and Agreed Minute #2

Mr. Chang said the Korean negotiators were now prepared to accept the U.S. draft of this paragraph and Agreed Minute, with the following understanding:

> "The termination of employment on account of the
> U.S. military requirements referred to in the second sentence
> of Agreed Minute #2 shall be referred to the Joint Committee,
> in advance whenever possible, for mutual agreement, as provided
> for in Agreed Minute #4. But such termination of employment as
> may be made in accordance with the relevant provisions of labor
> legislation of the Republic of Korea will not be subject to
> mutual agreement at the Joint Committee."

28. Paragraph 4(a)

Mr. Chang stated that the Korean negotiators were prepared to accept the U.S. draft of Paragraph 4(a) except for subparagraph (5). They proposed that subparagraph (5) be altered to read "as stipulated in subparagraph (2), above" instead of "subparagraph (3), above". Although they maintain that the cooling-off period should comprise 70 days after the dispute is referred for conciliation, the Korean negotiators now proposed, as a compromise, to fix the starting date of the cooling-off period at the second stage of the conciliation process, regardless of whether the Joint Committee deals with the dispute itself or refers it to a specially designated committee. The U.S. draft of this subparagraph does not clearly accommodate the case when the Joint Committee takes up the dispute itself without having referred t the matter to the special committee. Therefore, the Korean negotiators urge that their compromise proposal be accepted.

29. Paragraph 4(b) and (c)

0177

29. Paragraph 4(b) and (c)

Mr. Chang said the Korean negotiators accepted the U.S. draft of Paragraph 4 (b) and (c), relating to collective action and emergency measures, without any change of wording.

30. Paragraph 5(B)

Turning to Paragraph 5(b), Mr. Chang said the Korean negotiators were now prepared to accommodate the contention expressed by the U.S. negotiators by accepting the word "shall" instead of "will" and by substituting the words phrase "through mutual consultation" for the phrase "through mutual agreement". The language in question would then read as follows:

> ".... employees who have acquired new skills essential to the mission of the United States Armed Forces shall, upon request of the United States armed forces, be deferred through mutual consultation from Republic of Korea military service or other compulsory service."

The Korean negotiators hoped, Mr. Chang continued, that through amicable consultation no disagreement would arise between the appropriate authorities of both sides in deferring skilled employees essential to the mission of the U.S. armed forces.

31. Agreed Minute #5

Mr. Chang said the Korean negotiators believe that the "interests of the United States" referred to in the phrase "inimical to the interests of the United States" in the U.S. draft of Agreed Minute #5 do not imply interests in terms of wages, compensation, or other forms of payments and protection of workers. Rather, they imply those interests of a political nature, such as when the leadership of a union is dominated or influenced by leftist or communist elements. The Korean negotiators believe that if such an unlikely situation should develop, it would undoubtedly be inimical to the interests of the Republic of Korea. Therefore, they would like to change the language to read as follows:

> "... inimical to the common interests of the United States and the Republic of Korea. ..."

32. Paragraph 3 and Agreed Minute #4

0178

32. Paragraph 3 and Agreed Minute #4

The Korean negotiators tabled the following proposed revision of

Paragraph 3:

> "3. To the extent not inconsistent with the provisions of this Article or the military requirements of the U.S. armed forces (or except as may otherwise be mutually agreed) the conditions of employment, compensation, and labor-management relations established by the United States armed forces for their employees shall conform with provisions of labor legislation of the Republic of Korea."

They also tabled the following proposed revision of Agreed Minute #4:

> *changed*
> "4. When employers cannot conform with provisions of labor legislation of the Republic of Korea applicable under Paragraph 3 on account of the military requirements of the United States armed forces, the matter shall be referred, in advance whenever possible, to the Joint Committee for mutual agreement."

Mr. Chang noted that in order to meet the U.S. requirements, the proposed revision of the Agreed Minute retaines the phrase "whenever possible". However, the Korean negotiators believe that "under Paragraph 3" is preferable to "under this Article" because the latter phrase might lead to dual application of an already agreed-upon deviation which the Korean negotiators believes to be irrelevant and unnecessary. With regard to the phrase "whenever possible", Mr. Chang said the Korean negotiators wished to include in the Agreed Joint Summary the following understanding:

> *changed*
> "The deviation from Korean labor legislation shall be referred to the Joint Committee for mutual agreement in advance, except in the case when reaching advance agreement by the Joint Committee would seriously hamper military operations in an emergency."

Mr. Chang said the Korean negotiators believed this understanding would present no difficulty to the U.S. negotiators in view of the statement made by the latter at the 71st meeting.

0179

Ratification Article

33. Turning to the Ratification Article, Mr. Chang tabled the following proposed revisions:

"1. This Agreement shall enter into force sixty days after the date of a written notification from the Government of the Republic of Korea to the Government of the United States that it has approved the Agreement in accordance with its legal procedures.

"2. The Government of the Republic of Korea shall undertake to seek from its legislature all legislative and budgetary action necessary to give effect to its provisions of this Agreement.

"3. ...

"4. ~~Thexprexixienxxxefxthexprexentxty~~ Within the scope of this Agreement, Paragraph 13 of Article III of the Agreement on Economic Coordination between the Republic of Korea and the Unified Command of May 24, 1952, shall not apply to members of the U.S. armed forces, civilian component, invited contractors, or dependents thereof."

34. Mr. Chang said the Korean negotiators wished to modify the U.S. draft along the lines of other Status of Forces Agreements by separating the clause regarding legislative and budgetary action by the legislature, in view of the fact that the entry into force of the Agreement ~~xxx~~ (is) one thing and legislative and budgetary action is another. Furthermore, the Korean negotiators would like to point out that Article 5 of the ROK Constitution clearly stipulates that treaties duly ratified and promulgated in accordance with the Constitution have the same effective force as ~~~~ do domestic laws of the Republic of Korea. Therefore, the ROK Government is bound to enforce the Agreement as domestic law, regardless of whether legislative and budgetary actions necessary for the execution of its provisions have been taken.

35. The Korean negotiators, Mr. Chang continued, believe that the four-month interval following ratification and legal procedures, proposed by the U.S. negotiators, was not only too long but also contradictory to the desire expressed by both sides for early conclusion of the Agreement. Moreover, the Korean negotiators cannot find ~~any~~

0180

such a long interval in any other Status of Forces Agreement. They believe the Agreement should enter into force upon ratification. However, they were proposing sixty days in order to accommodate the U.S. negotiators. They accepted Paragraph 3 of the U.S. draft and hope that the U.S. negotiators would find it possible to accept their revisions of Paragraphs 1 and 2.

36. Mr. Chang said the Korean negotiators were proposing the additional Paragraph 4 in the belief that the Agreement was meant to cover the status of the U.S. armed forces in Korea and would have no relevance to the Unified Command per se. Therefore, the privileges, immunities and facilities granted to the U.S. armed forces as individuals or agencies of the Unified Command should ~~not~~ come under the provisions of the SOFA and no other agreement.

Criminal Jurisdiction Article

37. ~~Mr. Chang~~ Taking up the Criminal Jurisdiction Article, Mr. Chang said that the Korean negotiators were prepared to accept verbatim the following provisions of the U.S. draft: Paragraph 1(a), Paragraph 11, Paragraph 12, and the following Agreed Minutes: Preamble, #2 Re Paragraph 1(b) ~~2~~, Re Paragraph 2, Re Paragraph 6, all those Re Paragraph 9, except for the Agreed Minute Re Paragraph 9(g). They withdrew their proposal for an Agreed Minute Re Paragraph 4 regarding dual nationals. With modifications, they were prepared to accept the following provisions of the U.S. draft: Paragraph 1(b), Paragraph 7(b), and the following Agreed Minutes: Re Paragraph 3(a), Re Paragraph 3(b), Re Paragraph 9(a), Re Paragraph 10 (a) and 10(b).

38. <u>Paragraph 1(a)</u>

Mr. Chang said that with regard to persons subject to [the] jurisdiction ~~of~~ of the military authorities of the United States, it has been the position of the Korean negotiators that since 1960 dependents have been **excluded** from the categories of persons subject to the military law of the United States and that they should, therefore, be left out of the discussion of this article. However, taking into

0181

account, the oft-repeated concern of the United States negotiators, the Korean negotiators were now prepared to accept the U.S. proposal, thereby clearly spelling out that "members of the United States armed forces, civilian component, and their dependents" are covered by the provisions of this article, as proposed by the U.S. negotiators.

~~39. Paragraph 11~~

~~Mr. Chang said that the Korean negotiators, with a view to accommodating the U.S. requirements to the fullest extent, accepted the provisions Paragraph 11 of the U.S. draft, pertaining to suspension of the Article in time of hostilities.~~

~~40. Paragraph 12~~

39. Agreed Minute Re Paragraph 1(b) #2

Mr. Chang recalled that the Korean negotiators had maintained the position that the U.S. proposal with respect to offenses committed outside the Republic of Korea, in the Agreed Minute Re Paragraph 1(b) #2, had been unacceptable. First, Article 5 of the Korean Criminal Code clearly stipulates that this law shall apply to aliens who have committed certain offenses of a serious nature outside the territory of the Republic of Korea. Therefore, the provisions of this Agreed Minute are clearly contradictory to the legal system of the Republic of Korea. Secondly, since the United States does not have a similar provisions in its legal system, offenses committed outside the Republic of Korea or outside the territory of the United States cannot be punished under the provisions of the U.S. draft. However, in view of the fact that the presumption envisaged in the Agreed Minute is highly hypothetical and occurrence of such offenses would be exceptional and extremely rare, the Korean negotiators now accepted this Agreed Minute.

40. Agreed Minute Re Paragraph 2

Mr. Chang recalled that the Korean negotiators had proposed deletion

0182

of the Agreed Minute Re Paragraph 2 from the U.S. draft. The exclusive jurisdiction granted to the Korean authorities includes jurisdiction conferred on them with respect to offenses, including offenses relating to the security of the Republic of Korea, punishable only by the law of the Republic of Korea. The exclusive jurisdiction involved here would be exercised mostly over such offenses against the security of the receiving state as treason, sabotage, espionage, or violation of any law relating to official secrets or secrets relating to the national defense of the receiving state. In other words, Mr. Chang continued, the nature of such offenses is so serious that any mishandling thereof might result in grave danger to the very survival or existence of the government of the receiving state. Secondly, the U.S. draft calls for waiver of exclusive jurisdiction of the host country over offenders whom the U.S. military authorities have no legal right to punish equitably as required by the relevant laws of the Republic of Korea. Thirdly, the Korean negotiators had been unable to find any precedents xxxxxy for this language in any other Status of Forces Agreement.

41. However, Mr. Chang said, in the light of the U.S. concern that legal grounds should be provided fox in the Agreement so that if the Korean authorities do not wish to exercise their exclusive jurisdiction in specific cases they could waive in favor of the United States offenses of a minor naturefox, for disciplinary action, the Korean negotiators xxxxxpxxpxxxxxx accepted the Agreed Minute with the inclusion of the following understanding in the Agreed Joint Summary:

> "It is understood that the U.S. authorities shall exercise utmost restraint in requesting waivers of exclusive jurisdiction as provided for in the Agreed Minute Re Paragraph 2 of this Article."

42. Trial Safeguards

Mr. Chang said the Korean negotiators were now prepared to accept
in subjecting their personnel to Korea
all of those trial safeguards still at issue which the U.S negotiators felt to be juridiction
necessary for guaranteeing a fair trial. Their acceptance included reinsertion

of the second sentence in the Agreed Minute Re Paragraph 9(a), ~~acceptance of the~~ and in the Agreed Minute
Re Paragraph 9 acceptance of the following:

0183

the understanding proposed by the U.S. negotiators at the 80th meeting with regard to subparagraph (a) of the second unnumbered paragraph ~~of the Agreed Minute Re Paragraph~~ ~~acceptance of~~ subparagraph (d), ~~of the second unnumbered paragraph of that Agreed~~ ~~Minute, subparagraph~~ *and* (j), of the second unnumbered paragraph, the third unnumbered paragraph, and the fourth unnumbered paragraph.

43. *Agreed Minute Re Paragraph 9(g)*

However, Mr. Chang continued, with regard to the Agreed Minute Re Paragraph 9(g), the Korean negotiators had maintained that that portion of the Agreed Minute which would render inadmissible as evidence any statement taken from an accused in the absence of a U.S. representative should be deleted, on the ground that since a representative of the U.S. Government, a counsel, an interpreter, and the accused himself are all given the right to be present at all of the judicial proceedings, it is entirely within the discretion of the U.S. Government representative whether or not to appear in such cases. Furthermore, the absence of the U.S. Government representative from the judicial proceedings should not impair the admissibility of a statement. ~~It~~ ~~xxxxxx~~ Mr. Chang recalled also that when the two sides had been discussing the problem of trial safeguards pertaining to Agreed Minute Re Paragraph 9(g), the U.S. negotiators had insisted that a representative of the U.S. Government should be entitled to be present at all criminal proceedings, while the Korean negotiators had ojected, on the ground that the presence of ~~xxxxxxxxpxx~~ the representative in case of an in camera proceeding, however rare, would prejudice the provisions of the Korean Constitution as well as relevant laws of the Republic of Korea with respect to public trials. Nevertheless, Mr. Chang continued, the U.S. negotiators, contrary to their previous position, had recently proposed, in paragraph 6 of the Agreed Minute Re Paragraph 3(b), ~~ixix~~ language which states that "a Korean representative shall be entitled to be present at the trial, except where his presance is incompatible with the rules of the court of the United States or with the security requirements of the United States, which are not at the same time the security requirements of the Republic of Korea." In the light of ~~thxxtxxxx~~ previous statements by the U.S. negotiators that the representative of the

0184

U.S. Government has an affirmative duty to be present at the trial sessions, and will

be available at all times, and that the United States Government will ensure that he

fulfills this duty, the Korean negotiators, while accepting the U.S. position in prin-

ciple, in order to be consistent with the relevant portion of this Article, propose,

as a condition of their acceptance of Paragraph 6 of the Agreed Minute Re Paragraph 3(b),

the addition of the following language at the end of the Agreed Minute Re Paragraph 9(g):

> "... except where his presence is incompatible with
> the rules of the court of the Republic of Korea or with the
> security requirements of the Republic of Korea, which are
> not at the same time the security requirements of the United
> States."

Mr. Chang said predicted that cases of this type would be extremely rare and that

the Korean negotiators do not foresee any problem. The Republic of Korea and the United

States are both sovereign states and the ties between them are especially close. There-

fore, it is only reasonable that representatives of each government should have corre-

sponding rights and should not be discriminated against.

44. Paragraph 1(b) and Agreed Minute Re Paragraph 9(a)

Mr. Chang stated that the Korean negotiators preferred the deletion of

the word "civil" from Paragraph 1(b) to deletion of the second sentence of

the Agreed Minute Re Paragraph 9(a). Therefore, they proposed that the second sentence,

which had been deleted from the most recent U.S. draft, be reinserted and the word "civil"

be deleted. The sentence to be reinserted would read:

> "A member of the United States armed forces, or
> civilian component, or a dependent, shall not be tried
> by a military tribunal of the Republic of Korea."

By accepting the above trial safeguard, Mr. Chang said, the Korean

negotiators had fully met the U.S. concern that under existing Korean law a member of

the U.S. armed forces, civilian component, or a dependent may be tried by a Korean

military court. Accordingly.

45. Paragraph 7(b)

Mr. Chang stated that the Korean negotiators were prepared to accept

0185

Paragraph 7(b) of the U.S. draft, with the addition of the following language at the end of the paragraph:

> "In such cases, the authorities of the United States shall furnish relevant information on a routine basis to the authorities of the Republic of Korea, and a representative of the Government of the Republic of Korea shall have the right to have access to a member of the United States armed forces, the civilian component, or a dependent who is serving a sentence imposed by a court of the Republic of Korea in confinement facilities of the United States."

46. Mr. Chang explained that although the Korean negotiators are prepared to accept the unprecedented provisions of Paragraph 7(b) with respect to post-trial custody, they believe it necessary that the U.S. authorities routinely furnish to the Korean authorities such relevant information as the behavior and degree of repentance of those who are in penal servitude. In addition, the Korean authorities should be given the right of access to such persons not only for the purpose of seeing to it that they are carrying out their penal terms to the mutual satisfaction of the authorities of both governments but also in the interest of the persons in confinement. Denial by the U.S. negotiators of the Korean proposal would result in undue deprivation of those persons of such privileges as provisional release (parole) provided for in Article 72 of the Korean Criminal Code and Articles 49 to 52 of the Korean Prison Act.

47. Agreed Minute Re Paragraph 3(a)

Mr. Chang referred to the amended understanding pertaining to the issuance of duty certificates which the U.S. negotiators had proposed at the 80th meeting. He recalled that, in responding to a question at the 75th meeting, the U.S. negotiators had stated that "since there are only five Staff Judge Advocates assigned to the U.S. armed forces in Korea and since the lowest-ranking one is assigned at the division level, issuance of the duty certificate would take place at the division level or higher and the lowest-ranking competent authority issuing a duty certificate would be a Brigadier General." Taking this explanation in good faith, Mr. Chang continued,

0186

the Korean negotiators had proposed the understanding that:

> "A duty certificate shall be issued only upon the advice of a Staff Judge Advocate, and the competent ~~issuing~~ authority issuing the duty certificate shall be a General Grade Officer."

However, contrary to their previous explanation, the U.S. negotiators had proposed the addition of the words "or his designee" at the end of the understanding and ~~it~~ had further elaborated their position that a general officer must, of necessity, delegate many acts to his senior subordinates.

48. In view of the decisive role the duty certificate plays in determining whether or not a certain offense is done in the performance of official duty, the Korean negotiators had originally proposed the Staff Judge Advocate as the authority issuing the duty certificate. However, in the hope of concluding discussion of this point, the Korean negotiators had accepted ~~xxxxxx~~ in the text the wording "competent military authorities of the United States forces", coupled with the condition envisaged in the understanding which they had proposed. In the light of the lengthy discussion of the duty certificate question and the ~~xxxxxxx~~ (basic) agreement which had been reached thereon, the Korean negotiators consider that the proposed additional wording ~~xxxxxxxxxxxx~~ ~~xxxxxxxxx~~ will delay complete agreement on this issue. Therefore, they sincerely hope that the U.S. negotiators will voluntarily withdraw their proposed revision of the understanding.

49. ~~Xxxxxxxxxxxxxxxxxxxxxxxx~~ Colonel Crawford stated that he wished to correct the record to show that there are actually six Staff Judge Advocates assigned to the U.S. armed forces in Korea, instead of five as he had previously stated. The sixth is ~~xx~~ a U.S. Air Force officer assigned to Osan Air Base.

50. Mr. Chang resumed his remarks regarding official duty certificates by stating that the Korean negotiators maintained unchanged their position that the definition of offical duty should be incorporated in an Agreed Minute in order to eliminate any possibility of ambiguity regarding the question of what constitutes

0187

official duty. The Korean negotiators, Mr. Chang continued, are well aware of the difficulties and concern expressed by the U.S. negotiators in connection with this problem.
Nevertheless, they feel very strongly that if the U.S. negotiators would generously
accept their proposal, it would greatly help them in obtaining the understanding of the
Korean people and members of the National Assembly.

51. Agreed Minute Re Paragraph 3(b)

Mr. Chang stated that with regard to Paragraph 1 of the Agreed Minute
Re Paragraph 3(b) the Korean negotiators were now prepared to make one of their most
significant concessions by accepting the principle of the one-time, en masse waiver
of primary jurisdiction. Accordingly, they were withdrawing their proposal to insert
[at the beginning of]
the Paragraph 1 the words "At the request of the United States".

52. After taking into account the difficulties expressed by the U.S. negotiators at the 80th meeting with regard to the ~~proposed~~ 21-day limitation contained in
the ~~additional~~ sentence proposed by the Korean negotiators *for addition* ~~to be added~~ to Paragraph
4 of the Agreed Minute, Mr. Chang continued, the Korean negotiators withdrew their
previous proposal and now proposed instead the following additional sentence:

> "In case the Government of the Republic of Korea,
> in resolving disagreement in accordance with the foregoing
> provisions, determines that it is imperative that juris-
> diction be exercised by the authorities of the Republic of
> Korea, the recall of waiver shall be final and conclusive."

53. As the U.S. negotiators were aware, Mr. Chang said, the above proposal is patterned after the question raised by the Korean negotiators at the 78th
session and the affirmative reply given by the U.S. negotiators. Therefore, the Korean
negotiators believe that this proposal does not deviate from, but is consistent with,
the waiver formula proposed by the U.S. negotiators. Both sides are in agreement on the
principle involved but differ only ~~in~~ [over] the manner of stating the principle. Furthermore,
the Korean negotiators wished to point out that just as acceptance [their] ~~by certain~~ of the
principle of a blanket waiver will fully meet the U.S. requirements, reciprocal
acceptance by the U.S. negotiators of this proposed additional sentence would be

0188

very helpful to the ROK Government in securing the understanding and cooperation of the Korean people and the National Assembly. At the same time, it would dispel any misunderstanding or unnecessary dispute which might arise in the implementation of the waiver formula. The Korean negotiators hoped, therefore, that the U.S. negotiators would give full consideration to their proposal and accept it.

54. Mr. Chang said that,in view of the explanation by the U.S. negotiators that cases arising under the provisions of Paragraph 6 of the Agreed Minute Re 3(b) would be extremely rare and cannot be expected to present any problems, the Korean negotiators accepted the U.S. draft of that paragraph.

55. Agreed Minute Re Paragraph 10(a) and 10(b)

Mr. Chang said the Korean negotiators wished to propose some modifications of the Agreed Minute Re Paragraph 10(a) and 10(b). According to the U.S. draft, he pointed out, the Korean authorities are not allowed to make any arrest within facilities and areas. The Korean negotiators, he said, are not demanding any unconditional right of arrest; the Korean authorities would seek consent in advance from the U.S. military authorities when such arrest within facilities and areas is necessary. The Korean negotiators would also like to point out that the right of pursuit of a flagrant offender who has committed a serious crime is an established principle of international law. Furthermore, if ~~xxpxxxxxxxxxxxxxxxxxxxxxxxxxxxxxx~~ the arrest of a person who is within facilities and areas is desired by the Korean authorities, his arrest should be carried out by the U.S. authorities on request. ~~Ixxxkixxxxxxxxkxxx~~ The Korean negotiators believe ~~xxxxxifxxxxxffixxxxxxxxxxxxg~~ mutual cooperation in these matters, as envisaged in ~~xxxxxxxxx~~ their proposals, is essential. They wished to point out that the U.S. draft is also silent on the question of turning over to the Korean authorities persons arrested within facilities and areas. (In the light of the recent agreement of both sides on the custody provisions of this Article, the Korean negotiators believed the original U.S. position with regard to this Agreed Minute should ~~xxx~~ be modified accordingly.)

0189

56. Mr. Chang said that for the reasons just given, the Korean negotiators wished to propose the following modifications in the Agreed Minute:

      a. "... The authorities of the Republic of Korea will normally not exercise the right of <u>arrest</u>, search, seizure, or inspection with respect to any person or property within facilities and areas in use by the military authorities of the United States or with respect to ~~any~~ ~~personal~~ property ~~within facilities and areas in use by~~ ~~the military authorities~~ of the United States wherever situated, except in cases where the competent military authorities of the United States consent to such <u>arrest</u>, search, <u>seizure</u>, or inspection by the Korean authorities of such persons or property <u>or in cases of pursuit of a flagrant offender who has committed a serious crime</u>."

      b. "Where <u>arrest or detention</u>, search, seizure, or inspection with respect to persons or property within facilities and areas in use by the United States or with respect to property of the United States in the Republic of Korea is desired by the Korean authorities, the United States military authorities will undertake, upon request, to make such <u>arrest or detention</u>, search, seizure, or inspection. ..."

      c. "... <u>Any person arrested or detained by the U.S. military authorities within, or in the vicinity of, a facility or area</u> who is not a member of the United States armed forces, civilian component, or a dependent shall immediately be turned over to the authorities of the Republic of Korea."

57. Agreed Minute ~~Re Paragraph 1(b)~~ #1 Re Paragraph 1(b)

    Mr. Chang stated that the martial law clause, proposed by the U.S. negotiators in their Agreed Minute #1 Re Paragraph 1(b), would require that during a period of martial law the provisions of the Criminal Jurisdiction Article would be suspended in that part of the Republic of Korea under martial law and that during the period of martial law the military authorities of the United States would exercise exclusive jurisdiction over ~~the~~ U.S. personnel with respect to offenses committed in the area under martial law. The Korean negotiators are unable to understand the importance which the U.S. negotiators attach to this provision. In the light of the large concessions already made by the Korean negotiators with regard to other provisions of this Article, and for ~~the~~ reasons which they would now state, the Korean negotiators, Mr. Chang declared, are

0190

unable to accept ~~the~~ this ~~provisional~~ Agreed Minute.

58. First, Mr. Chang said, the Korean negotiators had already made an "unbearable" concession to the U.S. negotiators in accepting the U.S. proposal with regard to requests for waiver of exclusive jurisdiction by the ROK Government over offenses, including offenses against the security of the Republic, ~~and~~ which are punishable by its law but not by the law of the United States. They had made this concession in the earnest hope that the U.S. negotiators would accede to the Korean requirements with ~~respect~~ regard to martial law.

59. In the second place, Mr. Chang continued, the Korean negotiators had given assurances in the past that under no circumstances would members of the U.S. armed forces, the civilian component, or their dependents be subject to trial by military tribunals of the Republic of Korea. To further convince the U.S. negotiators of their sincerity, the Korean negotiators had, at this meeting, indicated their willingness to accept the reinsertion of the second sentence of the Agreed Minute Re Paragraph 9(a) rather than as an understanding in the Agreed Joint Summary as they had proposed at the 70th meeting. Furthermore, they had accepted the principle of waiver of primary jurisdiction. Finally, Mr. Chang said, they had been unable to find any precedents for this provision in any other Status of Forces Agreement. Therefore, the Korean negotiators proposed deletion of this Agreed Minute, which would open the way for full agreement on the Criminal Jurisdiction Article and, eventually, the entire SOFA.

Invited Contractors Article

60. Taking up the Invited Contractors Article, Mr. Chang recalled that full agreement had been reached on all of its provisions with the exception of Paragraph 8, relating to the question of criminal jurisdiction over contractors, their employees, and the dependents of such persons. The Korean negotiators had taken the position that the Republic of Korea should have the primary right to exercise juris-

0191

diction over such persons while the U.S. negotiators had argued that they should be subject to the provisions of the Criminal Jurisdiction Article.

61. Mr. Chang said the Korean negotiators were unable to accept Paragraph 8 for the following reasons. First, since the status of the persons under discussion was that of special commercial entrants with military contracts, if they were turned over to the military authorities of the United States in accordance with the relevant provisions of the Criminal Jurisdiction Article, the U.S. military authorities would have no legal grounds on which to apprehend and punish them equitably. Secondly, their status cannot be equated to the status of members of the civilian component because the former are civilians engaged in profit-seeking business in connection with a military contract, while the latter are employees of the Government of the United States, working for the U.S. armed forces. Consequently the members of the civilian component are under strict punitive regulations of the armed forces. Furthermore, the privileges which the Korean negotiators deem essential for the performance by the contractors of their contracts will be given to them under the provisions of Paragraph 3 of this Article. Finally, Mr. Chang said, the Korean negotiators had been unable to find any precedents for Paragraph 8 in other Status of Forces Agreements.

62. In view of the considerations which he had just stated, Mr. Chang continued, acceptance by the ROK Government of such a discriminatory and unprecedented proposal would result in added burdens to the Government and might eventually jeopardize its position with the people and the National Assembly at the time of ratification of the Agreement and during its implementation. Therefore, the Korean negotiators requested the U.S. negotiators to take into full account the relevant factors and generously accept the Korean position, thereby strengthening the position of the ROK Government in its efforts to cope with possible future difficulties.

63. Mr. Chang said the Korean negotiators wished to retain in the Agreed Joint Summary the following understandings which had already been agreed to:

a. The U.S. armed forces shall no longer bring 0192

into the Republic of Korea any employees of third-country nationality after the entry into force of this Agreement.

      b. If the U.S. authorities determine that there would be significant advantage for U.S.-ROK mutual defense to utilize one or more third-country corporations as USFK-invited contractors, the authorities of the Government of the Republic of Korea shall give sympathetic consideration to a U.S. request to extend the benefits of this Agreement to such non-U.S. corporations.

64. Mr. Chang stated that the Korean negotiators also wished to record their understanding that under the provisions of Paragraph 2 of this Article, designation as invited contractors of corporations and persons already located in the Republic of Korea at the time of entry into force of the Agreement shall be subject to review by the competent authorities of the Republic of Korea and the United States in the Joint Committee. Further, any future renewal of the designation or any new designation with respect to the corporations and persons referred to in Paragraph 1 the Article would be the subject of consultation in advance in the Joint Committee.

65. Mr. Fleck thanked Mr. Chang for the very detailed and comprehensive presentation made by the Korean negotiators and stated that the U.S. negotiators would give very careful and serious consideration to the [Korean] proposals.

0193

<u>JOINT SUMMARY RECORD OF THE 81ST SESSION</u>

1. Time and Place: 4:00-7:00 P.M., June 7, 1965 at the
                      Foreign Ministry's Conference Room
                      (No.1)

2. Attendance:

   ROK Side:

   Mr. Chang, Sang Moon   Director
                             European and American Affairs
                             Bureau
                             Ministry of Foreign Affairs

   Mr. Hur, Hyong Koo   Chief
                             Prosecutors Section
                             Ministry of Justice

   Mr. Lee, Nam Ki   Chief
                             America Section
                             Ministry of Foreign Affairs

   Mr. Choo, Moon Ki   Chief
                             Legal Affairs Section
                             Ministry of Justice

   Mr. Kim, Tai Chung   Chief
                             Labor Administration Section
                             Office of Labor Affairs

   Mr. Kim, Young Soo   Chief
                             Operations Section
                             Ministry of Finance

   Mr. Lee, Chai Sup   Customs Bureau
                             Ministry of Finance

   Maj. Lee, Kye Hoon   Military Affairs Section
                             Ministry of Foreign Affairs

   Mr. Kim, Kee Joe   3rd Secretary
                             Ministry of Foreign Affairs

   Mr. Lee, Keun Pal   3rd Secretary
   (Interpreter)   Ministry of Foreign Affairs

   Mr. Hwang, Young Jae   3rd Secretary
                             Ministry of Foreign Affairs

   Mr. Lee, Chung Bin   3rd Secretary
                             Ministry of Foreign Affairs

   Mr. Park, Won Chul   3rd Secretary
                             Ministry of Foreign Affairs

   U.S. Side:

   Mr. Benjamin A. Fleck   First Secretary
                             Aemrican Embassy

0194

0195

Col. Allan G. Pixton	Deputy Chief of Staff 8th U.S. Army
Capt. George Hagerman	Assistant Chief of Staff USN/K
Col. Kenneth C. Crawford	Staff Judge Advocate 8th U.S. Army
Mr. Frank R. LaMacchia	First Secretary American Embassy
Mr. Robert A. Kinney	J-5 8th U.S. Army
Mr. Goodwin Shapiro	Second Secretary American Embassy
Maj. Alton H. Harvey	Staff Judge Advocate's Office 8th U.S. Army
Mr. David Y.C. Lee (Interpreter)	Second Secretary American Embassy
Mr. Ogden C. Reed (Observer)	Civilian Personnel Director 8th U.S. Army
Mr. G.W. Flower (Observer)	8th U.S. Army
Col. Charles M. Thompson (Observer)	Claims Service 8th U.S. Army

1. Mr. Chang opened the meeting by stating that the Korean negotiators wished to articulate their position at this final stage of negotiations. Mr. Chang said that it has been the desire and intent of the Korean negotiators to reach full agreement and to conclude these long-pending negotiations as soon as possible. Taking cognizance of the different opinions between the two sides, they have exerted their utmost effort to accommodate the requirements of the U.S. negotiators as far as possible.

2. As the U.S. negotiators had stated at the 80th meeting, Mr. Chang continued, the leaders of the two governments, at the recent conference in Washington, had

0196

미도 113-4

0197

reached agreement in principle on the major outstanding issues of this Agreement. Therefore, it is the belief of the Korean negotiators that both sides should exert their utmost efforts to resolve the remaining differences which have been hindering an early conclusion of the Agreement.

3. Mr. Chang said the Korean negotiators were now prepared to propose their final, comprehensive draft of this Agreement. With appropriate understandings and minor modifications, they accepted the U.S. drafts of the following articles: Non-Appropriated Fund Organizations, Customs, Military Payment Certificates, Security Measures, Foreign Exchange Controls, Duration of the Agreement, Facilities and Areas, and Civil Claims.

4. However, Mr. Chang continued, after having given their most careful consideration to the rest of the articles (Criminal Jurisdiction, Labor, Invited Contractors, and Ratification of the Agreement), they were prepared to accept the U.S. drafts only after incorporating modifications of an important nature. These modifications are essential and imperative to the Government of the Republic of Korea. As had been pointed out by the Korean negotiators at the past discussions, the people and the National Assembly are deeply concerned and critical toward the possible outcome of these negotiations. This concern is clearly indicated in recent criticisms directed at both governments in the columns of the newspapers and voided by some eminent and responsible citizens. Mr. Chang stated that such embarrassing consequences would be in the interests of neither the host state nor the sending state. Keeping these facts in mind, Mr. Chang said, the Korean negotiators

0198

0199

wished to present their final position on each of the
as-yet unagreed upon articles of the SOFA.

Security Measures Article

5. Mr. Chang recalled that at the 55th meeting
the U.S. negotiators had proposed deletion of the phrase
"of the persons referred to in this paragraph, and their
property" if the Korean negotiators would agree to the
inclusion in the Agreed Joint Summary of the following
understanding:

> "In cooperating with each other under this
> Article, the two governments agree that each will
> take such measures as may be necessary to ensure
> the security and protection of the U.S. armed
> forces, the members thereof, the civilian component,
> the persons who are present in the Republic of Korea
> pursuant to the Article dealing with Invited
> Contractors, their dependents and their property."

Mr. Chang said the Korean negotiators accepted the U.S.
proposal and the U.S. draft of the Article as tabled
at the 80th meeting.

Non-Appropriated Fund Organizations Article

6. Mr. Chang noted that the only remaining issue
in the Non-Appropriated Fund Organizations Article was
the question of who should be granted the use of these
organizations under item (f) of the Agreed Minute proposed
by the U.S. negotiators. To meet the requirements expressed
by the U.S. negotiators, the Korean negotiators were now
prepared to accept the Agreed Minute. However, in
accepting, the Korean negotiators wished to include in
the Agreed Joint Summary the following understanding:

> "It is understood that the present use of
> Non-Appropriated Fund organizations by organizations
> and persons other than those referred to in items
> (a),(b),(c),(d), and (e) shall immediately be
> suspended at the time of the entry into force of
> this Agreement. The extent of organizations and
> persons to be granted the use of such organizations
> under item (f) of this Minute shall be left to

0200

마음 113-4

0201

further negotiations between the appropriate authorities of the two Governments."

7. Mr. Chang noted that agreement on the Non-Appropriated Funds Organizations Article meant automatic agreement on Agreed Minute #7 of the Customs Article. The negotiators had thereby reached full agreement on the latter article as well.

Foreign Exchange Controls Article

8. Mr. Chang stated that the Korean negotiators accepted the U.S. draft of the Agreed Minute to the Foreign Exchange Controls Article, thereby reaching full agreement on that article.

Military Payment Certificates Article

9. Mr. Chang recalled that at the 55th meeting both sides agreed to delete their respective drafts of an Agreed Minute and to include in the Agreed Joint Summary the following understanding:

> "The ROK and U.S. negotiators agree that nothing in the Status of Forces Agreement in any way prevents the appropriate authorities of either the Republic of Korea or the United States from raising any appropriate matter at any time with each other. The U.S. negotiators recognize the desire of the ROK authorities to discuss the disposal of Military Payment Certificates under custody of the ROK Government. However, both the ROK and U.S. negotiators have agreed to remove from the SOFA text any reference to the question of compensation for Military Payment Certificates held by unauthorized persons. This agreement does not prejudice the position of either party in connection with discussion of this question through other channels."

10. Mr. Chang noted that the remaining issue to be solved was whether to include the phrase "to the extent authorized by United States Law" proposed by the U.S. negotiators or the phrase "subject to the military law of the United States" proposed by the Korean negotiators. The Korean negotiators, he said, accepted the language of the U.S. draft, thereby reaching complete agreement on

0202

미·오113-나

0203

this article. However, the Korean negotiators wished to stress that their acceptance was made in the belief that the U.S. authorities would take every measure necessary to prevent abusive transactions of Military Payment Certificates by the persons authorized to use such certificates.

Facilities and Areas Articles

11. Mr. Chang recalled that discussion of the article relating to facilities and areas (U.S. draft article IV) had been deferred since the 42nd meeting, held on February 14, 1964. He recalled that there had been a difference in the positions of the two sides over the question of compensation to owners of private property. The Korean negotiators were now prepared to withdraw their previous contention with respect to compensation for privately-owned property extremely demolished as a result of use by the U.S. armed forces. The Korean negotiators accepted the three paragraphs and Agreed Minute of the U.S. draft. However, they wished to propose a second Agreed Minute reading as follows:

> "2. All removable facilities, equipment and material or portions thereof provided by the Republic of Korea under this Agreement and located within the areas and facilities referred to in this Article shall be returned to the Republic of Korea whenever they are no longer needed for the purpose of this Agreement."

12. Mr. Chang said the additional Agreed Minute was proposed with the same intent as the Agreed Minute already contained in the U.S. draft. The Korean negotiators consider it logical that all removable properties provided by their government and located in any area or facilities should be returned to the owners whenever the properties are no longer needed by the U.S. armed forces. This additional Agreed Minute should present no difficulty to

0204

기요 113-4

0205

the U.S. negotiators. Furthermore, it is also intended
to supplement the provisions of Paragraph 2 and 3 of
Article II because those provisions are merely related
to the return of the facilities and areas, as a whole or in
part, which are no longer needed. Those provisions,
therefore, do not refer to removable property located
within the areas or facilities.

13. Turning to Article V, relating to cost and
maintenance, Mr. Chang stated that the Korean negotiators
were now prepared to withdraw their draft regarding
compensation to owners of private property and to
accept the U.S. draft following clarification of the
language by the U.S. negotiators. Mr. Chang said the
Korean negotiators thought the language of Paragraph 1
was too broad. It spoke of "all expenditures incident to
the maintenance of the U.S. armed forces in the Republic
of Korea" rather than expenditures incident to the
maintenance of facilities and areas. Since this article
was intended to deal with facilities and areas only,
why should the language not be more restrictive?

14. Mr. Fleck replied that this language was identical
with the language of the similar article in the SOFA
with Japan. Therefore, the U.S. negotiators did not
understand why the Korean negotiators should object to it,
inasmuch as the Korean negotiators had frequently
expressed the desire to obtain language in other parts
of this agreement which would be identical or similar
to the language of the SOFA with Japan. Furthermore,
since the language was broader, it gave the ROK Government
a broader exemption from maintenance costs. The term
"maintenance of the U.S. armed forces" included maintenance
of the facilities and areas occupied by those forces.

0206

여.요.113-4

0207

The Korean negotiators, therefore, should have no difficulty in agreeing to this language.

15. Mr. Chang thanked Mr. Fleck for this explanation and said that the Korean negotiators accepted the U.S. draft of the article.

Claims Article

16. Mr. Chang stated that the Korean negotiators, with a view to reaching full agreement, were prepared to accept the revised draft of the Claims Article tabled by the U.S. negotiators at the 80th meeting, subject only to minor modifications.

17. With regard to Paragraph 5(e)(i), the Republic of Korea accepts the standard 25% - 75% distribution ration, as proposed by the U.S.

18. With regard to Paragraph 5(e)(iii), Mr. Chang continued, the Korean negotiators are prepared to withdraw their proposed Agreed Minute if the U.S. negotiators will agree to modify the subparagraph as follows (proposed changes underlined):

> "iii. Every half year, a statement of the sums paid by the Republic of Korea in the course of the half-yearly period in respect of every case regarding which the liability, amount, and proposed distribution on a percentage basis has been approved by both governments shall be sent to the appropriate authorities of the United States, together with a request for reimbursement. Such reimbursement shall be made in won within the shortest possible time. The approval by both governments as referred to in this subparagraph shall not prejudice any decision taken by the arbitrator or adjudication by a competent tribunal of the Republic of Korea as set forth in paragraphs 2(c) and 5(c) respectively."

19. Mr. Chang said the proposed modifications are necessary to clarify the contradictory provisions in the U.S. draft. Paragraph 5(c) of that draft provides that all the payments made by the Korean government, whether made pursuant to a settlement or to an adjudication, shall be binding upon the Parties, whereas Paragraph 5(e)(iii) implies that none of the payments made by the Korean

0208

이·묘113-4

0209

government, regardless of whether the payment was made pursuant to a settlement or to an adjudication, shall be binding unless the U.S. authorities approve the payment in advance. Therefore, the Korean negotiators propose the above modifications to Paragraph 5(e)(iii) in order to avoid possible misunderstanding.

20. With regard to Paragraph 12, Mr. Chang said the Korean negotiators would accept the U.S. proposal to delete the final clause and to include an understanding in the Agreed Joint Summary, with a minor modification. The Korean negotiators believe that any decision as to whether claims generated by Korean Service Corps members should or should not come under the provisions of this article cannot be made until the status of the KSC personnel is determined. Therefore, the Korean negotiators propose deletion of the first sentence of the understanding, which would then read as follows:

> "The liability for claims generated by KSC personnel will be determined by other negotiations between the Republic of Korea and the United States."

21. With regard to Paragraph A2 of the Agreed Minute, Mr. Chang said the Korean negotiators accepted the principle that the effective date of the claims provisions in areas other than that of the Seoul Special City shall be determined by the Joint Committee, as proposed by the U.S. negotiators at the previous session. However, to meet the requirements of both sides, the Korean negotiators proposed the following modified draft of Paragraph A2:

> "The provisions of paragraphs five, six, seven, and eight will be extended, at the earliest date practicable, to other areas of the Republic of Korea as determined by the Joint Committee."

22. As the U.S. negotiators were well aware, Mr. Chang continued, the Korean Claims Service has recorded

0210

이克 113나

0211

an efficient operation since 1962. The State Compensation
Committee is manned with qualified commissioners and
investigators who have ample experience in legal affairs.
For the equitable settlement of claims, proper laws and
regulations are provided. At the present time, the Claims
Service is processing and settling the claims arising out
of various cases of damage caused by members of the
Korean armed forces as well as by government officials,
to the satisfaction of the claimants concerned. This
effectiveness of the Korean Claims Service had been demonstrated
by the Korean negotiators, Mr. Chang stated, in previous
formal and informal negotiating meetings. Therefore,
the Korean negotiators are certain that the Korean Claims
Service is capable of assuming all of the claims
responsibilities from the date the SOFA enters into force.

    23. Mr. Chang recalled that the U.S. negotiators had
agreed to adopt the proposed system in the Seoul Special
City area automatically six months after the entry into
force of this agreement without any decision of the Joint
Committee. This acceptance, in the belief of the Korean
negotiators, was nothing but an admission on the part of
the U.S. negotiators that the Republic of Korea has a working
and efficient claims system, applicable to other parts
of the Republic. Moreover, the authority of the Korean
State Compensation Committee extends to the entire territory
of the Republic of Korea, as does that of the U.S. armed
forces Claims Service. The Korean negotiators cannot
understand the insistence of the United States that the
application of the Korean system be limited to a specific
area.

0212

미·로 113-4

0213

24. However, to expedite the negotiations and reach full agreement on this article at the earliest possible date, the Korean negotiators were making an important concession regarding this provision, Mr. Chang continued. The Korean negotiators believe that the United States would give due consideration, in the Joint Committee, to the capability of the Korean Claims Service, so that the provisions of paragraphs five, six, seven and eight could be extended to other areas of the Republic of Korea at the earliest date practicable.

Labor Article

25. Turning to the Labor Article, Mr. Chang said that the Korean negotiators, with a view to reaching prompt agreement, were prepared to accept the U.S. draft as a whole, with modifications of the following provisions: Paragraphs 1(b), 3, 4(a), 5(b), and Agreed Minutes #4 and #5. Most of the proposed modifications, he pointed out, were technical in nature rather than substantive and the Korean negotiators believed they would present no difficulty to the U.S. negotiators since they are all valid and reasonable.

26. Paragraph 1 (a) and (b)

Mr. Chang stated that the Korean negotiators were now prepared to agree to inclusion of the invited contractors in the provisions of this article. The Korean negotiators were prepared to accept subparagraph (b) of the U.S. draft if the U.S. negotiators would agree to the addition of the following sentence:

"Such civilian personnel shall be nationals of the Republic of Korea."

By accepting the U.S. draft of subparagraph (b), Mr. Chang stated, the Korean negotiators were acceeding to the specific exclusion of KSC personnel and domestics from

0214

기로 113-4

0215

the definition of employee. In making this most
significant concession, the Korean negotiators wished to
the Agreed Joint Summary to clearly indicate that
exclusion of KSC personnel from the definition of
employee shall not be construed as a change in the position
taken by the Korean negotiators with regard to the
status of KSC personnel. Moreover, the addition of the
second sentence, proposed by the Korean negotiators, with
regard to the nationality of employees is considered necessary
by the Korean negotiators to minimize the employment
of third-country nationals in Korea.

27. Paragraph 2 and Agreed Minute #2

Mr. Chang said the Korean negotiators were
now prepared to accept the U.S. draft of this paragraph
and Agreed Minute, with the following understanding:

> "The termination of employment on account
> of the U.S. military requirements referred to in
> the second sentence of Agreed Minute #2 shall be
> referred to the Joint Committee, in advance whenever
> possible, for mutual agreement, as provided for
> in Agreed Minute #4. But such termination of
> employment as may be made in accordance with the
> relevant provisions of labor legislation of the
> Republic of Korea will not be subject to mutual
> agreement at the Joint Committee."

28. Paragraph 4(a)

Mr. Chang stated that the Korean negotiators
were prepared to accept the U.S. draft of Paragraph 4(a)
except for subparagraph (5). They proposed that
subparagraph (5) be altered to read "as stipulated in subparagraph (2), above" instead of "subparagraph (3), above."
Although they maintain that the cooling-off period should
comprise 70 days after the dispute is referred for
conciliation, the Korean negotiators now proposed, as
a compromise, to fix the starting date of the cooling-off
period at the second stage of the conciliation process,

0216

기문 113-4

0217

regardless of whether the Joint Committee deals with
the dispute itself or refers it to a specially designated
committee. The U.S. draft of this subparagraph does not
clearly accommodate the case when the Joint Committee
takes up the dipute itself without having referred
the matter to the special committee. Therefore, the Korean
negotiators urge that their compromise proposal be
accepted.

29. Paragraph 4(b) and (c)

Mr. Chang said the Korean negotiators accepted
the U.S. draft of Paragraph 4 (b) and (c), relating to
collective action and emergency measures, without any
change of wording.

30. Paragraph 5(b)

Turning to Paragraph 5(b), Mr. Chang said the
Korean negotiators were now prepared to accommodate the
contention expressed by the U.S. negotiators by accepting
the word "shall" instead of "will" and by substituting the
phrase "through mutual consultation" for the phrase "through
mutual agreement". The language in question would then
read as follows:

"....employees who have acquired skills
essential to the mission of the United States Armed
Forces shall, upon request of the United States
armed forces, be deferred through mutual consultation
from Republic of Korea military service or other
compulsory service.".... "

The Korean negotiators hoped, Mr. Chang continued, that
through amicable consultation no disagreement would
arise between the appropriate authorities of both sides
in deferring skilled employees essential to the mission
of the U.S. armed forces.

31. Agreed Minute #5

Mr. Chang said the Korean negotiators believe
that the words "interests of the United States" referred

0218

마 문 113-4

0219

to in the phrase "inimical to the interests of the United States" in the U.S. draft of Agreed Minute #5 do not imply interests in terms of wages, compensation, or other forms of payments and protection of workers. Rather, they imply those interests of a political nature, such as when the leadership of a union is dominated or influenced by leftist or communist elements. The Korean negotiators believe that if such an unlikely situation should develop, it would undoubtedly be inimical to the interests of the Republic of Korea. Therefore, they would like to change the language to read as follows:

> "...inimical to the common interests of the United States and the Republic of Korea......"

32. Paragraph 3 and Agreed Minute #4

The Korean negotiators tabled the following proposed revision of Paragraph 3:

> "3. To the extent not inconsistent with the provisions of this Article or the military requirements of the U.S. armed forces or except as may otherwise be mutually agreed, the conditions of employment, compensation, and labor-management relations established by the United States armed forces for their employees shall conform with provisions of labor legislation of the Republic of Korea."

They also tabled the following proposed revision of Agreed Minute #4:

> "4. When employers cannot conform with provisions of labor legislation of the Republic of Korea applicable under Paragraph 3 on account of the military requirements of the United States armed forces, the matter shall be referred, in advance whenever possible, to the Joint Committee for mutual agreement."

Mr. Chang noted that in order to meet the U.S. requirements, the proposed revision of the Agreed Minute retaines the phrase "whenever possible". However, the Korean negotiators believe that "under Paragraph 3" is preferable to "under this Article" because the latter phrase might lead to dual application of an already agreed-upon deviation which the Korean negotiators believe to be irrelevant and

0220

0221

unnecessary. With regard to the phrase "whenever possible", Mr. Chang said the Korean negotiators wished to include in the Agreed Joint Summary the following understanding:

"The deviation from Korean labor legislation shall be referred to the Joint Committee for mutual agreement in advance, except in the case when reaching advance agreement by the Joint Committee would seriously hamper military operations in an emergency."

Mr. Chang said the Korean negotiators believed this understanding would present no difficulty to the U.S. negotiators in view of the statement made by the latter at the 71st meeting.

Ratification Article

33. Turning to the Ratification Article, Mr. Chang tabled the following proposed revisions:

"1. This Agreement shall enter into force sixty days after the date of a written notification from the Government of the Republic of Korea to the Government of the United States that it has approved the Agreement in accordance with its legal procedures.

"2. The Government of the Republic of Korea shall undertake to seek from its legislature all legislative and budgetary action necessary to give effect to its provisions of this Agreement.

"3......

"4. Within the scope of this Agreement, Paragraph 13 of Article III of the Agreement on Economic Coordination between the Republic of Korea and the Unified Command of May 24, 1952, shall not apply to members of the U.S. armed forces, civilian component, invited contractors, or dependents thereof."

34. Mr. Chang said the Korean negotiators wished to modify the U.S. draft along the lines of other Status of Forces Agreements by separating the clause regarding legislative and budgetary action by the legislature, in view of the fact that the entry into force of the Agreement is one thing and legislative and budgetary action is another. Furthermore, the Korean negotiators would like to point out that Article 5 of the ROK Constitution clearly stipulates that treaties duly ratified and promulgated in accordance with the Constitution have the same effective force

0222

기픈 1134

0223

as do domestic laws of the Republic of Korea. Therefore,
the ROK Government is bound to enforce the Agreement as
domestic law, regardless of whether legislative and budgetary
actions necessary for the execution of its provisions
have been taken.

35. The Korean negotiators, Mr. Chang continued,
believe that the four-month interval following ratification
and legal procedures, proposed by the U.S. negotiators,
was not only too long but also contradictory to the
desire expressed by both sides for early conclusion of the
Agreement. Moreover, the Korean negotiators cannot find
such a long interval in any other Status of Forces
Agreement. They believe the Agreement should enter into
force upon ratification. However, they were proposing
sixty days in order to accommodate the U.S. negotiators.
They accepted Paragraph 3 of the U.S. draft and hope
that the U.S. negotiators would find it possible to accept
their revisions of Paragraph 1 and 2.

36. Mr. Chang said the Korean negotiators were
proposing the additional Paragraph 4 in the belief that the
Agreement was meant to cover the status of the U.S.
armed forces in Korea and would have no relevance to the
Unified Command per se. Therefore, the privileges,
immunities and facilities granted to the U.S armed forces
as individuals or agencies of the Unified Command should
come under the provisions of the SOFA and no other agreement.

Criminal Jurisdiction Article

37. Taking up the Criminal Jurisdiction Article,
Mr. Chang said that the Korean negotiators were prepared to
accept verbatim the following provisions of the U.S. draft:
Paragraph 1(a), Paragraph 11, Paragraph 12, and the following
Agreed Minutes: Preamble #2 Re Paragraph 1(b), Re Paragraph 2,

미·문 113-4

0225

Re Paragraph 6, all those Re Paragraph 9, except for the
Agreed Minute Re Paragraph 9(g). They withdrew their
proposal for an Agreed Minute Re Paragraph 4 regarding
dual nationals. With modifications, they were prepared to
accept the following provisions of the U.S. draft:
Paragraph 1(b), Paragraph 7(b), and the following Agreed
Minutes: Re Paragraph 3(a), Re Paragraph 3(b), Re Paragraph
9(a), Re Paragraph 10 (a) and 19(b).

38. Paragraph 1(a)

Mr. Chang said that with regard to persons
subject to the jurisdiction of the military authorities
of the United States, it has been the position of the
Korean negotiators that since 1960 dependents have been
excluded from the categories of persons subject to the
military law of the United States and that they should,
therefore, be left out of the discussion of this article.
However, taking into account the oft-repeated concern
of the United States negotiators, the Korean negotiators
were now prepared to accept the U.S. proposal, thereby
clearly spelling out that "members of the United States
armed forces, civilian component, and their dependents"
are covered by the provisions of this article, as proposed
by the U.S. negotiators.

39. Agreed Minute #2 Re Paragraph 1(b)

Mr. Chang recalled that the Korean negotiators
had maintained the position that the U.S. proposal
with respect to offenses committed outside the Republic
of Korea, in the Agreed Minute #2 Re Paragraph 1(b),
had been unacceptable. First, Article 5 of the Korean
Criminal Code clearly stipulates that this law shall
apply to aliens who have committed certain offenses of
a serious nature outside the territory of the Republic
of Korea. Therefore, the provisions of this Agreed

0226

미.므 113-4

0227

Minute are clearly contradictory to the legal system of the Republic of Korea. Secondly, since the United States does not have a similar provisions in its legal system, offenses committed outside the Republic of Korea or outside the territory of the United States cannot be punished under the provisions of the U.S. draft. However, in view of the fact that the presumption envisaged in the Agreed Minute is highly hupothetical and occurence of such offenses would be exceptional and extremely rare, the Korean negotiators now accepted this Agreed Minute.

40. Agreed Minute Re Paragraph 2

Mr. Chang recalled that the Korean negotiators had proposed deletion of the Agreed Minute Re Paragraph 2 from the U.S. draft. The exclusive jurisdiction granted to the Korean authorities includes jurisdiction conferred on then with respect to offenses, including offenses relating to the security of the Republic of Korea, punishable only by the law of the Republic of Korea, The exclusive jurisdiction involved here would be exercised mostly over such offenses against the security of the receiving state as treason, sabotage, espionage, or violation of any law relating to official secrets or secrets relating to the national defense of the receiving state. In other words, Mr. Chang continued, the nature of such offenses is so serious that any mishandling thereof might result in grace danger to the very survival or existence of the government of the receiving state. Secondly, the U.S. draft calls for waiver of exclusive jurisdiction of the host country over offenders whom the U.S. military authorities have no legal right to punish eqitably as required by the relevant laws of the Republic of Korea. Thirdly, the Korean negotiators had been unable

0228

to find any precedents for this language in any other Status of Forces Agreement.

41. However, Mr. Chang said, in the light of the U.S. concern that legal grounds should be provided in the Agreement so that if the Korean authorities do not wish to exercise their exclusive jurisdiction in specific cases they could waive in favor of the United States offenses of a minor nature, for disciplinary action, the Korean negotiators accepted the Agreed Minute with the inclusion of the following understanding in the Agreed Joint Summary:

> "It is understood that the U.S. authorities shall exercise utmost restraint in requesting waivers of exclusive jurisdiction as provided for in the Agreed Minute Re Paragraph 2 of this Article."

42. Trial Safeguards

Mr. Chang said the Korean negotiators were now prepared to accept all of those trial safeguards still at issue which the U.S. negotiators, in subjecting their personnel to Korean jurisdiction, felt to be necessary for guaranteeing a fair trial. Their acceptance included reinsertion of the second sentence in the Agreed Minute Re Paragraph 9(a), and in the Agreed Minute Re Paragraph 9 acceptance of the following the understanding proposed by the U.S. negotiators at the 80th meeting with regard to subparagraph (a) of the second unnumbered paragraph, subparagraphs (d) ands (j) of the second unnumbered paragraph, the third unnumbered paragraph, and the fourth unnumbered paragraph.

43. Agreed Minute Re Paragraph 9(g)

However, Mr. Chang continued, with regard to the Agreed Minute Re Paragraph 9(g), the Korean negotiators had

0230

마.모113-4

0231

maintained that that portion of the Agreed Minute which
would render inadmissible as evidence any statement
taken from an accused in the absence of a U.S. representative
should be deleted, on the ground that since a representative
of the U.S. Government, a counsel, an interpreter, and
the accused himself are all given the right to be present
at all of the judicial proceedings, it is entirely within
the discretion of the U.S. Government representative
whether or not to appear in such sases. Furthermore, the
absence of the U.S. Government representative from the
judicial proceedings should not impair the admissibility
of a statement. Mr. Chang recalled also that when the two
sides had been discussing the problem of trial safeguards
pertaining to Agreed Minute Re Paragraph 9(g), the U.S.
negotiators had insisted that a representative of the U.S.
Government should be entitled to be present at all criminal
proceedings, while the Korean negotiators had ojected,
on the ground that the presence of the representative in
case of an in camera proceeding, however rare, would
prejudice the provisions of the Korean Constitution
as well as relevant laws of the Republic of Korea with respect
to public trials. Nevertheless, Mr. Chang continued, the
U.S. negotiators, contrary to their previous position,
had recently proposed, in paragraph 6 of the Agreed Minute
Re Paragraph 3(b), language which states that "a Korean
representative shall be entitled to be present at the
trial, except where his presence is incompatible with the
rules of the court of the United States or with the
security requirements of the United States, which are not
at the same time the security requirements of the Republic
of Korea." In the light of previous statements by the U.S.
negotiators that the representative of the U.S. Government

0232

마.모 113-4

0233

한·미국 간의 상호방위조약 제4조에 의한 시설과 구역 및 한국에서의 미국군대의 지위에 관한 협정(SOFA)
전59권. 1966.7.9 서울에서 서명 : 1967.2.9 발효(조약 232호) (V.33 실무교섭회의, 제81차, 1965.6.7)   239

has an affirmative duty to be present at the trial
session and will be available at all times, and that the
United States Government will ensure that he fulfills
this duty, the Korean negotiators, while accepting the
U.S. position in principle, in order to be consistent with
the relevant portion of this Article, propose, as a condition
of their acceptance of Paragraph 6 of the Agreed Minute
Re Paragraph 3(b), the addition of the following language
at the end of the Agreed Minute Re Paragraph 9(g):

> ".....except where his presence is incompatible
> with the rules of the court of the Republic of Korea
> or with the security requirements of the Republic
> of Korea, which are not at the same time the security
> requirements of the United States."

Mr. Chang predicted that cases of this type would be
extremely rare and the Korean negotiators do not foresee
any problem. The Republic of Korea and the United States
are both sovereign states and the ties between them are
especially close. Therefore, it is only reasonable that
representatives of each government should have corresponding rights and should not be discriminated against.

44. Paragraph 1(b) and Agreed Minute Re Paragraph 9(a)

Mr. Chang stated that the Korean negotiators
preferred the deletion of the word "civil" from Paragraph
1(b) to deletion of the second sentence of the Agreed Minute
Re Paragraph 9(a). Therefore, they proposed that the
second sentence, which had been deleted from the most
recent U.S. draft, be reinserted and the word "civil"
be deleted. The sentence to be reinserted would read:

> "A member of the United States armed forces,
> or civilian component, or a dependent, shall not be
> tried by a military tribunal of the Republic of Korea."

By accepting the above trial safeguard, Mr. Chang said,
the Korean negotiators had fully met the U.S. concern that
under existing Korean law a member of the U.S. armed forces,
civilian component, or a dependent may be tried by a Korean

0234

마흔113-4

0235

military court.

45. Paragraph 7(b)

Mr. Chang stated that the Korean negotiators were prepared to accept Paragraph 7(b) of the U.S. draft, with the addition of the following language at the end of the paragraph:

"In such cases, the authorities of the United States shall furnish relevant information on a routine basis to the authorities of the Republic of Korea, and a representative of the Government of the Republic of Korea shall have the right to have access to a member of the United States armed forces, the civilian component, or a dependent who is serving a sentence imposed by a court of the Republic of Korea in confinement facilities of the United States."

46. Mr. Chang explained that although the Korean negotiators are prepared to accept the unprecedented provisions of Paragraph 7(b) with respect to post-trial custody, they believe it necessary that the U.S. authorities routinely furnish to the Korean authorities such relevant information as the behavior and degree of repentance of those who are in penal servitude. In addition, the Korean authorities should be given the right of access to such persons not only for the purpose of seeing to it that they are carrying out their penal terms to the mutual satisfaction of the authorities of both governments but also in the interest of the persons in confinement. Denial by the U.S. negotiators of the Korean proposal would result in undue deprivation of those persons of such privileges as provisional release (parole) provided for in Article 72 of the Korean Criminal Code and Articles 49 to 52 of the Korean Prison Act.

47. Agreed Minute Re Paragraph 3(a)

Mr. Chang referred to the amended understanding pertaining to the issuance of duty certificates which the U.S. negotiators had proposed at the 80th meeting.

0236

미·흥 113-4

0237

한·미국 간의 상호방위조약 제4조에 의한 시설과 구역 및 한국에서의 미국군대의 지위에 관한 협정(SOFA)
전59권. 1966.7.9 서울에서 서명 : 1967.2.9 발효(조약 232호) (V.33 실무교섭회의, 제81차, 1965.6.7) 243

He recalled that, in responding to a question at the 75th meeting, the U.S. negotiators had stated that "since there are only five Staff Judge Advocates assigned to the U.S. armed forces in Korea and since the lowest-ranking one is assigned at the division level, issuance of the duty certificate would take place at the division level or higher and the lowest-ranking competent authority issuing a duty certificate would be a Brigadier General." Taking this explanation in good faith, Mr. Chang continued, the Korean negotiators had proposed the understanding that:

> "A duty certificate shall be issued only upon the advice of a Staff Judge Advocate, and the competent authority issuing the duty certificate shall be a General Grade Officer."

However, contrary to their previous explanation, the U.S. negotiators had proposed the addition of the words "or his designee" at the end of the understanding and had further elaborated their position that a general officer must, of necessity, delegate many acts to his senior subordinates.

48. In view of the decisive role the duty certificate plays in determining whether or not a certain offense is done in the performance of official duty, the Korean negotiators had originally proposed the Staff Judge Advocate as the authority issuing the duty certificate. However, in the hope of concluding discussion of this point, the Korean negotiators had accepted in the text the wording "competent military authorities of the United States forces", coupled with the condition envisaged in the understanding which they had proposed. In the light of the lengthy discussion of the duty certificate question and the basic agreement which had been reached thereon, the Korean negotiators consider that the proposed additional wording will delay complete agreement on this issue.

0238

마.모.113-4

0239

Therefore, they sincerely hope that the U.S. negotiators
will voluntarily withdraw their proposed revision of the
understanding.

49. Colonel Crawford stated that he wished to
correct the record to show that there are actually six
Staff Judge Advocates assigned to the U.S. armed forces
in Korea, instead of five as he had previously stated.
The sixth is a U.S. Air Force officer assigned to Osan
Air Base.

50. Mr. Chang resumed his remarks regarding official
duty certificates by stating that the Korean negotiators
maintained unchanged their position that the definition
of official duty should be incorporated in an Agreed Minute
in order to eliminate any possibility of ambiguity regarding
the question of what constitutes official duty. The Korean
negotiators, Mr. Chang continued, are well aware of the
difficulties and concern expressed by the U.S. negotiators
in connection with this problem. Nevertheless, they feel
very strongly that if the U.S. negotiators would generously
accept their proposal, it would greatly help them in
obtaining the understanding of the Korean people and
members of the National Assembly.

51. Agreed Minute Re Paragraph 3(b)

Mr. Chang stated that with regard to Paragraph 1
of the Agreed Minute Re Paragraph 3(b) the Korean
negotiators were now prepared to make one of their most
significant concessions by accepting the principle of the
one-time, **en masse** waiver of primary jurisdiction.
Accordingly, they were withdrawing their proposal to insert
at the beginning of Paragraph 1 the words "At the request
of the United States."

52. After taking into account the difficulties expressed
by the U.S. negotiators at the 80the meeting with

0240

미·믈113-4

0241.

regard to the 21-day limitation contained in the sentence proposed by the Korean negotiators for addition to Paragraph 4 of the Agreed Minute, Mr. Chang continued, the Korean negotiators withdrew their previous proposal and now proposed instead the following additional sentence:

"In case the Government of the Republic of Korea, in resolving disagreement in accordance with the foregoing provisions, determines that it is imperative that jurisdiction be exercised by the authorities of the Republic of Korea, the recall of waiver shall be final and conclusive."

53. As the U.S. negotiators were aware, Mr. Chang said, the above proposal is patterned after the question raised by the Korean negotiators at the 78th session and the affirmative reply given by the U.S. negotiators. Therefore, the Korean negotiators believe that this proposal does not deviate from, but is consistent with, the waiver formula proposed by the U.S. negotiators. Both sides are in agreement on the principle involved but differ only over the manner of stating the principle. Furthermore, the Korean negotiators wished to point out that just as their acceptance of the principle of a blanket waiver will fully meet the U.S. requirements, reciprocal acceptance by the U.S. negotiators of this proposed additional sentence would be very helpful to the ROK Government in securing the understanding and cooperation of the Korean people and the National Assembly. At the same time, it would dispel any misunderstanding or unnecessary dispute which might arise in the implementation of the waiver formula. The Korean negotiators hoped, therefore, that the U.S. negotiators would give full consideration to their proposal and accept it.

54. Mr. Chang said that, in view of the explanation by the U.S. negotiators that cases arising under the provisions of Paragraph 6 of the Agreed Minute Re 3(b)

0242

미 은 113-4

0243

would be extremely rare and cannot be expected to present any problems, the Korean negotiators accepted the U.S. draft of that paragraph.

55. Agreed Minute Re Paragraph 10(a) and 10(b)

Mr. Chang said the Korean negotiators wished to propose some modifications of the Agreed Minute Re Paragraph 10(a) and 10(b). According to the U.S. draft, he pointed out, the Korean authorities are not allowed to make any arrest within facilities and areas. The Korean negotiators, he said, are not demanding any unconditional right of arrest; the Korean authorities would seek consent in advance from the U.S. military authorities when such arrest within facilities and areas is necessary. The Korean negotiators would also like to point out that the right of pursuit of a flagrant offender who has committed a serious crime is an established principle of international law. Furthermore, if the arrest of a person who is within facilities and areas is desired by the Korean authorities, his arrest should be carried out by the U.S. authorities on request. The Korean negotiators believe mutual cooperation in these matters, as envisaged in their proposals, is essential. They wished to point out that the U.S. draft is also silent on the question of turning over to the Korean authorities persons arrested within facilities and areas. (In the light of the recent agreement of both sides on the custody provisions of this Article, the Korean negotiators believed the original U.S. position with regard to this Agreed Minute should be modified accordingly.)

56. Mr. Chang said that for the reasons just given, the Korean negotiators wished to propose the following modifications in the Agreed Minute:

0244

0245

a. "....The authorities of the Republic of Korea will normally not exercise the right of <u>arrest</u>, search, seizure, or inspection with respect to any person or property within facilities and areas in use by the military authorities of the United States or with respect to property of the United States wherever situated, except in cases where the competent military authorities of the United States consent to such <u>arrest</u>, search, seizure, or inspection by the Korean authorities search, seizure, or inspection by the Korean authorities of such persons or property <u>or in cases of pursuit of a flagrant offender who has committed a serious crime</u>."

b. "Where arrest or detention, search, seizure, or inspection with respect to persons or property within facilities and areas in use by the United States or with respect to property of the United States in the Republic of Korea is desired by the Korean authorities, the United States military authorities will undertake, upon request, to make such <u>arrest or detention</u>, search, seizure, or inspection....."

c. ".....Any person arrested or detained by the U.S. military authorities within, or in the vicinity of, a facility or area who is not a member of the United States armed forces, civilian component, or a dependent shall immediately be turned over to the authorities of the Republic of Korea."

57. <u>Agreed Minute #1 Re Paragraph 1(b)</u>

Mr. Chang stated that the martial law clause, proposed by the U.S. negotiators in their Agreed Minute #1 Re Paragraph 1(b), would requrie that during a period of martial law the provisions of the Criminal Jurisdiction Article would be suspended in that part of the Republic of Korea under martial law and that during the period of martial law the military authorities of the United States would exercise exclusive jurisdiction over U.S. personnel with pespect to offenses committed in the area under martial law. The Korean negotiators are unable to understand the importance which the U.S. negotiators attach to this provision. In the light of the large concessions already made by the Korean negotiators with regard to other provisions of this Article, and for reasons which they would now state, the Korean negotiators, Mr. Chang declared, are unable to accept this Agreed Minute.

0246

미-문 113-4

0247

58. First, Mr. Chang said, the Korean negotiators had already made an "unbearable" concession to the U.S. negotiators in accepting the U.S. proposal with regard to requests for waiver of exclusive jurisdiction by the ROK Government over offenses, including offenses against the security of the Republic, which are punishable by its law but not by the law of the United States. They had made this concession in the earnest hope that the U.S. negotiators would accede to the Korean requirements with regard to martial law.

59. In the second place, Mr. Chang continued, the Korean negotiators had given assurances in the past that under no circumstances would members of the U.S. armed forces, the civilian component, or their dependents be subject to trial by military tribunals of the Republic of Korea. To further convince the U.S. negotiators of their sincerity, the Korean negotiators had, at this meeting, indicated their willingness to accept the reinsertion of the second sentence of the Agreed Minute Re Paragraph 9(a) rather than as an understanding in the Agreed Joint Summary as they had proposed at the 70th meeting. Furthermore, they had accepted the principle of waiver of primary jurisdiction. Finally, Mr. Chang said, they had been unable to find any precedents for this provision in any other Status of Forces Agreement. Therefore, the Korean negotiators proposed deletion of this Agreed Minute, which would open the way for full agreement on the Criminal Jurisdiction Article and, eventually, the entire SOFA.

0248

기록113-4

0249

Invited Contractors Article

60. Taking up the Invited Contractors Article,
Mr. Chang recalled that full agreement had been reached
on all of its provisions with the exception of Paragraph 8,
relating to the question of criminal jurisdiction over
contracters, their employees, and the dependents of such
persons. The Korean negotiators had taken the position that
the Republic of Korea should have the primary right to
exercise jurisdiction over such persons while the U.S.
negotiators had argued that they should be subject to the
provisions of the Criminal Jurisdiction Article.

61. Mr. Chang said the Korean negotiators were
unable to accept Paragraph 8 for the following reasons.
First, since the status of the persons under discussion
was that of special commercial entrants with military
contracts, if they were turned over to the military authorities
of the United States in accordance with the relevant
provisions of the Criminal Jurisdiction Article, the U.S.
military authorities would have no legal grounds on which
to apprehend and punish them equitably. Secondly, their
status cannot be equated to the status of members of the
civilian component because the former are civilians
engaged in profit-seeking business in connection with
a military contract while the latter are employees of the
Government of the United States, working for the U.S.
armed forces. Consequently the members of the civilian
component are under strict punitive regulations of the
armed forces. Furthermore, the privileges which the
Korean negotiators deem essential for the performance by
the contractors of their contracts will be given to them

0250

가-211-3-4

0251

under the provisions of Paragraph 3 of this Article. Finally, Mr. Chang said, the Korean negotiators had been unable to find any precedents for Paragraph 8 in other Status of Forces Agreements.

62. In view of the considerations which he had just stated, Mr. Chang continued, acceptance by the ROK Government of such a discriminatory and unprecedented proposal would result in added burdens to the Government and might eventually jeopardize its position with the people and the National Assembly at the time of ratification of the Agreement and during its implementation. Therefore, the Korean negotiators requested the U.S. negotiators to take into full account the relevant factors and generously accept the Korean position, thereby strengthening the position of the ROK Government in its efforts to cope with possible future difficulties.

63. Mr. Chang said the Korean negotiators wished to retain in the Agreed Joint Summary the following understandings which had already been agreed to:

> a. The U.S. armed forces shall no longer bring into the Republic of Korea any employees of third-country nationality after the entry into force of this Agreement.

> b. If the U.S. authorities determine that there would be significant advantage for U.S. -ROK mutual defense to utilize one or more third-country corporations as USFK-invited contractors, the authorities of the Government of the Republic of Korea shall give sympathetic consideration to a U.S. request to extend the benefits of this Agreement to such non-U.S. corporations.

64. Mr. Chang stated that the Korean negotiators also wished to record their understanding that under the provisions of Paragraph 2 of this Article, designation as invited contractors of corporations and persons already located in the Republic of Korea at the time of entry into force of the Agreement shall be subject to review by the competent

0252

0253

authorities of the Republic of Korea and the United States in the Joint Committee. Further, any future renewal of the designation or any new designation with respect to the corporations and persons referred to in Paragraph 1 of the Article would be the subject of consultation in advance in the Joint Committee.

65. Mr. Fleck thanked Mr. Chang for the very detailed and comprehensive presentation made by the Korean negotiators and stated that the U.S. negotiators would give very careful and serious consideration to the Korean proposals.

0254

마흐로 113-4 (내)

0255

1. <u>GENERAL REMARKS</u>

The Korean negotiators now open the 81st session
of SOFA negotiation. At the outset of this session,
the Korean negotiators would like to articulate their
position at this final stage of negotiations.

It has been the desire and intent of the Korean
negotiators to reach full agreement and conclude this
long-pending negotiations as soon as possible. Taking
cognizance of the different opinion between both sides
we have exerted our utmost effort to accommodate the
requirement of the US negotiators as far as possible,

As the US negotiators stated at the 80th session,
the leaders of our two governments at the recent conference
in Washington reached agreement in principle on the major
outstanding issues of this agreement.

Therefore, it is our belief that both sides should
exert their utmost efforts to resolve the remaining
difference)which have been hindering an early conclusion
of this Agreement.

The Korean negotiators now are prepared to propose
their comprehensive and final draft of this agreement.
First of all the Korean negotiators accept the US draft
of Non-Appropriated Fund Organizations, Customs, MP and
Security Measures, Foreign Currency Controls, Duration,
Facilities and Areas, and Civil Claims. articles with certain
understanding and minor modification

The Korean negotiators, however, after having given
their most careful consideration to the rest of the

0256

Articles: Criminal Jurisdiction, Labor, Invited Contractors,
and Ratification, are prepared to accept the U.S. drafts
with modifications of important nature. This modifications
are essential and imperative to the Government of the
Republic of Korea. As has been pointed out by the
Korean negotiators at the past discussions, the people
and the National Assembly are deeply concerned and
critical toward the possible outcome of this negotiations.
This concern is clearly indicates in recent criticisms
directed to both Governments as appeared in the newspaper
columns and voiced by some eminent and responsible citizens.
Such embarrassing consequences will be neither for the
interests of the host state nor for the interests of
the sending state.

In keeping these facts in mind, the Korean negotiators
present the final position on entire articles of SOFA.

<u>2, Security Measures Article</u>

     Regarding the Security Measures Article, the U.S.
negotiators proposed at the 55th session that the U.S.
were prepared to agree to adoption of the original U.S.
draft of this Article, with the deletion of the phrase
"of the persons referred to in this paragraph, and
their property" provided the Korean negotiators would
agree to the inclusion in the Joint Agreed Summary
of an understanding that:

     "In cooperating with each other under this Article
     the two governments agree that each will take
     such measures as may be necessary to ensure the
     security and protection of the U.S. armed forces,
     the members thereof, the civilian component, the
     persons who are present in the Republic of Korea
     pursuant to the Article dealing with Invited
     Contractors, their dependents and their property."

The Korean negotiators accept the aforesaid U.S.
proposal.

0258

3. Non-Appropriated Fund Organizations Article and Customs Article

With respect to the Article dealing with Non-Appropriated Fund Organizations, the only remaining issue is the question as to who should be granted the use of Non-Appropriated Fund Organizations under item(f) of the Agreed Minute proposed by the U.S. negotiators.

To meet the requirements expressed by the U.S. negotiators, the Korean negotiators are now prepared to accept the U.S. Agreed Minute. However, in accepting the U.S. Agreed Minute, the Korean negotiators wish to retain in the Joint Summary Record the following understanding:

"It is understood that the present use of Non-Appropriated Fund Organizations by those organizations and persons other than those referred to in items (a),(b), (c), (d), and (e) shall immediately be suspended at the time of the entry into force of this Agreement. The extent of organizations and persons to be granted the use of such organizations under item (f) of this Minute shall be left to further negotiations between the appropriate authorities of the two Governments."

As we have agreed on NAFO problem, we have also automatically agreed upon Agreed Minute 7 of the Customs Article, thereby reaching full agreement on Customs Article.

Foreign Exchange Controls Article

The Korean negotiators are also prepared to accept the only remaining problem of Foreign Exchange Controls Article with respect to Agreed Minute proposed by the U.S. negotiators.

0259

42 Military Payment Certificate Article

Regarding the Military Payment Certificate Article, the two sides agreed to delete their respective Agreed Minute with the following understanding to be placed in the Agreed Joint Summary at the 55th session:

"The ROK and US negotiators agree that nothing in the Status of Forces Agreement in any way prevents the appropriate authorities of either the Republic of Korea or the United States from raising any appropriate matter at any time with each other. The US negotiators recognize the desire of the ROK authorities to discuss the disposal of Military Payment Certificates under custody of the ROK Government. However, both the ROK and US negotiators have agreed to remove from the SOFA text any reference to the question of compensation for Military Payment Certificates held by unauthorized persons. This agreement does not prejudice the position of either party in connection with discussion of this question through other channels."

Therefore, the remaining issues to be solved with respect to this article are the phrase "to the extent authorized by United States law" in the original US draft Para 1(b), and the phrase "subject to the military law of the United States" proposed by the Korean negotiators in lieu of the aforesaid US phrase. The Korean negotiators accept the US phrase, thereby reaching a complete agreement on this article.

However, it is to be stressed that this acceptance is made in our belief that the US authorities would take every measures necessary to prevent abusive transactions of MPC by the persons who are authorized to use such certificate.

0260

5. FACILITIES AND AREAS
(To be presented at 81st session)

1. The discussion on this Article relating to facilities and areas has been deferred since the 42nd session held on February 14 last year. It is recalled that there had been difference in their positions over the question of compensation to private property. The Korean side is now prepared to withdraw our previous contention with respect to compensation for private-owned property extremely demolished by the use of U.S. armed forces and accepts three paragraphs and Agreed Minute #1 provided for in Article V. However, the Korean side proposes additional Agreed Minute #2 which reads:

"All removable facilities, equipment and material or portions thereof provided by the Republic of Korea under this Agreement and located within the areas and facilities referred to in this Article shall be returned to the Republic of Korea whenever they are no longer needed for the purpose of this Agreement."

This additional Agreed Minute is made in the same intent of Agreed Minute of Article IV of the U.S. draft. The Korean side considers it logical that all removable properties provided by our Government and located in any area or facilities should be returned to the owners whenever they are no longer needed for the U.S. armed forces. Therefore, we propose this Agreed Minute in our belief that this would present no difficulty on the part of the U.S. side. Furthermore, this provision is also intended to supplement the provisions of Paragraph 2 and 3 of Article II, because those are merely related with the return of the facilities and areas as a whole or

0261

in part which are no longer needed and therefore do not
refer the removable property located within the areas
or facilities.

2. Turning to Article V relating to cost and
maintenance, the Korean side is now prepared to withdraw
our draft with regard to the compensation to the private-
owned property and accepts the U.S. draft upon clarification to be made by the U.S. side on certain wordings.

6. ✓ <u>CLAIMS ARTICLE</u>

With respect to the claims article, the Korean
negotiators, with a view to reaching full agreement, are
prepared to accept the revised drafts recently proposed
by the US negotiators, subject to only minor modifications.

Regarding Para 5(e)(i), the Republic of Korea accepts
the standard 25% - 75% distribution percentages as proposed
by the United States.

Regarding Para 5(e)(iii), the Korean negotiators
will withdraw their proposed Agreed Minute, if the US
side agrees to modify the Para 5(e)(iii) as follows:

"Every half year, a statement of the sums paid by
the Republic of Korea in the course of the half-yearly period
in respect of every case regarding which the liability,
amount, and proposed distribution on a percentage basis has
been approved by <u>both governments</u> shall be sent to the
appropriate authorities of the United States, together
with a request for reimbursement. Such reimbursement
shall be made in won within the shortest possible time.
The approval by both governments as referred to in this
subparagraph shall not prejudice any decision taken by
the arbitrator or adjudication by a competent tribunal
of the Republic of Korea as set forth in paragraphs 2(c)
and 5(c) respectively."

Although the Korean negotiators believe that their
Agreed Minute clearly sets forth the agreed principle that
there should be a mutual agreement on the settlement of
the Korean Government, and that the decision of a competent
tribunal of the Republic of Korea should be binding, they
are willing to accept the US proposal with minor modifications.

0263

The proposed Korean modifications are necessary to
define the contradictory provisions in the US draft.
Paragraph 5(c) provides that all the payment made by the
Korean government, whether made pursuant to a settlement
or to a adjudication, shall be binding the Parties, whereas
paragraph 5(e)(iii) implies that all the payment made by
the Korean government, regardless of whether the payment
was made pursuant to a settlement or to a adjudication,
shall not be binding unless the US authorities approves
in advance.

Therefore, the Korean negotiators propose to modify
the paragraph 5(e)(iii) of the US draft to avoid possible
misunderstanding.

Regarding Para 12, the Korean negotiators will
accept the US proposal with a minor modification of the
UNDERSTANDING to be included in the Agreed Joint Summary.
The modified UNDERSTANDING proposed by the Korean negotiators is
as follows: *The liability for claims generated by KSC personnel*

"~~The status of the KSC members~~ will be determined
by other negotiations between the Republic of Korea
and the United States."

The Korean negotiators believe that any decision as
to whether claims generated by KSC members should be
applied to this article or not can not be made until
the status of the KSC personnel are determined. Therefore,
the Korean negotiators propose to delete the first sentence
of the UNDERSTANDING proposed by the US negotiators.

0264

Regarding Para A2 of the Agreed Minute, the Korean negotiators are accepting the principle that the effective date of the claims provisions in other areas shall be determined by the Joint Committee, as the US side proposed at the previous session. However, to meet the requirement of both sides, the Korean negotiators propose following modified draft as Para A2 of the Agreed Minute:

"The provisions of paragraphs five, six, seven and eight will be extended, at the earliest date practicable, to other areas of the Republic of Korea as determined by the Joint Committee."

As the US negotiators are well aware, the Korean claims service has recorded an efficient operation since 1962. The State Compensation Committee manned with qualified commissioners and investigators who have ample experience in legal affairs. For equitable settlement of claims, proper laws and regulations are provided. And at the present time, the claims service is processing and settling the claims arising out of various damages caused by members of the Korean armed forces as well as government officials, to the satisfaction of the claimant concerned. This effectiveness of the Korean claims service has been demonstrated by the Korean negotiators in the previous formal and informal meetings.

Therefore, the Korean negotiators are certain that the Korean claims service is capable of assuming all the claims responsibilities from the date this agreement enters into force.

The US negotiators have agreed to adopt the proposed system automatically six months after the entry into force of this agreement without any decision of the Joint

0265

Committee in the Seoul Special City area. The US acceptance
of the Korean Claims Service system for application in
Seoul City area is, the Korean negotiators believe,
nothing but an admission on the part of the US side
that the Republic of Korea has a working and efficient claims
system, applicable to other part of the Republic of Korea.

Moreover, the authority of the Korean State Compensation
Committee extends to entire territory of the Republic
of Korea as that of the US armed forces claims service in
Korea does. The Korean negotiators simply cannot understand
the insistency of the United States that the application
of Korean system be limited to specific area.

However, to expedite the negotiation within the
earliest time possible by reaching full agreement on
this article, the Korean negotiators are making an
important concession to the United States regarding this
provision. The Korean negotiators believe that the United
States would give due consideration, at the Joint Committee,
to the capability of the Korean Claims Service so that
the provisions of paragraphs five, six, seven and eight
could be extended to other areas of the Republic of Korea
at the earliest date preacticable.

With this brief explanation of the Korean negotiators
regarding their position on claims article, the Korean
negotiators believe that the United States side would fully
understand the Korean position and accept the Korean
proposal without any further discussion.

0266

/7 LABOR ARTICLE

1. With regard to the Labor Article, the Korean negotiators with a view to reaching a prompt agreement are prepared to accept the U.S. draft as a whole with the following modifications thereof which are shown in the separate sheet: The proposed modifications touch upon six paragraphs of U.S. draft, namely; Paragraph 1(b), 3, 4(a), 5(b) and Agreed Minutes #4 and #5.

However, the most of ~~the~~ our modifications are made on the merit of technical ground rather than principle and we believe they will present no difficulty on the U.S. side since all of them are reasonable and valid.

a. Paragraph 1(a) and (b)

As Paragraph 1(a), the Korean side is prepared to agree to inclusion of the "invited contractors", and withdraw ~~our former contention~~ on the condition that the U.S. side accepts our new understanding on the Contractors Article.

With regard to sub-paragraph (b) relating to definition of employee, the Korean side is prepared to accept the U.S. version with an addition of sentence "Such civilian personnel shall be nationals of the Republic of Korea." By accepting the U.S. version of sub-paragraph (b), we concede to inclusion of KSC and domestics in the definition of employee. In making this most significant concession, the Korean side should like to propose certain understandings. As for the case of KSC, "exclusion of KSC from the definition of employee in this article shall not be ~~regarded~~ construed as ~~discard~~ of the position taken by the Korean negotiators with regard to the KSC status."

0267

In connection with the domestic, ~~We~~ accept the U.S. proposal on the ground that Article 10 of the Labor Standard Act excludes the domestic from its application. However, the rights and claims of the domestic within the scope of the Korean Civil Code and Labor Union Act are not impaired." ~~In addition, the insertion of the second sentence in respect of nationality of employees is requisite on our part to minimise the third nationals employment in Korea.~~ *strike out*

2. Paragraph 2 and Agreed Minute #2

Turning to Paragraph 2 and second sentence of Agreed Minute #2, the Korean side is now prepared to accept the U.S. versions with the following understanding: that

"The termination of employment on account of the U.S. military requirements referred to in the second sentence of Agreed Minute #2 shall be referred to the Joint Committee, in advance whenever possible, for mutual agreement, as provided for in Agreed Minute #4. ~~But~~ However such termination of employment as may be made in accordance with the relevant provisions of labor legislation of the Republic of Korea will not be subject to mutual agreement at the Joint Committee."

3. Paragraph 4(a)

As is shown in our modification the Korean side is prepared to accept almost every line of U.S. version of this paragraph with a change of wording which reads sub-paragraph (2) in place of sub-paragraph (3). Although we maintain that the cooling-off period shall be 70 days after the dispute is referred for conciliation, the Korean side now propose, as a compromise, to fix the starting date of cooling-off period at the second

0268

stage whether the dispute is dealt by the Joint Committee
itself or referred it to its specially-designated
committee. The U.S. draft paragraph 4(a)(5) does not
clearly accommodate the case when the Joint Committee
takes up the dispute itself without having referred the
matter to its special committee. Therefore, we urge
that insofar as the cooling-off period is concerned,
our compromised proposal ~~shall~~ should be accepted.

4. Paragraph 4(b) and (c)

The Korean side accepts paragraph 4(b) and (c) /relating
to collective action and emergency measures /without any change of wording.

5. Paragraph 5(b)

Turning to paragraph 5(b) regarding the deferment
of essentially skilled employees, the Korean side is
now prepared to accommodate the contention expressed
by the U.S. side by accepting the U.S. word "shall"
in place of "will" and by substituting the phrase "and
through mutual consultation" for the Korean phrase "and
through mutual agreement". We hope that through
amicable mutual consultation, there would arise no
disagreement between the appropriate authorities of
both sides in making deferment of skilled employees
essential to the mission of the U.S. armed forces.

6. Agreed Minute #5

The Korean side believes that the "interest"
of U.S. as appeared in the phrase "inimical to the
interests of the United States" in the U.S. draft, Agreed
Minute #5 does not imply those interests in terms of
wages, compensation or other forms of payments protection,
but rather imply those interest in terms of political
nature, such as the case when the leadership of the labor
group is dominated or influenced by leftist or communist

0269

elements. We maintain that if such an unlikely situation
develops, it would be undoubtedly inimical to the
interests of the Republic of Korea. Therefore, we
would like to add a word "common" and we believe the
U.S. side has no difficulty in agreeing on this
additional word.

   7. Paragraph 3 and Agreed Minute #4

      This is the paragraph the Korean side earnestly
maintain our original formula under which the deviation
from our labor legislation shall be referred to the
Joint Committee for mutual agreement. In order to
meet the U.S. requirements, we keep the U.S. phrase
"whenever possible" in our revised Agreed Minute, by
which the Korean version meets substantial requirements of the U.S. side. At the same time, the Korean
draft incorporates many phrases of the U.S. draft.
However, we maintain the phrase "under paragraph 3"
in lieu of "under this Article", because the latter
sometimes may lead to dual application of already
agreed deviation, which we consider irrelevant and
unnecessary. Regarding the phrase "whenever possible",
the Korean negotiators would like to have following
understanding recorded in the Joint Summary:

      "The deviations from Korean labor legislation shall
be referred to the Joint Committee for mutual agreement
in advance, except in the case when reaching an advance
agreement at Joint Committee would seriously hamper
military operation, particularly in an emergency."
We believe this understanding would present no difficulty
on the part of U.S. side in the light of the statement made
by the U.S. side at the 71st session.

0270

In conclusion the Korean side holds the view that
we have made significant concession in order to
meet the U.S. requirement as well as to come to complete
agreement on this Article. Therefore the Korean side
hope that the U.S. side would accept our proposal thus
paving the way for further close cooperation between
both sides.

0271

8. RATIFICATION OF AGREEMENT

(To be present at 81st session)

1. The Korean side modifies the US draft along the lines of other SOFA's by separating the clause with respect to legislative and budgetary action from the legislature in light of the fact that the entry into force of the Agreement is one thing and legislative and budgetary action is another. Furthermore, the Korean side would like to point out that Article 5 of the our Constitution clearly stipulates that the Treaties duly ratified and promulgated in accordance with the Constitution have the same effective force as those of the domestic laws of the Republic of Korea. Therefore, our Government is bound to enforce the Agreement as the domestic law regardless whether legislative and budgetary actions necessary for the execution of the provisions have been taken.

2. Regarding the four months intervals after legal procedures have been taken for entry into force of this Agreement, we believe that it is not only too long but contradictory to the expressed desire of an early conclusion of this Agreement, which has been maintained by both negotiators. Moreover, the Korean side cannot find such a long intervals in other SOFA's, and the Agreement should enter into force upon its ratification. However, we propose thirty days interval in order to accommodate the U.S. proposal. We hope the US side will find it possible to accept our revised Paragraphs 1 and 2. As for paragraph 2 of US draft, we accept the US version, being read as paragraph 3.

3. The Korean negotiators table this new paragraph 4 in the belief that this Agreement covers the Status US armed forces in Korea and has no relevance to the Unified Command per se, and that the privileges, immunities and facilities granted to the US armed forces as individuals or agencies of

0272

the unified command shall come under the provisions of the SOFA not other agreement.

At the ~~Sixth~~ session the US negotiators made the statement in connection with the applicability of SOFA to US armed forces personnel. We quote the statement "Within the scope of the matters agreed to, the provisions of the SOFA will apply to US armed forces and their members, while in the Republic of Korea pursuant to the resolutions of the United Nations Security Council or pursuant to the Mutual Defense Treaty. They will not, however, apply to members of the US armed forces for whom status is provided in the MAAG Agreement signed on Jan. 26, 1950 and personnel of service attache offices in the Embassy of the United States." and our proposal is drafted in line with this statement.

Therefore, the Korean negotiators consider that the US side would have no difficulty in accepting the proposed new paragraph 4 which reads:

"The provisions of the present Agreement shall apply to US armed forces, their members, civilian component, invited contractors or their dependents thereof, while in the Republic of Korea pursuant to the resolution of the United Nations Security Council or pursuant to the Mutual Defense Treaty. Such provisions will not, however, apply to members of the United States armed forces for whom status is provided in the Agreement for the Establishment of the United States Military Advisory Group to the Republic of Korea, signed on January 26, 1950 and personnel of the United States armed forces attached to the Embassy of the United States.

한·미국 간의 상호방위조약 제4조에 의한 시설과 구역 및 한국에서의 미국군대의 지위에 관한 협정(SOFA)
전59권. 1966.7.9 서울에서 서명 : 1967.2.9 발효(조약 232호) (V.33 실무교섭회의, 제81차, 1965.6.7)   279

9. Criminal Jurisdiction Article

(1) The Korean negotiators are prepared to accept the following provisions of the U.S. draft verbatim:

   a. Paragraph 1(a) with reference to persons subject to the jurisdiction of the military authorities of the United States.

   b. Agreed Minute Re Paragraph 2 with respect to request for waiver of Exclusive Jurisdiction of the Republic of Korea.

   c. Paragraph 11 with respect to suspension of This Article in time of Hostilities.

   d. Paragraph 12 with reference to Offenses Committed before the entry into force of this Agreement.

   e. Preamble of the Agreed Minute with reference to existing agreements relating to the exercise of jurisdiction over Personnel of the United Nations forces.

   f. Agreed Minute Re Paragraph 6 with respect to Appearance of Witness or Defendents.

   g. Agreed Minute Re Paragraph 1(b)(2) with respect to Offenses committed outside the Republic of Korea.

   h. The Second Sentence of Agreed Minute Re Paragraph 9(a) with respect to Korean Military Tribunal.

   i. Agreed Minutes Re Paragraph 9 with respect Trial Safeguards Except Agreed Minute Re Paragraph 9(g).

(2) They with-draw their provision of Agreed Minute Re Paragraph 4 with respect to Dual Nationals.

(3) The Korean negotiators accept the following provisions of the U.S. draft with modifications:

   a. Paragraph 1(b) with respect to the Korean authorities having jurisdiction.

   b. Paragraph 7(b) with respect to Post-Trial Custody

   c. Agreed Minute Re Paragraph 10(a) and 10(b) with reference to arrests within or in the vicinity of Facilities and Areas.

   d. Agreed Minute Re Paragraph 3(a) with respect to Official Duty Certificate.

   e. Agreed Minute Re Paragraph 3(b) with respect to Waiver of Primary Right to exercise Jurisdiction.

0274

1. <u>Persons subject to jurisdiction of the military authorities of the United States, Paragraph 1(a)</u>

With respect to persons subject to jurisdiction of the military authorities of the United States, it has been our position that since 1960 dependents are excluded from the categories of persons subject to the military law of the United States, and that they should, therefore, be left out of scope of our discussions. However, taking into account the oft-repeated concern of the United States side, the Korean negotiators are now prepared to accept the U.S. proposal, thereby clearly spelling out that "members of the United States armed forces, or civilian component, and their dependents" throughout the Article as proposed by the U.S. negotiators.

2. <u>Exclusive Jurisdiction, Agreed Minute Re Paragraph 2</u>

With respect to the U.S. Agreed Minute Re Paragraph 2, pertaining to requests in the Joint Committee for waivers of its exclusive jurisdiction, the Korean negotiators had proposed deletion of that Agreed Minute from the U.S. draft for the following reasons:

First; the exclusive jurisdiction granted to the Korean authorities covers the jurisdiction conferred on them with respect to offenses, including offenses relating to its security, only punishable by the law of the Republic of Korea. Exclusive jurisdiction involved here is mostly to be exercised over such offenses against the security of the receiving state as treason against the state, sabotage, espionage or violations of any law relating to official secrets or secrets relating to the national defense of the receiving state. In other words, the

- 2 -

0275

nature of such offenses are so serious that any mishandling thereof may result in grave danger to the very survival or existence of the Government of the receiving state itself.

Secondly, the U.S. negotiators are asking, under their proposal, for waiver of exclusive jurisdiction of the host country over offenders whom the U.S. military authorities have no law to punish equitably as required by relevant laws of the Republic of Korea.

Thirdly; the Korean negotiators are unable to find any similar international precedents in any other SOFA.

However, in the light of the U.S. concern that legal grounds should be provided for in the Agreement so that if the Korean authorities do not wish to exercise their exclusive jurisdiction in specific cases, they could waive, in favor of the United States, offenses of minor nature, for disciplinary sanction, by the Korean negotiators accept the U.S. Agreed Minute Re Paragraph 2 with the following Understanding in the Joint Summary Record:

"It is understood that the U.S. authorities shall exercise its utmost restraint in requesting for waivers of exclusive cases.provided for in Agreed Minute Re Paragraph 2 of this Article."

3. Suspension of Criminal Jurisdiction Article in time of Hostilities, Paragraph 11

With respect to paragraph 11 pertaining to suspension of Criminal Jurisdiction Article in time of hostilities, the Korean negotiators, with a view to accommodate the U.S. requirements to the fullest extent, accept the provision of paragraph 11 of the U.S. draft.

- 3 -

0276

4. <u>Offenses Committed before the entry into force of this Agreement, Paragraph 12</u>

With respect to paragraph 12 of this Article, the Korean negotiators accept the provision of paragraph 12. It is self-explanatory that the provisions of this Article shall not apply to any offenses committed before the entry into force of this Agreement.

<u>Preamble of the Agreed Minute</u>

The Korean negotiators also accept the preamble of the Agreed Minute proposed by the U.S. negotiators.

5. <u>Appearance of Witness or Defendents, Agreed Minute Re Paragraph 6</u>

The Korean negotiators are prepared to accept the U.S. proposal with respect to appearances of a witness or a defendent before a Korean court.

6. <u>Korean Agreed Minute Re Paragraph 4</u>

The Korean negotiators are now prepared to delete from their draft their Agreed Minute Re Paragraph 4 regarding dual nationals, if the U.S. negotiators have any objection to inclusion of that Agreed Minute.

7. <u>Jurisdiction over Offenses Committed outside the Republic of Korea, Agreed Minute Re Paragraph 1(b)(2)</u>

With respect to offenses committed outside the Republic of Korea, the Korean negotiators had maintained their position that the U.S. proposal provided for in Agreed Minute Re Paragraph 1(b)(2) was unacceptable for the following reasons:

First; the Article 5 of the Korean Criminal Code clearly stipulates that this law shall apply to aliens who have committed certain offenses of serious nature outside the territory of the Republic of Korea. Therefore, the paragraph 1(b)(2) is clearly contradictory to the legal system of the Republic of Korea.

- 4 -

0277

Secondly; since the United States does not have
similar provision in its legal system, offenses committed
either outside the Republic of Korea or outside the
territory of the United States can not be punished under
the proposed U.S. draft.

However, in view of the fact that the U.S. presumption Envisaged in the Agreed Minute Re Paragraph 1(b)(2)
is highly hypothetic and occurrence of such offenses
would be exceptional and extremely rare, and, therefore,
the provision would not carry much weight in its actual
implementation, the Korean negotiators accept the
provision of the Agreed Minute Re Paragraph 1(b)(2).

8. <u>The Korean authorities to have jurisdiction,
Paragraph 1(b), and Trial Safeguard, Agreed
Minute Re Paragraph 9(a)</u>

Provided that the U.S. negotiators delete the word
"civil" from the provision of paragraph 1(b) pertaining
to the Korean authorities having criminal jurisdiction,
the Korean negotiators are now prepared to accept the
second sentence of the Agreed Minute Re Paragraph 9(a)
which reads as following:

"<u>A member of the United States armed forces, or
civilian component, or a dependent, shall not be tried
by a military tribunal of the Republic of Korea.</u>"

By accepting the above trial safeguard, the Korean
negotiators have fully met the U.S. concern that under
existing Korean law, a member of the U.S. armed forces,
civilian component, or a dependent may be tried by a
Korean court. Accordingly, the Korean negotiators request
that the U.S. negotiators take into full account the
Korean position and delete the word "civil" from paragraph

- 5 -

0278

1(b) of the U.S. draft.

9. Post-trial Custody, Paragraph 7(b)

The Korean negotiators are prepared to accept the U.S. proposal with regard to post-trial custody provided for in paragraph 7(b) with the following additional sentences at the end of the U.S. provision:

"In such cases, the authorities of the United States shall furnish relevant information on a routine basis to the authorities of the Republic of Korea, and a representative of the Government of the Republic of Korea shall have the right to have access to a member of the United States armed forces, the civilian component, or a dependent who is serving a sentence imposed by a court of the Republic of Korea in confinement facilities of the United States."

Although the Korea negotiators are prepared to accept the unprecedented provision of paragraph 7(b) with respect to post-trial custody, they believe it necessary that the U.S. authorities routinely furnish to the Korean authorities such relevant information as behavior, degree of repentance of those who are under penal servitude. In addition to such information, the Korean authorities should be given the right of access to such persons not only for the purpose of seeing to it that they are carrying out penal terms to the mutual satisfaction, but also for the interests of the persons in confinement. Denial of our proposal by the U.S. side would result in undue deprivation from those persons of such privileges as provisional release (parole) provided for in Article 72 of the Korean Criminal Code, and Articles from 49 to 52 of the Korean Prison Act.

- 6 -

0279

9　10. Arrests within or in the vicinity of Facilities and Areas, Agreed Minute Re Paragraph 10(a) and 10(b)

With reference to the Agreed Minute Re Paragraph 10(a) and 10(b), the Korean negotiators propose the modified version by incorporating additional sentences into the U.S. draft.

First; according to the U.S. draft, the Korean authorities are not allowed to make any arrest within facilities and areas. The Korean negotiators are not demanding any unconditional right of arrest but Korean authorities will seek consent in advance from the U.S. military authorities when such arrest within facilities and areas is necessary. It is also to be pointed out that the right of pursuit of a flagrant offender who has committed a serious crime is an established principle of international law.

Furthermore, if a person is within facilities and areas and his arrest is desired by the Korean authorities, such person should on request be arrested by the U.S. authorities. In this connection, the Korean negotiators believe that if an efficient policing within facilities and areas are to be achieved, such mutual cooperation invisaged in the Korean proposal is essential.

The U.S. draft is also silent on the problem of turning over to the Korean authorities (such) *any* person, arrested within or in the vicinity of Facilities and areas, and (whose custody should, in accordance with *who is not a member of the United States armed forces, civilian component, or a dependent.* paragraph 5, be in the hands of the Republic of Korea.) (In the light of our recent agreement on the problem of custody, the original position of the U.S. side with

- 7 -

0280

respect to the Agreed Minute Re Paragraph 10(a) and 10(b)
should likewise be modified correspondingly. For instance,
paragraph 5(d) states, among other things, that any
member of the United States armed forces, the civilian
component, or a dependent committed an offense against
the security of the Republic of Korea, shall remain
under the custody of the authorities of the Republic of
Korea, whereas the last sentence of the Agreed Minute
Re Paragraph 10(a) and 10(b) states simply that any
person other than a member of the U.S. armed forces, the
civilian component, or a dependent arrested by the U.S.
military authorities shall immediately be turned over
to the authorities of the Republic of Korea, thereby,
contradicting each other as to transfer of those persons
whose custody should rest with the authorities of the
Republic of Korea.) Therefore, (to preclude any ambiguity
which may arise over the interpretation of relevant
portions of this Article,) the Korean negotiators propose
some additional sentences to be incorporated into the
U.S. Agreed Minute Re Paragraph 10(a) and 10(b). *so that the
modified version should read as following :*
    (1) Additional sentences to be incorporated into
the U.S. Agreed Minute between the first sentence and
the second sentence:

    "This shall not preclude the authorities of the
Republic of Korea from making arrests within facilities
and areas in cases where the competent authorities of
the United States armed forces have given consent, or in
cases of pursuit of a flagrant offender who has committed
a serious crime.

- 8 -

0281

6. o <u>Re Paragraph 10(a) and 10(b)</u>

o   The United States military authorities will normally make all
arrests within facilities and areas in use by the United States *armed*
forces. The Korean authorities will normally not exercise the
right of <u>arrest</u>, search, seizure, or inspection with respect to
any person or property within facilities and areas in use by the
military authorities of the United States or with respect to
property of the United States wherever situated, except in cases
where the competent military authorities of the United States
consent to such <u>arrest</u>, search, seizure, or inspection by the
Korean authorities of such persons or property, <u>or in case of
pursuit of a flagrant offender who has committed a serious crime</u>.

        Where <u>arrest</u>, search, seizure, or inspection with respect to
persons or property within facilities and areas in use by the
United States or with respect to property of the United States in
Korea is desired by the Korean authorities, the United States
military authorities ~~shall~~ *will* undertake, upon request, to make such
<u>arrest</u>, detention, search, seizure, or inspection. In the event
of a judgement concerning such property, except property owned or
utilized by the United States Government or its instrumentalities,
the United States will in accordance with its laws turn over such
property to the Korean authorities for disposition in accordance
with the judgement.

        The United States military authorities may arrest or detain
in the vicinity of a facility or area any person in the commission or
attempted commission of an offense against the security of that
facility or area. Any
        Any ~~such~~ person ~~who is~~ arrested or detained by the United
States military authorities, within or in the vicinity of a facility
<u>or area and</u> who is not a member of the United States armed forces
or civilian component or a dependent shall immediately be turned
over to the Korean authorities.

/(Proposed to the U.S. side on June 10, 1965, replacing the Korean
/   modified version of the Agreed Minute Re Paragraph 10(a) and 10(b)
\   tabled at the 81st Session, June 7, 1965)

                                                    0282

Where persons whose (arrests) is desired by the
authorities of the Republic of Korea and who are not
subject to the jurisdiction of the United States military
authorities within facilities and areas in use by the
United States armed forces, the United States military
authorities shall undertake, upon request, to arrest such
persons. [Any such person whose custody is to be in the
hands of the authorities of the Republic of Korea in
accordance with paragraph 5 of this Article, or any such
person who is not a member of the United States armed
forces, civilian component, or a dependent shall immediately be turned over to the authorities of the Republic
of Korea.]

    (2) Additional sentence to be placed at the beginning
of the last sentence of the Agreed Minute Re Paragraph 10(a)
and 10(b).

    (Any such person whose custody is to be in the hands
of the authorities of the Republic of Korea in accordance
with paragraph 5 of this Article, or".)

    11. Official Duty Certificate, Agreed Minute Re
        Paragraph 3(a)

    (1) With reference to the amended understanding
pertaining to the U.S. military authorities issuing
duty certificate proposed by the U.S. negotiators at
the 80th session, it is recalled that the U.S. negotiators,
in responding to the question raised by the Korean
negotiators at the 75th session, had clarified that
"since there are only five Staff Judge Advocates assigned
to the U.S. armed forces in Korea and since the lowest-
ranking one is assigned at the division level, issuance
of duty certificate would take place at the division
level or higher and the lowest-ranking competent authority
issuing a duty certificate would be a Brigadier General."

Taking in good faith the explanation, the Korean
negotiators had proposed the understanding that "A duty
certificate shall be issued only upon the advice of a
Staff Judge Advocate, and the competent authority issuing
the duty certificate shall be a General Grade Officer."
However, contrary to their previous explanation, the
U.S. negotiators had proposed the addition of the words
"or his designee" at the end of the understanding originally
proposed by the Korean negotiators, and had further
elaborated their position that a general officer must,
of necessity, delegate many acts to be done by his
senior subordinates.

In view of the decisive role the certificate play
in determination as to whether or not a certain offense
is done in the performance of official duty, the Korean
negotiators had originally proposed Staff Judge Advocate
as the authority issuing duty certificate. However, in
the hope of completing discussion thereon, the Korean
negotiators had accepted the wording in the U.S. draft
"competent military authorities of the United States
forces" coupled with the condition envisaged in our
understanding on compromising basis.

In the light of our lengthy discussions on the duty
certificate, and subsequent essential agreement thereon,
the Korean negotiators consider that the proposed addition
is obvious breach of our mutual understanding in solving
this problem of duty certificate, and we are forced to
be under an impression that the U.S. side is delaying the
complete agreement on this issue. Therefore, we
sincerely hope that the U.S. side voluntarily withdraw their
additionally proposed words.

- 10 -

0284

(2) With reference to the definition of official
duty, it is our unchanged position that the definition
of official duty should be incorporated into Agreed
Minute, and that since the definition is a guideline
and therefore, the definition be adopted as an Agreed
Minute so that it could wipe out any ambiguity over the
interpretation as to what constitute official duty.
Here again, both sides are in essential agreement with
respect to its content, but differ only in formality.

The Korean negotiators are well aware of the
difficulties and concern expressed by the U.S. side in
connection with this problem. Nevertheless, we feel
very strongly that if the U.S. side generously accept
our proposal, it will greatly help us in obtaining
understanding of the people and the National Assembly.
Therefore, we sincerely hope that the U.S. side generously
accept our proposal as an Agreed Minute.

Additional Sentence to paragraph 4. of she)

12. Waiver of Primary Right to exercise Jurisdiction;
Agreed Minute Re Paragraph 3(b)

(1) Regarding paragraph 1 of the Agreed Minute Re
Paragraph 3(b), the Korean negotiators, are now prepared
to make one of the most significant concessions by
accepting the principle of waiver not in each case but
en masse to the United States of the primary jurisdiction
provided for in paragraph 3(b) of this Minute. Accordingly,
the Korean negotiators withdraw their proposed phraseology
"At the request of the United States," at the beginning
of the provision of paragraph 1.

(2) With reference to the additional sentence proposed
by the Korean negotiators at the end of paragraph 4 of
the U.S. draft, the Korean negotiators, after taking into

- 11 -

0285

account the difficulties expressed by the U.S. negotiators
at the 80th session, regarding 21 day limitation, propose
in place of the previous proposal, the following additional
sentence;

"In case where the Government of the Republic of
Korea, in resolving disagreement in accordance with the
foregoing provisions, determines that it is imperative
that jurisdiction be exercised by the authorities of the
Republic of Korea the recall of waiver shall be final
and conclusive."

As the U.S. negotiators are aware, the above proposal
is patterned after the question raised by the Korean
negotiators and affirmative clarification thereon by the
U.S. negotiators at the 78th session. Therefore, it is
the belief of the Korean negotiators that this proposal
does not deviate from, but is consistent with the principles
of waiver formula proposed by the U.S. negotiators. In
this regards, both sides are in essential agreement with
respect to its content, but differ only in formality.

Furthermore, the Korean negotiators wish to point
out that while the acceptance by the Korean negotiators
of the principle of general waiver will fully meet the
U.S. requirements, the reciprocal acceptance by the U.S.
negotiators of the proposed additional sentence to
paragraph 4 will be very helpful to the Korean Government
in securing the understanding and cooperation from the
National Assembly and the people.

And at the same time, it will dispel any misunderstanding or unnecessary dispute which may arise in the
actual implementation of this formula.

The Korean negotiators sincerely hope that the
U.S. negotiators give full consideration to our proposal
and accept it favorably.

0286

(3) With respect to the paragraph 6 of the Agreed
Minute Re Paragraph 3(b), in view of the U.S. clarification that cases of offenses, to which the exceptional
clauses apply, would be extremely rare and they do not,
therefore, expect it to present any problem, the Korean
negotiators are now prepared to accept the U.S. version
in place of our previously agreed provision.

Additional Sentence is

13. Trial Safeguards, Agreed Minute Re Paragraph 9(g)

(1) The Korean negotiator are now prepared to accept
all of those trial safeguards still at issue which
the U.S. negotiators felt necessary for guaranteeing
a fair trial in subjecting their personnel to the Korean
jurisdiction.

The acceptance by the Korean negotiators, therefore,
include the second sentence of Agreed Minute Re Paragraph
9(a), the understanding proposed by the U.S. side at the
previous session with respect to subparagraph (a) of the
second sentence of Agreed Minute Re Paragraph 9, subparagraph (d) of the second unnumbered paragraph and the
4th unnumbered paragraph of Agreed Minute Re Paragraph 9,
sub-paragraph (j) of the second paragraph of Agreed Minute
Re Paragraph 9, and the third unnumbered papagraph of
Agreed Minute Re Paragraph 9.

(2) With respect to Agreed Minute Re Paragraph 9(g),
it is, however, recalled that the Korean negotiatorss
had maintained their position that the portion of the
Agreed Minute rendering inadmissible as evidence any
statement taken from an accused in the absence of a
United States representative should be deleted on the
ground that since a representative of the Government, a
counsel, an interpreter, and the accused himself are all

- 13 -

0287

given the right to be present at all of the judicial proceedings, it is entirely within the discretion of the Government representative whether or not to appear in such cases. Furthermore, the absence of the Government representative from the judicial proceedings should not impair the admissibility of a statement. It is also recalled that when the two sides were discussing the problem of trial safeguards pertaining to the Agreed Minute Re Paragraph 9(g), the U.S. side insisted that a representative of the U.S. Government should be entitled to be present at all criminal proceedings, while the Korean negotiators raised their objection on the ground that the presence of such representative in case of in camera proceeding would, however, rare the case may be, prejudice the provisions of the Korean Constitution as well as relevant laws of the Republic of Korea with respect to public trials. Nevertheless, contrary to their previous position, the U.S. negotiators have recently proposed in their paragraph 6 of the waiver formula, the language which reads that "a Korean representative shall be entitled to be present at the trial, except where his presence is incompatible with the rules of the court of the United States or with the security requirements of the United States, which are not at the same time the security requirements of the Republic of Korea." In the light of the U.S. statement in the past that the representative has an affirmative duty to be present at the sessions, and he will be available at all times and the United States will insure that he fulfills this duty, while accepting in principle the U.S. position, the Korean negotiators, to be consistent with relevant portion of this Article, propose as a condition to our

- 14 -

0268

acceptance of the U.S. paragraph 6, inclusion of additional sentence at the end of Agreed Minute Re Paragraph 9(g) that "except where his presence is incompatible with the rules of the court of the Republic of Korea or with the security requirements of the Republic of Korea, which are not at the same time the security requirements of the United States."

Cases of this type would be extremely rare and the Korean negotiators do not foresee any problem.

Republic of Korea as well as the United States are both sovereign states having specially close ties between them. Therefore, it is only reasonable that not discriminatory, but corresponding right should be accorded to a representative of each Government.

14. Martial Law and Jurisdiction, Agreed Minute Re Paragraph 1(b)(1)

The martial law clause proposed by the U.S. negotiators in their Agreed Minute Re Paragraph 1(b)(1) requires that during the period of martial law, the provisions of Criminal Jurisdiction Article should be suspended in the part of the Republic of Korea under martial law, and that in such time, the military authorities of the United States shall exercise exclusive jurisdiction over the U.S. personnel with respect to offenses committed in such part until martial law is lifted.

The Korean negotiators do understand the import of the U.S. concern envisaged in their proposal. Nevertheless, in the light of our already made big concessions elsewhere in the Article and for the following number of reasons, the Korean negotiators are unable to accept the U.S. proposal:

- 15 -

0289

First; the Korean negotiators have already made ~~unbearable~~ concession to the U.S. side in accepting the U.S. proposal with respect to request for waiver of exclusive jurisdiction over offenses, including offenses against the security of the Republic of Korea, and which are only punishable by its law but not by the law of the United States, in the earnest hope that the U.S. side will generally accede to the Korean requirements with respect to martial law.

Secondly; the Korean negotiators have given assurances in the past that under no circumstances, members of the U.S. armed forces, the civilian component, or their dependents will be subject to the military tribunal of the Republic of Korea. To further convince the U.S. side of our sincerity, the Korean negotiators have accepted the second sentence of Agreed Minute Re Paragraph 9(a) as an Agreed Minute rather than as an understanding in the Joint Summary Record as proposed ~~by the U.S. side at the 80th session.~~

Thirdly; it is also to be noted that the Korean side had accpeted the principle of general waiver of primary jurisdiction conferred on it.

Fourth; we are unable to find any similar precedents in other SOF Agreements.

Therefore, the Korean negotiators propose that the U.S. negotiators delete their Agreed Minute, and thereby, opening the way for reaching in full agreement on Criminal Jurisdiction Article, and eventually the Agreement itself.

- 16 -

0290

Thus, with a view to complete the current negotiations as expeditiously as possible, the Korean negotiators have made very important concessions to the U.S. side, and at the same time proposed some modifications we believe essential. Therefore, the Korean negotiators request that the U.S. side give favorable consideration to these modifications.

10. Invited Contractors Article

With respect to Invited Contractors Article, it is reminded that the both sides had reached in full agreement on the Article dealing with Invited Contractors except paragraph 8. Regarding paragraph 8 relating to Criminal Jurisdiction over contractors, their employees, and the dependents of such persons, the Korean negotiators had held their position that the authorities of the Republic of Korea should have the primary right to exercise jurisdiction over contractors, their employees, and the dependents of such persons referred to in paragraph 1 of this Article, whereas the U.S. negotiators had held their position that such persons referred to in paragraph 1 should be subject to those provisions of Criminal Jurisdiction Article with respect to members of the civilian component, and their dependents.

However, the Korean negotiators are unable to accept the U.S. draft for the following reasons:

First; their status being a special commercial entrant with military contract, if they are turned over to the military authorities of the United States in accordance with relevant provisions of the Criminal Jurisdiction Article, the U.S. military authorities will have no legal grounds to apprehend and punish such persons equitably according to the nature of offenses.

Secondly; Furthermore, their status should not be equated to the status of the civilian component simply because they are civilians engaged in profit-seeking business in connection with military contract, while members of the civilian component are employees of the

0292

Government of the United States working for their armed forces, and consequently being placed under strict punitive regulations relating to the armed forces.

Thirdly; those privileges deemed essential for their performance of contracts for the U.S. armed forces are already given to them under paragraph 3 of this Article.

Fourth; the Korean negotiators are unable to find any similar international precedents in other SOFA.

Consequently, the acceptance by the Korean Government of such discriminatory and unprecedented proposal will result in added burdens to the Government and may eventually jeopardize its position toward the people and the National Assembly in time of ratification of the Agreement and following implementation thereof.

Therefore, the Korean negotiators request that the U.S. side take into full account the relevant factors involved here and generously accept the Korean proposal, thereby, strengthening the position of the Korean Government in its effort to cope with possible future difficulties.

Further, the Korean negotiators wish to summarize their position and to retain in the Joint Summary Record the following understandings as guidelines for future implementation of this Article:

1. The U.S. armed forces shall no longer bring into the Republic of Korea any employees of third-country nationality after the entry into force of this Agreement.

2. Under the provisions of paragraph 2 of this Article, designation of such corporations and persons

0293

한·미국 간의 상호방위조약 제4조에 의한 시설과 구역 및 한국에서의 미국군대의 지위에 관한 협정(SOFA) 299
전59권. 1966.7.9 서울에서 서명 : 1967.2.9 발효(조약 232호) (V.33 실무교섭회의, 제81차, 1965.6.7)

already existing in the Republic of Korea before the
entry into force of this Agreement shall be subjec to
review between the competent authorities of the Republic
of Korea and the United States at the Joint Committee,
and any future renewal of designation upon termination
of such contracts or any new designation with respect
to corporations and persons referred to in paragraph 1
of this Article shall be the subject of consultation
in advance at the Joint Committee between both parties
to this Agreement.

    3. If the U.S. authorities determines that there
would be significant advantage for U.S.-ROK mutual
defense to utilize one or more third-country corporations
as USFK-invited contractors, the authorities of the
Government of the Republic of Korea shall give sympathetic
consideration to a U.S. request to extend the benefits
of this Agreement to such non-U.S. corporations.

    4. Those corporations, and persons providing
materials or services to the Organizations referred to
in paragraph 1 of Non-Appropriated Fund Organizations
Article in the form of concession, shall in no way be
construed as those corporations and persons provided
for in paragraph 1 of this Article.

    Those understandings being consistent with the
provisions of this Article, the Korean negotiators hope
that they are acceptable to the U.S. negotiators.

0294

정/리/보/존/문/서/목/록

기록물종류	문서-일반공문서철	등록번호	933 9606	등록일자	2006-07-27
분류번호	741.12	국가코드	US	주제	
문서철명	한.미국 간의 상호방위조약 제4조에 의한 시설과 구역 및 한국에서의 미국군대의 지위에 관한 협정 (SOFA) 전59권. 1966.7.9 서울에서 서명 : 1967.2.9 발효 (조약 232호) *원본				
생산과	미주과/조약과	생산년도	1952 - 1967	보존기간	영구
담당과(그룹)	조약	조약		서가번호	--
참조분류					
권차명	V.35 체결 교섭 및 준비, 1965.5-12월				

내용목차	1. 교섭 * 6.16-18 실무자 비공식 회의 2. 준비 * 일지 : 1953.8.7　　　이승만 대통령-Dulles 미국 국무장관 공동성명 　　　　　　　- 상호방위조약 발효 후 군대지위협정 교섭 약속 1954.12.2　　　정부, 주한 UN군의 관세업무협정 체결 제의 1955.1월, 5월　미국, 제의 거절 1955.4.28　　　정부, 군대지위협정 제의 (한국측 초안 제시) 1957.9.10　　　Hurter 미국 국무차관 방한 시 각서 수교 (한국측 제의 수락 요구) 1957.11.13. 26　정부, 개별 협정의 단계적 체결 제의 1958.9.18　　　Dawling 주한미국대사, 형사재판관할권 협정 제외 조건으로 행정협정 체결 의사 전달 1960.3.10　　　정부, 토지, 시설협정의 우선적 체결 강력 요구 1961.4.10　　　장면 국무총리-McConaughy 주한미국대사 공동성명으로 교섭 개시 합의 1961.4.15, 4.25　제1, 2차 한.미국 교섭회의 (서울) 1962.3.12　　　정부, 교섭 재개 촉구 공한 송부 1962.5.14　　　Burger 주한미국대사, 최규하 장관 면담 시 형사재판관할권 문제 제기 않는 조건으로 　　　　　　　교섭 재개 통고 1962.9.6　　　한.미국 간 공동성명 발표 (9월 중 교섭 재개 합의) 1962.9.20~　　제1-81차 실무 교섭회의 (서울) 　1965.6.7 1966.7.8　　　제82차 실무 교섭회의 (서울) 1966.7.9　　　서명 1967.2.9　　　발효 (조약 232호)

마/이/크/로/필/름/사/항

촬영연도	*롤 번호	화일 번호	후레임 번호	보관함 번호
2006-11-23	I-06-0070	03	1-226	

0001

1. 교섭

0002

<table>
<tr><td colspan="2" align="center"># 협 조 전</td><td>응신기일</td></tr>
</table>

분류기호 외방조 295 —제목 군대 지위 협정 조항에 대한 의견 회보

(협조제의)

수신 구미국장   발신일자 1965. 5. 31.

한·미 군대 지위 협정 조항중 효력 존속 조항, 비준 조항 및 개정
조항에 대한 당국의 의견을 아래와 같이 회보 합니다.

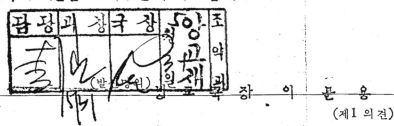

조약과장 이 문 용

(제1 의견)

효력 존속 조항에 관하여

1. 미국이 타국과 체결한 군대 지위 협정의 효력 존속 조항을
하여 볼때, 다음의 두 가지로 구별할수 있음.

가. 타국에 군대를 파견할시 동 파견의 근거를 어떠한 협정에 둠으
로써 군대 지위 협정의 효력을 군대 파견의 근거를 형성하고 있는 동 협
정의 효력 기간과 동일하게 하는 경우.

(제2 의견)

나. 군대 지위 협정의 효력기간 자체를 기한부로 정하는 경우.

2. 한미 군대 지위 협정에 있어서 미측이 제의 하는바는, 상기 (가)의
경우로써 한미 상호 방위 조약의 효력기간과 동일하게 규정하고 있으나,
이에 대하여 문제되는 점은 다음과 같음.

가. 본건 군대 지위 협정 서문에서 밝힌바와 같이, 주한미군 주둔의

한·미국 간의 상호방위조약 제4조에 의한 시설과 구역 및 한국에서의 미국군대의 지위에 관한 협정(SOFA)
전59권. 1966.7.9 서울에서 서명 : 1967.2.9 발효(조약 232호) (V.35 체결 교섭 및 준비, 1965.5-12월) 303

근거를 1953년 한미 상호 방위 조약 제4조에만 국한시키는 것이 아니고 국제연합 안전보장 이사회의 제 결의에도 또한 두고 있는것임.

나. 한미 상호 방위조약의 효력 기간은 미국이 타국과 체결한 방위조약의 효력기간과는 상이하게 무기한으로 하고 있으나 1년전의 통고로써 종결시킬수 있게 되어 있으므로, 동조약의 근거조항을 엄격히 해석할때(정치적인 면을 떠나서), 동조약의 효력 기간은 불안정한 상태에 있다고 할수 있음.

3. 상술한바와 같이, 외국에 주둔하고 있는 미군의 근거가 규각 상이하고, 주둔군 지위 협정의 규율 대상이 동 미군의 설치 근거 협정 자체가 아니라 주둔하고 있는 미군이며 또한 협정의 개정은 일반적으로 별도 규정이 없는한 원협정과 동일한 효력을 가지고 있다는 사실에 비추어, 미측이 제시한 본건 협정 존속 기간 조항을 다음과 같이 수정함이 좋을것임.

This Agreement shall remain in force while the United States forces are stationed in the Republic of Korea under the relevant resolutions of the United Nations Security Council and the Mutual Defense Treaty between the Republic of Korea and the United States of America signed on October 1, 1953 unless terminated earlier by agreement between the two Governments.

개정조항에 관하여

미측안에 대하여 이의 없음.

0004

비준조항에 관하여
_____

1. 미측의 비준조항에 대하여 문제시되는점은 다음과 같음.

가. 미측은 동조항 1항에서 밝힌바와 같이, 본건 협정의 발효 조치를 취할 의무를 아국 정부에 대하여 일방적으로 부담시키고 있는바, 여사한 심례는 미측이 체결한 군대지위 협정 가운데 " 리비아"와 " 아이스랜드" 경우 이외에는 찾어볼수 없는 극히 비평등적인 조항이라고 할수 있음. 조약이 양국 정부를 그 주체로 하여 상호간의 권리의무를 규율하는 문서 행위인 이상, 발효조치를 취할 의무를 아국 정부에게만 일방적으로 부담 시킴은 상호주의 원칙에 비추어서도 부당한것임.

나. 아국 정부로서는 본건 협정의 조속한 시행을 바라는 입장인바, 전기 1항에서 밝힌 발효를 위한 4 개월의 유예기간은 하등의 실질적 의의 가 없는것으로 사료됨.

다. 아국 정부로써 " 본 협정의 승인과 필요한 제반 입법 및 예산 조치의 완료 통고"를 협정의 발효 요건으로 하고 있는바, 여사한 조항 또한 아국 정부에게 일방적 부담을 과하고 있을뿐만 아니라 여사한 조치의 이행에는 상당한 시간이 요할것으로 사료되며, 이로써 협정 불이행에 대한 책임을 아국 정부에 귀속 시키는 결과가 될것임.

2. 상술한바를 고려하여 본건에 관한 미측제의 가운데 2항은 그대로 수락하고 1항은 다음과 같이 수정함이 가할것임.

1. This Agreement shall enter into force on the thirtieth day after the date on which the two Governments shall have notified each other to the effect that all legal requirements for the entry into force of this Agreement have been met.

0005

2. The Government of each Party to this Agreement undertakes to seek from its legislative necessary budgetary and legislative action with respect to for their execution..

(제 2 안)

1. This Agreement shall enter into force on the thirtieth day after the date on which the Government of the Republic of Korea shall have notified to the Government of the United States of America to the effect that all legal requirements for the entry into force of this Agreement have been met.
2. The Government of each Party to this Agreement undertakes to seek from its legislature necessary budgetary and legislative action with respect to for their execution.

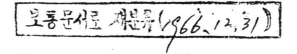

0006

협 조 전	응신기일

분류기호 외방조 195   제목 군대 지위 협정 조항에 대한 의견 회보

수신구 미국장   발신일자 1965. 5. 31.   (협조제의)

한·미 군대 지위 협정 조항중 효력 존속 조항, 비준 조항 및 개정 조항에 대한 당국의 의견을 아래와 같이 회보 합니다.

(발신명의) 방 교 국 장 이 문 용

(제1 의견)

효력 존속 조항에 관하여

1. 미국이 타국과 체결한 군대 지위 협정의 효력 존속 조항을 대별 하여 볼때, 다음의 두 가지로 구별할수 있음.

가. 타국에 군대를 파견할시 동 파견의 근거를 어떠한 협정에 둠으로써 군대 지위 협정의 효력을 군대 파견의 근거를 형성하고 있는 동 협정의 효력 기간과 동일하게 하는 경우,

(제2 의견)

나. 군대 지위 협정의 효력기간 자체를 기한부로 정하는 경우.

2. 한미 군대 지위 협정에 있어서 미측이 제의 하는 바는, 상기 (가)의 경우로서 한미 상호 방위 조약의 효력기간과 동일하게 규정하고 있으나, 이에 대하여 문제되는 점은 다음과 같음.   0007

가. 본건 군대 지위 협정 서문에서 밝힌바와 같이, 주한미군 주둔의

공통서식 1—23   (16절지)

근거를 1953년 한미 상호 방위 조약 제 4조에만 국한시키는것이 아니고 국제연합 안전보장 이사회의 제 결의에도 또한 두고 있는것임.

나. 한미 상호 방위조약의 효력 기간은 미국이 타국과 체결한 방위조약의 효력기간과는 상이하게 무기한으로 하고 있으나 1년전의 통고로써 종결시킬수 있게 되어 있으므로, 동조약의 관계조항을 엄격히 해석할때(정치적인 면을 떠나서), 동조약의 효력 기간은 불안정한 상태에 있다고 할수 있음.

3. 상술한바와 같이, 외국에 주둔하고 있는 미군의 근거가 각각 상이 하고, 주둔군 지위 협정의 규율대상이 동 미군의 설치 근거 협정 자체가 아니라 주둔하고 있는 미군이며 또한 협정의 개정은 일반적으로 별도 규정 이 없는한 원협정과 동일한 효력을 가지고 있다는 사실에 비추어, 미측이 제시한 본건 협정 존속 기간 조항을 다음과 같이 수정함이 좋을것임.

and agreed revision during

This Agreement shall remain in force while the United States forces are stationed in the Republic of Korea under the relevant resolutions of the United Nations Security Council and the Mutual Defense Treaty between the Republic of Korea and the United States of America signed on October 1, 1953 unless terminated earlier by agreement between the two Governments.

개정조항에 관하여

미측안에 대하여 이의 없음.

비준조항에 관하여

1. 미측의 비준조항에 대하여 문제시되는점은 다음과 같음.

가. 미측은 동조항 1항에서 밝힌바와 같이, 본건 협정의 발효 조치를 취할 의무를 아국 정부에 대하여 일방적으로 부담시키고 있는바, 여사한 실예는 미측이 체결한 군대지위 협정 가운데 " 리비아"와 " 아이스랜드" 경우 이외에는 찾어볼수 없는 극히 비평등적인 조항이라고 할수 있음. 조약이 양국 정부를 그 주체로 하여 상호간의 권리의무를 규율하는 문서행위인 이상, 발효조치를 취할 의무를 아국 정부에게만 일반적으로 부담시킴은 상호주의 원칙에 비추어서도 부당한것임.

나. 아국 정부로서는 본건 협정의 조속한 시행을 바라는 입장인바, 전기 1항에서 밝힌 발효를 위한 4개월의 유예기간은 하등의 실질적 의의가 없는것으로 사료됨.

다. 아국 정부로서 " 본 협정의 승인과 필요한 제반 입법 및 예산조치의 완료 통고"를 협정의 발효 요건으로 하고 있는바, 여사한 조항 또한 아국 정부에게 일방적 부담을 과하고 있을뿐만 아니라 여사한 조치의 이행에는 상당한 시간이 요할것으로 사료되며, 이로써 협정 불이행에 대한 책임을 아국 정부에 귀속 시키는 결과가 될것임.

2. 상술한바를 고려하여 본건에 관한 미측제의 가운데 2항은 그대로 수락하고 1항은 다음과 같이 수정함이 가할것임.

1. This Agreement shall enter into force on the thirtieth day after the date on which the two Governments shall have notified each other to the effect that all legal requirements for the entry into force of this Agreement have been met.

0009

2. The Government of each Party to this Agreement
undertakes to seek from its legislative necessary budgetary
and legislative action with respect to for their
execution.

(제 2 안)

1. This Agreement shall enter into force on the
thirtieth day after the date on which the Government
of the Republic of Korea shall have notified to the
Government of the United States of America to the
effect that all legal requirements for the entry
into force of this Agreement have been met.
2. The Government of each Party to this Agreement
undertakes to seek from its legislature necessary
budgetary and legislative action with respect to for
their execution.

보통문서로 재분류(1966. 12. 31)

It is has approved or agreement in accordance with their its legal procedures.

0010

RATIFICATION OF AGREEMENT
ARTICLE (XXX)

1. This agreement shall enter into force four months after the date of a written notification from the Government of the Republic of Korea to the Government of the United States that it has approved the agreement and has taken all legislative and budgetary action necessary to give effect to its provisions.

2. Subject to the provisions of Article XXII, Paragraph 12, this agreement shall, upon its entry into force, supersede and replace the agreement between the Government of the United States and the Government of the Republic of Korea on jurisdictional matters, effected by an exchange of notes at Taejon on July 12, 1950.

DURATION OF AGREEMENT
ARTICLE (XXIX)

This Agreement, and agreed revisions thereof, shall remain in force while the Mutual Defense Treaty between the United States and the Republic of Korea remains in force unless terminated earlier by agreement between the two Governments.

5-5   0011

RATIFICATION OF AGREEMENT

1. This Agreement shall enter into force thirty days
    after the date of a written notification from the
    Government of the Republic of Korea to the Government
    of the United States that it has approved the Agreement
    in accordance with its legal procedures.

2. The Government of the Republic of Korea shall undertakes to
    seek from its legislature all legislative and budgetary
    action necessary to give effect to its provisions
    of this Agreement.

3.

보통문 제개분(1966.12.31.

5-5

0012

RATIFICATION OF AGREEMENT

1. This Agreement shall enter into force <u>thirty days</u> after the date of a written notification from the Government of the Republic of Korea to the Government of the United States that it has approved the Agreement <u>in accordance with its legal procedures.</u>

2. <u>The Government of the Republic of Korea shall undertake to seek from its legislature</u> all legislative and budgetary action necessary to give effect to its provisions of this Agreement.

3. Subject to the provisions of Article XXII, Paragraph 12, this agreement shall, upon its entry into force, supersede and replace the agreement between the Government of the United States and the Government of the Republic of Korea on jurisdictional matters, effected by an exchange of notes at Taejon on July 12, 1950.

4. The provisions of the present Agreement shall apply to the United States armed forces, their members, civilian component, invited contractors or ~~their~~ dependents *thereof*, while in the Republic of Korea pursuant to the resolution of the United ~~States~~ Nations Security Council or pursuant to the ~~resolutions of the United~~ ~~Nations Security~~ Mutual Defense Treaty. Such provisions will not, however, apply to members of the United States armed forces for whom status is provided in the Agreement for the Establishment of the United States Military Advisory Group to the Republic of Korea, signed on January 26, 1950, and personnel of *the United States armed forces* ~~service attache officers~~ *attached to the* ~~in the~~ Embassy of the United States.

5-1

0013

1. The Korean side modifies the U.S. draft along the lines of other SOFAs by separating the clause with respect to legislative and budgetary action from the legislature in light of the fact that the entry into force of the Agreement is one thing and legislative and budgetary action is another. ~~We maintain the legislative and budgetary action is not necessary for all but the provisions which require such action for their execution.~~ Furthermore, the Korean side would like to point out that Article 5 of the our Constitution clearly stipulates that the Treaties duly ratified and promulgated in accordance with the Constitution have the same effective force as those of the domestic laws of the Republic of Korea. Therefore, our Government is bound to enforce the Agreement as the domestic law ~~and will expedite to take all legislative~~ and ~~budgetary action necessary to give effect to its provisions of this Agreement.~~

2. Regarding the four months intervals after legal procedures have been taken for entry into force of this Agreement, we believe that it is not only too long but contradictory to the expressed desire of an early conclusion of this agreement, which has been maintained by both negotiators. Moreover, the Korean side can't find such a long intervals in other SOFAs, and the Agreement ~~shall~~ should enter into force in thirty day's period which is standard formula in many Status of Forces Agreements. We hope the U.S. side will find it possible to accept our revised Paragraph 1 and 2. As for paragraph 2 of U.S. draft, we accept the U.S. version, being read as paragraph 3.

5-7

0014

3. The Korean negotiators table this new paragraph 4 in
the belief that this Agreement covers the Status of U.S.
armed forces in Korea and has no relevance to the Unified
Command per se, and that the privileges, immunities and
facilities granted to the U.S. armed forces as individuals
or agencies of the unified command shall come under the
provisions of the SOFA not other agreement.

At the 8th session the U.S. negotiators made the
statement in connection with the applicability of SOFA
to U.S. armed forces personnel. We quote the statement
"Within the scope of the matters agreed to, the provisions
of the SOFA will apply to U.S. Armed Forces and their
members, while in the Republic of Korea pursuant to the
resolutions of the United Nations Security Council or
pursuant to the Mutual Defense Treaty. They will not,
however, apply to members of the U.S. Armed Forces for
whom status is provided in the MAAG Agreement signed on
January 26, 1950 and personnel of service attache offices
in the Embassy of the United States." an Our to Korean
side they Our proposal provides as (this statement)
Therefore, the Korean negotiators consider that the
U.S. side would have no difficulty in accepting the proposed
new paragraph 4. which reads:

is drafted in line with

5—3

0015

"4. Within the scope of this Agreement, Paragraph 13 of Article III of the Agreement on Economic Coordination between the Republic of Korea and the Unified Command of May 24, 1952 shall not apply to members of the United States armed forces, civilian component or dependents thereof, as stipulated in Article I of this Agreement."

The provisions of the present agreement shall apply to U.S. Armed forces, and their members, civilian component, invited contractors and their dependents, while in the Republic of Korea pursuant to the resolutions of the United Nations Security Council or pursuant to the Mutual Defense Treaty. They will not, however, apply to members of the U.S. Armed forces for whom status is provided in the MAAG Agreement signed on January 26, 1950 and personnel of service attache offices in the Embassy of the United States.

0016

~~0015~~

<table>
<tr><td colspan="2" style="text-align:center">**협 조 전**</td><td>응신기일</td></tr>
</table>

분류기호 외방교-~~~ 제목 **군대지위협정의 조항 체제**

수신 **구미국장**   발신일자 **방교국장**   (협조제의)

　　지난번 제 80 차 군대지위협정 교섭 실무자회의(1965.5.26)에서
미측에서 제시한 제안의 조항 체제에 관하여, 별첨과 같이
당국의 의견을 제시하오니 동 협정 체결의 교섭에 있어서
참고하여 주시기 바랍니다.

　　유 첨. 조항 체제표. **1**통 (발춘명의) **끝.**

　　　　　방 교 국 장   이   문   용   (제1 의견)

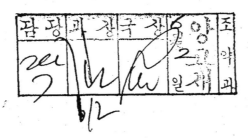

(제2 의견)

0017

0016

협 조 전	응신기일

분류기호 외방조-<s>50</s>	제목 군대지위협정의 조항 체제

수신 **구미국장**   발신일자 **방교국장**   (협조제의)

지난번 제 80 차 군대지위협정 교섭 실무자회의(1965.5.26)에서
미측에서 제시한 제안의 조항 체제에 관하여, 별첨과 같이
당국의 의견을 제시하오니 동 협정 체결의 교섭에 있어서
참고하여 주시기 바랍니다.

유 첨. 조항 체제표, 1 통, <u>끝</u>.
(발신명의)

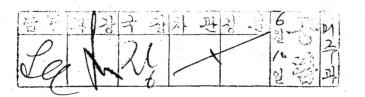

방 교 국 장   이   문   용

(제1 의견)

(제2 의견)

우리들이 제의한 안

Facilities and Area I grant and return
Facilities and Areas – Security Measures

0020

| 분류기호 | 제 목 주둔군 지위 협정의 결문에 관한 |
| 외방조 74 | 교섭자료 제시 |

수신 구미국장　　　　　발신일자 1965. 6. 10.　　（협조제의）

표기건에 관한 다음 2개안을 제시 하오니 참고 하시기 바랍니다.

다만 국가의 검위면을 고려하여서도 제 1 안이 소망되는바나. 이를 채택

하기 위하여서는 합동위원회가 본건 협정의 운영상 야기되는 행정 문제를

처리하는 행정 기관이라는 성격을 떠나서 본 협정 관계조항에 관한 한·미
　　　　　　　　　　　　　　（발신명의）

양국간의 해석상의 차이가 생길때 이를 다루는 법적인 기관이다고 볼수

있는 직접적인 근거가 없는 이상. 이에 대한 양국간의 양해 사항（1의견）

이 필요 합것으로 사료 됩니다.

제 1 안 :

　　　IN WITNESS WHEREOF, the undersigned, being duly
　　　authorized by their respective Governments, have
　　　signed the present Agreement.

　　　DONE in duplicate, in the Korean and English（의견）
　　　languages, both equally authentic, at Seoul,
　　　this　　　day of　　　, one thousand nine hundred
　　　and sixty five.

　　　For the Government of the Republic of Korea:
　　　For the Government of the United States of America:

공통서식　1-23　　　　　　　　　0021　　（16절 지）

한·미국 간의 상호방위조약 제4조에 의한 시설과 구역 및 한국에서의 미국군대의 지위에 관한 협정(SOFA) 321
전59권. 1966.7.9 서울에서 서명 : 1967.2.9 발효(조약 232호) (V.35 체결 교섭 및 준비, 1965.5-12월)

제 2 안 :

IN WITNESS WHEREOF, the undersigned, being duly
authorized by their respective Governments, have signed
the present Agreement.

DONE in duplicate, in the Korean and English languages,
at Seoul, this   day of   , one thousand nine hundred
and sixty five. The Korean and English texts shall have
equal authenticity, but in the case of divergence in
interpretation, the English text shall prevail.

For the Government of the Republic of Korea:
For the Government of the United States of America:

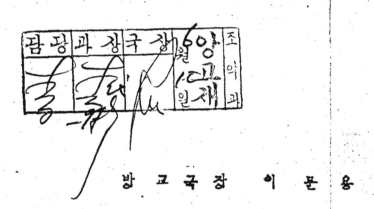

방 교 국 장 이 문 용

0022

협 조 전	응신기 일

분류기호 외방조 74	제 목	주둔군 지위 협정의 결문에 관한 교섭자료 제시

수신 구미국장   발신일자 1965. 6. 10.   (협조제의)

　　표기견에 관한 다음 2개안을 제시 하오니 참고 하시기 바랍니다.

다만 국가의 권위면을 고려하여서도 제 1 안이 소망되는 바나. 이를 채택

하기 위하여서는 합동위원회가 본건 협정의 운영상 야기되는 행정 문제를

처리하는 행정 기관이라는 성격을 떠나서 본 협정 관계 조항에 관한 한. 미

양국간의 해석상의 차이가 생길 때 이를 다루는 법적인 기관이라고 볼수

（발신명의）

있는 직접적인 근거가 없는 이상. 이에 대한 양국간의 양해 사항 (제1의견)

이 필요 할것으로 사료 됩니다.

제 1 안 :

　　IN WITNESS WHEREOF, the undersigned, being duly

authorized by their respective Governments, have

signed the present Agreement.

　　DONE in duplicate, in the Korean and English
(제2의견)
languages, both equally authentic, at Seoul,

this 　　　 day of 　　　 , one thousand nine hundred

and sixty five.

For the Government of the Republic of Korea:

For the Government of the United States of America:

공통서식 1—23   2-1   0023   (16절 지)   9h

제 2 안 :

    IN WITNESS WHEREOF, the undersigned, being duly
authorized by their respective Governments, have signed
the present Agreement.

    DONE in duplicate, in the Korean and English languages,
at Seoul, this   day of   , one thousand nine hundred
and sixty five. The Korean and English texts shall have
equal authenticity, but in the case of divergence in
interpretation, the English text shall prevail.

For the Government of the Republic of Korea:

For the Government of the United States of America:

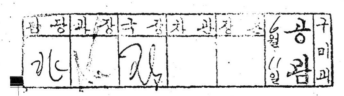

방 교 국 장   이 문 용

2-2   0024

기 안 지

기안자	미주과 이근팔	전화 번호		공보	필요	불필요

	과장	국장	차관	장관		

협조 서명	자명안	법무부: 검찰과장	검찰국장	차관	장관	보존 년한	
기안 년 월 일		65.6.15.	시행 년월일			정서기장	
분류기호 문서번호		외구미 722.2					

경유					
수신		건 의		발신	
참조					

제 목	주둔군지위협정 체결 교섭 실무자회의에 임할
	우리측 입장

　　　당부에서는 한·미간 주둔군지위협정 체결 교섭

실무자회의에서 한·미양측의 의견차이로 말미아마

형사재판관할건조항 중 상금 해결을 보지 못하고 있는

계엄령 선포지역의 관할건 행사문제에 관하여 다음과

같이 해결방안을 수립코저 하오니 재가하여 주시기

바랍니다.

　　　　　　　　형사재판관할건에 관한 해결방안

계엄령 선포지역의 관할건 행사

　1. 양측입장

　　(1) 한국측 : 삭제 주장.

　　(2) 미국측 : 대한민국이 계엄령을 선포한 경우에는

　　　　　　본조의 규정이 즉시 정지되고 미군당국은

공통서식 1—2 (갑)　　　　　　　　　　　0025　　　　(16절지)

계엄령이 해제될때 까지 계엄령 선포지역내

에서 미군인, 군속 및 그들의 가족에 대하여

전속적 관할권을 갖는다.

2. 해결방안 : 미측안 수락. 끝

보통문서로 재분류(1966.12.31.)

0026

기 안 지

기 안 자	미주과 이근팔	전 화 번 호		공 보	필 요	불필요

	과 장	국 장	차 관	장 관			
	11/6	6/16					

협 조 서 명 자					보 년	존 한	
기 안 년 월 일	1965. 6. 16.	시 행 년월일		통 제 관	검열 1965.6.17 통제관	정서 기	기 장
분류기호 문서번호	외구미 722. 2 —						
경 유 수 신 참 조	대 통 령 참조: 비서실장 국무총리 참조: 비서실장		발 신		장 관		
제 목	한.미간 주둔군지위협정 체결 교섭에 관한 특별보고						

1965 년 6 월 16 일 상오 9 시 15 분부터 동 10 시 15 분 가지

당부에서 개최된 한.미 양측 실무자단 간의 비공식회담에서 토의된

내용을 별첨과 같이 보고합니다.

유 첨: 주둔군지위협정 체결 교섭에 관한 특별보고 1 부. 끝

0027

공통서식 1—2 (갑)　　　　　　　　0026　　(16절지)

한·미간 주둔군지위협정 체결교섭 실무자
회의 특별보고

1. 일시   1965년 6월 16일 상오 9시 15분부터 동 10시까지
2. 장소   외무부 구미국장실
3. 토의내용

　　　　한·미간의 의견차이로 말미아마 실무자 교섭회의
에서 상금 합의를 보지못하고 있는 계엄령 선포지역내의
형사재만관할건 조항의 효력문제에 관하여 미측이 우리측
삭제주장을 완강히 거부하고 있음에 감하여 우리측은
교섭의 조속한 타결을 위하여 미측안대로 "대한민국이
계엄령을 선포한 경우에는 본조의 규정이 즉시 정지되고
미군당국은 계엄령이 해제될때까지 계엄령선포지역내에서
전속적인 관할건을 행사한다" 라는 미측합의의사록의
규정을 수락한다면 우리측이 제 81 차 회의에서 제안한
기타 문제에 관한 입장을 일괄 수락할 것인지 여부를
문의한바, 미측 현지교섭단으로서는 그러한 경우에도
기타 문제에 대하여는 다음과 같이 해결되어야 할것을
본국정부에 건고할것이라는 입장을 밝혔다.

　　가. <u>군초청계약자</u>

　　　　미측은 군초청계약자와 그들의 가족도 미군속과
그들의 가족과 동등하게 형사재만관할건 조항의 규정이
적용되어야 한다고 주장하여 왔으나 우리측이 이를
삭제할 것을 주장한데 대하여 미측은 우리측안 대로
군초청계약자 및 그들의 가족을 한국의 재만관할건에
복하게 하되 형사재만관할건 조항에 열거된 피의자의
건리와 신병구금에 관한 규정이 적용되어야 한다.

　　나. <u>노동조건의 적용범위</u>

　　　　우리측은 미군이 고용조건에 있어 한국법령을
준수치 못할 경우 가능한한 사전에 "상호합의" 를
위하여 합동위원회에 회부되어야 한다는 우리측 입장에
대하여 미측은 군사상의 필요성이 항상 선행하여야

0028

하며 따라서 한국측이 상호 합의하여야 한다는 입장은
수락할수 없으나 가능한 한 사전에 "협의와 적절한
조치"를 위하여 합동위원회에 회부되어야 한다는 방향
으로 수정되어야 한다.

다. 협정의 발효사항

미측이 제안한 발효기간인 4개월은 너무 길기
때문에 우리측은 60일로 단축할 것을 제안하고 입법
및 예산조치는 발효후 취할 것을 제안하였는데 대하여
미측은 우리안이 국회의 비준동의와 필요한 입법 및
예산조치를 취한후 90일 이후에 발효하는 것으로 수정
되어야 한다는 것임.

라. 당부의견

상기와 같은 미측 현지 교섭 실무자단의 의견으로
보아 우리정부가 계엄령에 관한 미측안을 그대로 수락
한다하여도 군초청계약자 및 노무조항등에서 미측은
계속 양보를 요구할 것이며 이에 대하여 우리측은
계엄령에 관한 미측안을 수락하는 경우에도 군초청계약자
및 노무조항등에서 우리측의 입장을 주장하려면 조기
타결은 불가능하며 앞으로 시일이 더욱 소요될 것으로
봅니다.

0029

경제·과학심의회의사무국

경사임—1753—456   (74—9451)   1965. 6. 17

수 신   외무부장관
참 조   구미국장
제 목   자료송부의뢰

　　　　당심의회의 정책 수립에 자하고자 하오니 한·미 행정협정중
노무조항과 관계되는 제반 자료를 송부하여 주시기 바랍니다. 끝

　　　　　사 무 국 장   김   정

0030

기 안 지

기 안 자	미주과 김기조	전화번호		공보	필요	불필요
과 장		국 장 전결		차 관		장·관

협조	자명				보존년한	
기안	년월일	1965.6.21.	시행년월일	통제관	1965.6.22	정서 기장
분류	기호 문서번호	외구미 722.2-				
경수 참	유신 조	경제·과학심의회 사무국장		발신	장 관	

제 목 한·미주둔군지위협정중 노무조항에 관한 자료

1. 대:1965. 6. 17. 검사입 1753-456

2. 대호로 요청하신 자료를 별첨과 같이 보내드립니다.

유첨: 1. 노무조항 설명서

· 2. 합의될 예정인 노무조항(영문) 끝

1965. 6. 31에 예고문에 의거 일반문서로 재분류함

노 무 조 항

우리의 노무조항은 그 체제상 일본이나 "나토" 제국의 주둔군 지위협정이 채택한 "간접 고용제" 와는 다른 "직접 고용제" 를 토대로 제규정이 마련되게 되어있다. 이러한 제도의 차이는 일본이나 독일이 전후 주둔군에 대한 노동자의 제공이 전쟁배상의 일환으로 피 점령국 당국에 의하여 이루어 졌음에 반하여 우리나라는 미군이 해방후 진주 부터 그들의 필요에 따라 직접 노동자를 채용하였던 전통에 따라 이룩된 것이다. 따라서 각 항목에 있어서 우리나라의 노무조항은 다른 나라와 근본적으로 상이하다.

이러한 "직접 고용제" 의 토대에서 우리 조항은 고용주가 미군과 그 기관 및 미군에 의한 초청계약자로 확정되었으며 고용인은 KSC 및 가사 사용인을 제외한 한국 국적을 가진 민간인으로 정하였다. 이러한 고용주는 그들 한국인 고용인을 직접 고용하고 관리하게 된다. 그 고용과 관리에 있어서 고용주와 고용인은 특별한 경우를 제외하고는 한국 노동법령을 준수하여야할 것을 규정하고 있다. 미군은 주지하는 바와 같이 한국에 방위 목적을 위하여 주둔하고 있음으로 한국 노동 법령을 준수함에 있어서 특별한 경우 예컨대 군사 작전상 불가피한 경우에는 한국 노동법령을 준수할수 없을때가 있을 것이다. 이러한 경우를 예상하고 노동조항은 그러한 경우에는 한국 법령을 그대로 준수하지 않아도 무방하다고 규정하였다. 그러나 그러한 특별한 경우를 제외하고 한국 법령을 준수치 못할 경우에는 한국측의 사전합의를 얻어서만 가능하도록 규정하고 있다.

한편, 노동쟁의 절차, 단체 행동권의 비행사자, 비상시의 노동력 배정, 비상시의 기술자 병역 연기, 고용인의 소득세 납부, 노동조합의 승인등 문제에 관하여 별도의 규정을 마련하였다. 그 내용은 대체로 다음과 같다.

1. 노동쟁의 해결절차로서 쟁의가 발생하면 한국 노동청, 합동위원회 혹 그가 지정하는 특별 분과위원회 , 합동 위원회의

8-2

0032

손으로 회부되어 조정되며 제2단계에 회부 됨 날로부터 70 일이 경과되지 않는한 단체 행동권을 행사할수 없도록 규정되어 있다.

2. 단체 행동권에 있어서 합동 위원회에서 미군의 사명 수행과 한국의 관계법령을 참작하여 파업등 단체 행동권을 행사하지 못할자의 범위를 결정하기로 되어 있다. 이 경우 파업권 행사를 미리 제한 받지 아니한 모든 고용인은 단체 행동권을 향유하는 것이 된다.

3. 한국 정부가 노동력을 배정하게 될 경우 미군에게도 한국군 에게 주는 배정 특권을 동일하게 부여하도록 규정하였으며 비상시 미군 업무 수행에 불가결한 기술을 습득한 긴요한 자에 대하여는 미군이 요청하면 상호 합의하에 병역 의무를 연기하여 주기로 되어 있다.

4. 미군 고용인의 소득세 납부에 있어서 본 협정발효 후 부터 고용주는 고용인에 대한 급료중에서 한국 소득세법에 규정된 원천 과세액을 공제하여 한국 정부에 납부하기로 되었다.

5. 노동 조합은 한국법에 의하여 설립되면 승인되도록 되었다. 그러나 한미 공동 이익에 배치하는 조합은 인정하지 않기로 하였다. 그리고 고용인이 조합에 가입하였다거나 가입하지 않았다고 해서 고용에 있어서 차별대우를 하는등과 같은 부당 노동행위를 금하고 있다.

현재까지 이상과 같은 내용으로 노무조항은 대체로 합의에 도달하였다.

영구문서 - 재분류 (1966. 12. 31.)

0033

8-3

기 안 지

기 안 자	미주과 김기조	전 화 번 호		공 보	필 요	불필요
	과 장	국 장		차 관 전결	장 관	
협 조 자 서 명					보 존 년 한	
기 안 일 년 월 일	1965. 6. 19.	시 행 년월일	통 제 관	정 서	기 장	
분류기호 문서번호	외구미					
경 수 참	유신 조	~~대통령 참조 . 비서실장~~ ~~국무총리 참조 . 비서실장~~	발신	장 관		
제 목	한미 주둔군 지위협정 미결사항에 대한 한미 비공식 실무자회의 개최보고					

한미 주둔군 지위협정 교섭에 있어서 미해결로 있는 문제에

대하여 한미 양측의 실무자들은 6월 17일과 6월 18일 양차에 걸쳐

외무부 구미국장실에서 비공식 회의를 개최하였는바 그 경위를

다음과 같이 보고합니다.

    1. 일시

        가. 1965. 6. 18.   10:00 - 12:30

        나. 1965. 6. 19.   14:00 - 16:00

    2. 참석자

        가. 한국측

            구미국장   장 상 문

            미주과장   이 남 기

            미주과사무관   김 기 조

        나. 미국측   0034

공통서식 1-2 (갑)   4-1   (16절지)

미대사관   후텝 1등 서기관

미 8 군   킨 니

미8군 쇼텅   하 - 비

3. 노무조항에 관한 토의와 합의 사항.

　　가. 미국측은 6. 18 노무조항 합의 의사록 제 4항에 관하여

　　　　한국안을 수락할수 없음을 밝히고 다음과 같은 안의

　　　　수락을 제안함.

　　　　4. When employers cannot conform with provisions
of labor legislation of the Republic of Korea applicable
under this Article on account of the military
requirements of the United States armed forces, the
matter shall be reported, in advance whenever possible,
to the Joint Committee for consideration and appropriate
action.

　　　　이에 대하여 우티측은 소위 "적절한 조치" 란 일방적으로

　　　　결정될 우려가 있음으로 이를 반대하였음. 그에 대하여

　　　　미측은 다음과 같은 대안을 제시함.

4............, the matter shall be referred to the
Joint Committee for mutual agreement whenever possible.

UNDERSTANDING

　　　　The deviation from Korean labor legislation
shall be referred to the Joint Committee for mutual
agreement whenever possible, except in the case
when such referral would seriously hamper military
operations.

4 - 2

0035

이에 대하여 우믜측은 양해 사항중에서 "가능한 한 "(whenever

possible) 을 삭제할 것을 요구하자 미측은 그를 수락할수 없다고

밝혔음. 이에 대하여 우믜측은 다시 다음과 같은 🔲안을 제시하였음.

4........., the matter shall be referred to the
Joint Committee for mutual agreement. In the event that
an agreement cannot be reached on the matter in the
Joint Committee, it may be made the subject of review
for appropriate action through consultation between
the appropriate authorities of both Governments.

UNDERSTANDING

It is understood that the deviation from Korean
labor legislation may not be referred to the Joint
Committee in the case when such referral would seriously
hamper military operations.

나. 미측은 상기 우믜안을 도매또 검토한후 6. 19 재차 내방하여

다음과 같은 안을 제시하면서 토의하자고 요청함.

4. When employers cannot conform with provisions
of labor legislation of the Republic of Korea applicable
under this Article on account of the military
requirements of the United States armed forces, the matter
shall be reported, in advance whenever possible, to
the Joint Committee for consideration and appropriate
action. In the event mutual agreement cannot be
reached in the Joint Committee regarding appropriate
action, the issue may be made the subject of review

4--3   0036

through discussions between appropriate officials of
the Government of the Republic of Korea and the
diplomatic mission of the United States of America.

　　　이상안에 대하여 장시간 토의끝에 우티측은 "보고되어야 한다"
(shall be reported) 를 "회부되어야 한다"
(shall be referred) 로 수정할것과 양해 사항으로 다음
사항을 추가할것을 요청하였음.

　　　1. 한국 노동법령을 준수치 못하는것은 합동위원회에 회부
　　　　　함에 있어서 그러한 회부가 군사 작전을 극심하게 저해할
　　　　　경우에는 회부하지 아니할수 있다.

　　　2. 본문중 "적접한 조치" (appropriate action)
　　　　　는 상호 합의 하였을 경우에 한하여 취할수 있다.

이상 우티측 제안을 미측에서 전부 수락함으로서 일단락을 보고
노무 조항 전체에 걸쳐 일단의 합의가 이루어 졌음. 이상의
합의 내용을 차기회의에서 공식화 하기로 함.　　　끝.

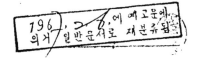

4-4　　　　　　　　　　　　　　0037

In the event a labor dispute is not resolved by the foregoing procedures, the Joint Committee shall restrict exercise of the right of further collective action by the essential employees in order to safeguard the military operations of the United States armed forces for the joint defense of the Republic of Korea. ~~The categories of the~~ the essential employees referred above shall be determined by the Joint Committee.

In the event a labor dispute is not resolved by the foregoing procedures, the Joint Committee, in cases deemed necessary for the military mission in the joint defense of the Republic of Korea, shall restrict exercise of the right of further collective action by the essential employees, who shall be determined by the Joint Committee in consideration of the role of the employees of the United States armed forces in the defense of the Republic of Korea and pertinent provisions of legislation of the Republic of Korea.

0038

In the event a labor dispute is not resolved
by the foregoing procedures, the Joint Committee shall
restrict exercise of the right of further collective
action by the essential employees in order to ~~so as not to~~
~~t~~safeguard the military operations of the United States
armed forces for the joint defense of the Republic
of Korea. The essential employees referred above
shall be determined by the Joint Committee.

In the event an agreement cannot be
reached on this question in the Joint Committee,
it may be made the subject of review through discussions
between appropriate officials of the Government
of the Republic of Korea and the diplomatic mission
of the United States of America.

0039

(b) The Joint Committee, taking into consideration the role of the employees of the United States armed forces in the defense of the Republic of Korea and pertinent provisions of legislation of the Republic of Korea, shall determine those categories of essential employees who shall not exercise the right of further collective action in the event a labor dispute is not resolved by the foregoing procedures. In the event an agreement cannot be reached on this question in the Joint Committee, it may be made the subject of review through discussions between appropriate officials of the Government of the Republic of Korea and the diplomatic mission of the United States of America.

0040

ARTICLE XVII Labor

In the event a labor dispute is not resolved by the foregoing procedures, exercise of the right of further collective action by ~~essential~~ employees ~~may~~ *shall* be restricted by the decision of the Joint Committee

※ ~~where such action~~ ~~in cases deemed necessary for the military mission~~ ~~in the joint defense of the Republic of Korea.~~

Understanding

The *categories of* ~~essential~~ employees ~~referred to in~~ *who shall not exercise the right of further collective action under* paragraph 4(b) of Article XVII shall be determined by the Joint Committee in consideration of the role of the employees of the United States armed forces in the defense of the Republic of Korea and pertinent provisions of legislation of the Republic of Korea.

※ *in cases where such collective action would seriously hamper military operations in the joint defense of the Republic of Korea.*

0041

4. (b) In the event a labor dispute is not resolved by
the foregoing procedures, the Joint Committee, in cases
deemed necessary for the ^military mission in the defense of the Republic of Korea,
may restrict exercise of the right of further collective
action by the essential employees, ^who ~~the categories of which~~
shall be determined by the Joint Committee in consideration
of the role of the employees of the United States armed
forces in the defense of the Republic of Korea and pertinent
provisions of legislation of the Republic of Korea.

X~ In the event a labor dispute is not resolved by the
foregoing procedures, the Joint Committee, shall restrict
exercise of the right of further collective action by
the essential employees, the categories of which shall
be determined by the Joint Committee.

*so as not to seriously hamper the military operation
of U.S. Armed Forces in Korea for the Joint defence of R.O.K.*

K   The Joint Committee, taking into consideration
the role of the employees of the United States armed
forces in the defense of the Republic of Korea, shall
determine those categories of essential employees
whose exercise of the right of further collective
action shall be restricted in the event a labor
dispute is not resolved by the foregoing procedures.

0043

In the event a labor dispute is not resolved by the
foregoing procedures, the Joint Committee, taking into
consideration the role of the employees of the United
States armed forces in the defense of the Republic of
Korea and pertinent provisions of legislation of the
Republic of Korea, shall determine those categories of
essential employees who shall not exercise the right of
further collective action(in cases where such collective
action would seriously hamper military operations in the
joint defense of the Republic of Korea.)..........

of the U.S. armed

In the event a labor dispute is not resolved

by the foregoing procedures, the Joint Committee, in

cases deemed necessary for the military mission

in the defense of the Republic of Korea, may restrict

exercise of the right of further collective action

by the essential employees, who shall be determined

by the Joint Committee in consideration of the role of

the employees of the United States armed forces

in the defense of the Republic of Korea and pertinent

provisions of legislation of the Republic of Korea.

— 0044

In the event a labor dispute is not resolved by the foregoing procedures, exercise of the right of further collective action by *(essential)* employees shall be restricted by the decision of the Joint Committee in cases where such collective action would seriously hamper military operations in the joint defense of the Republic of Korea. ....

<u>Understanding</u>

The categories of *(essential)* employees who shall not exercise the right of further collective action under paragraph 4(b) of Article XVII shall be determined by the Joing Committee in consideration of the role of the employees of the United States armed forces in the defnese of the Republic of Korea and pertinent provisions of legislation of the Republic of Korea.

0045

ARTICLE XVII (LABOR)

(Underlined parts are modifications.)

Present Draft	New Draft
3. To the extent not inconsistent with the provisions of this Article or the military requirements of the United States armed forces, the conditions of employment, compensation, and labor management relations established by the United States armed forces for their employees shall conform with provisions of labor legislation of the Republic of Korea.	3. To the extent not inconsistent with the provisions of this Article, or except as may otherwise be mutually agreed, the conditions of employment, compensation, and labor-management relations established by the United States armed forces for their employees shall conform with provisions of labor legislation of the Republic of Korea.
4. (b) The Joint Committee, taking into consideration the role of the employees of the United States armed forces in the defense of the Republic of Korea and pertinent provisions of legislation of the Republic of Korea, shall determine those categories of essential employees who shall not exercise the right of further collective action in the event a labor dispute is not resolved by the foregoing procedures. In the event an agreement cannot be reached on this question in the Joint Committee, it may be made the subject of review through discussions between appropriate officials of the Government of the Republic of Korea and the diplomatic mission of the United States of America.	4. Employees or any employee organization shall have the right of further collective action in the event a labor dispute is not resolved by the foregoing procedures, except in cases where the Joint Committee determines such action seriously hampers military operations of the United States armed forces for the joint defense of the Republic of Korea. In the event an agreement cannot be reached on this question in the Joint Committee, it may be made the subject of review through discussions between appropriate officials of the Government of the Republic of Korea and the diplomatic mission of the United States of America.

0046

Present Draft

New Draft

AGREED MINUTES

2. The undertaking of the Government of the United States to conform to the provisions of labor legislation of the Republic of Korea does not imply any waiver by the Government of the United States of its immunities under international law. The Government of the United States may terminate employment at any time the continuation of such employment is inconsistent with the military requirements of the United States armed forces.

4. When employers cannot conform with provisions of labor legislation of the Republic of Korea applicable under this Article on account of the military requirements of the United States armed forces, the matter shall be referred, in advance whenever possible, to the Joint Committee for consideration and appropriate action. In the event mutual agreement can not be reached in the Joint Committee regarding appropriate action, the issue may be made the subject of review through discussions between

2. The undertaking of the Government of the United States to conform to the provisions of labor legislation of the Republic of Korea does not imply any waiver by the Government of the United States of its immunities under international law. The Government of the United States may terminate _through mutual agreement_ employment at any time the continuation of such employment is inconsistent with the military requirements of the United States armed forces.

4. When employers cannot conform with provisions of labor legislation of the Republic of Korea applicable under this Article on account of the military requirements of the United States armed forces, the matter shall be referred, _in advance_, to the Joint Committee _for mutual agreement_. In the event mutual agreement cannot be reached in the Joint Committee regarding appropriate action, the issue may be made the subject of review through discussions between appropriate officials of the Government

0047

appropriate officials of the
Government of the Republic of Korea
and the diplomatic mission of the
United States of America.

5. A union or other employee
group shall be recognized by the
employers unless its objectives
are inimical to the common interests
of the Republic of Korea and the
United States. Membership or non-
membership in such groups shall
not be a factor in employment or
other actions affecting employees.

of the Republic of Korea and the
diplomatic mission of the United
States of America.

5. A union or other employee
group shall be recognized by the
employers unless its objectives
are inimical to the common interests
of the Republic of Korea and the
United States. Membership or non-
membership in any employee organization
or engaging in any collective action
applicable under this Article shall
not be a factor in employment or
other actions affecting employees.

0048

LABOR ARTICLE

Agreed Minute

4. When employers cannot conform with provisions of labor legislation of the Republic of Korea applicable under this Article on account of the military requirements of the United States armed forces, the matter shall be <u>referred</u>, in advance whenever possible, to the Joint Committee for consideration and appropriate action. In the event mutual agreement cannot be reached in the Joint Committee regarding appropriate action, the issue may be made the subject of review through discussions between appropriate officials of the Government of the Republic of Korea and the diplomatic mission of the United States of America.

(Presented by U.S. side and agreed with an understanding on June 18, 1965)

LABOR ARTICLE

Article (XXV)

1. In this Article the expression:

    (a) "employer" refers to the United States Armed Forces (including nonappropriated fund activities) and the persons referred to in the first paragraph of Article (XVIII).

    (b) "employee" refers to any civilian (other than a member of the civilian component) employed by an employer (except (1) a member of the Korean Service Corps and (2) a domestic employed by an individual member of the United States Armed Forces, civilian component or dependent thereof.)

2. Employers may recruit, employ and administer their personnel. Recruitment services of the Government of the Republic of Korea will be utilized insofar as is practicable. In case employers accomplish direct recruitment of employees, employers will provide such relevant information as may be required for labor administration to the Office of Labor Affairs of the Republic of Korea.

3. To the extent not inconsistent with the provisions of this article or the military requirements of the United States Armed Forces, the conditions of employment, compensation, and labor-management practices established by the United States Armed Forces for their employees will conform with the labor laws, customs and practices of the Republic of Korea.

4. (a) In consideration of provision for collective action in ROK labor legislation, any dispute between employers and employees or any recognized employee organization, which cannot be settled through the use of labor relations procedures of the United States armed forces shall be settled as follows:

(1) The dispute shall be referred to the Office of Labor Affairs, ~~XXXXXXXXXXXXXXXXXXXXXXXXXXXXXX~~ Republic of Korea, for conciliation.

(2) In the event that the dispute is not settled by the procedure described in (1) above within 20 days, the matter will be referred to the Joint Committee, which may refer the matter to a special committee designated by the Joint Committee for further conciliation efforts.

(3) In the event that the dispute is not settled by the procedures outlined above, the Joint Committee will resolve the dispute, assuring that expeditious procedures are followed. The decisions of the Joint Committee shall be binding.

(5) (4) Failure of any recognized employee organization or employee to bide by the decision of the Joint Committee on any dispute, or engaging in practices disruptive of normal work requirements during the in violation of provisions settlement procedures, shall be considered just cause for the withdrawal of recognition of that organization and the discharge of that employee.

(4) (5) Neither employee organizations nor employees shall engage in any practices disruptive of normal work requirements unless a consultation right

2

0051

period of at least ~~70~~ days has elapsed after the dispute is referred to ~~the Joint Committee~~, as stipulated in subparagraph (1), above.

(b) The Joint Committee, taking into consideration the role of the employees of the United States armed forces in the defense of the Republic of Korea and pertinent provisions of legislation of the Republic of Korea, shall determine those categories of essential employees who shall not exercise the right of further collective action in the event a labor dispute is not resolved by the foregoing procedures. In the event an agreement cannot be reached on this question in the Joint Committee, it may be made the subject of review through discussions between appropriate officials of the Government of the Republic of Korea and the diplomatic mission of the United States of America.

(c) In the event of a national emergency, such as war, hostilities or situations where war or hostilities is imminent, the application of this Article shall be limited in accordance with emergency measures taken by the Government of the Republic of Korea in consultation with the military authorities of the US.

5. (a) Should the Republic of Korea adopt measures allocating labor, the United States Armed Forces shall be accorded allocation privileges no less favorable than those enjoyed by the Armed Forces of the Republic of Korea.

3

0052

(b) In the event of a national emergency, such as war, hostilities, or situations where war or hostilities ~~may be~~ imminent, employees who have acquired skills essential to the mission of the United States Armed Forces, shall, upon request of the United States armed forces, be deferred ~~from Republic of Korea~~ military service or other compulsory service. The United States Armed Forces shall furnish in advance to the Republic of Korea lists of those employees deemed essential.

6. Members of the civilian component shall not be subject to Korean laws or regulations with respect to their terms and condition of employment.

AGREED MINUTES

1. It is understood that the Government of the Republic of Korea shall be reimbursed for direct costs incurred in providing assistance requested pursuant to paragraph 2.

2. The undertaking of the United States Government to conform to Korean labor laws, customs, and practices, does not imply any waiver by the United States Government of its immunities under international law. The United States Government may terminate employment at any time the continuation of such employment is inconsistent with the military requirements of the United States Armed Forces.

3. Employers will withhold from the pay of their employees, and pay over to the Government of the Republic of Korea withholdings required by the income tax legislation of the Republic of Korea.

4

21-4

0053

4. When employers cannot conform with provisions of labor legislation of the Government of the Republic of Korea applicable under ~~this Article~~ on account of the military requirements of the United States Armed Forces, the matter shall be reported in advance whenever possible, to the Joint Committee for ~~its consideration and review.~~

5. A union or other employee group will be recognized unless its objectives are inimical to the interests of the United States. Membership or non-membership in such groups shall not be a factor in employment or other actions affecting employees.

Para (3) of

mutual or mutual agreement

(Common)

for consideration and appropriate action.

5

21-5

AGREED MINUTES

1. The Republic of Korea will make available, at designated induction points, qualified personnel for Korean Service Corps units in numbers sufficient to meet the requirements of United States Armed Forces.

2. It is understood that the Government of the Republic of Korea shall be reimbursed for direct costs incurred in providing assistance requested pursuant to paragraph 2.

3. The undertaking of the United States Government to conform to Korean labor laws, customs, and practices, does not imply any waiver by the United States Government of its immunities under international law. The United States Government may terminate employment at any time the continuation of such employment is inconsistent with the military requirements of the United States Armed Forces.

4. Employers will withhold from the pay of their employees, and pay over to the Government of the Republic of Korea withholdings required by the income tax legislation of the Republic of Korea.

5. When employers cannot conform with provisions of labor legislation of the Government of the Republic of Korea applicable under this Article on account of the military requirements of the United States Armed Forces, the matter shall be reported, in advance whenever possible, to the Joint Committee for its consideration and review.

0055

LABOR ARTICLE
Article (XXV)

1. In this Article the expression:

     (a) "employer" refers to the United States Armed Forces (including nonappropriated fund activities) and the persons referred to in the first paragraph of Article (XVIII).

     (b) "employee" refers to any civilian (other than a member of the civilian component) employed by an employer, except (1) a member of the Korean Service Corps and (2) a domestic employed by an individual member of the United States Armed Forces, civilian component or dependent thereof. *Such civilian personnel shall be nationals of the Republic of Korea.*

2. Employers may recruit, employ and administer their personnel. Recruitment services of the Government of the Republic of Korea <u>shall</u> be utilized insofar as is practicable. In case employers accomplish direct recruitment of employees, employers <u>shall</u> provide such revelant information as may be required for labor administration to the Office of Labor Affairs of the Republic of Korea.

3. To the extent not inconsistent with the provisions of this Article or <u>except as may otherwise be mutually agreed</u>, the conditions of employment <u>and work, such as those relating to wages and supplementary payments, the conditions for the protection and welfare of employees, compensations, and the rights of employees, concerning labor relations shall</u> conform with <u>those laid down by the labor legislation</u> of the Republic of Korea

0056

4. (a) In consideration of provision for collective action in ROK labor legislation, any dispute between employers and employees or any recognized employee organization, which cannot be settled through grievance or labor relations procedures of the United States armed forces, shall be settled as follows:

(1) The dispute shall be referred to the Office of Labor Affairs of the Republic of Korea for conciliation.

(2) In the event that the dispute is not settled by the procedures described in (1) above within twenty (20) days, the dispute shall be referred to the Joint Committee, which may refer the matter to a special committee designated by the Joint Committee, for further conciliation efforts.

(3) In the event that the dispute is not settled by the procedures outlined above, the Joint Committee will resolve the dispute, assuring that expeditious procedures are followed. The decisions of the Joint Committee shall be binding.

(4) Neither employee organizations nor employees shall engage in any practice disruptive of normal work requirements during settlement procedures, unless a period of 70 days has elapsed after the dispute is referred to the Joint Committee mentioned in (2) above.

(5) Failure of any recognized employee organization or employee to abide by the decision of the Joint Committee on any dispute, or engaging in practices disruptive of normal work requirements in violation of the provisions stipulated in (4) above, shall be considered just cause for the withdrawal of recognition of that organiztion and the discharge of that employee.

0057

organization and the discharge of that employee.

(b) The Joint Committee, taking into consideration the role of the employees of the United States armed forces in the defense of the Republic of Korea and pertinent provisions of legislation of the Republic of Korea, shall determine those categories of essential employees who shall not exercise the right of further collective action in the event a labor dispute is not resolved by the foregoing procedures. In the event an agreement cannot be reached on this question in the Joint Committee, it may be made the subject of review through discussions between appropriate officials of the Government of the Republic of Korea and the diplomatic mission of the United States of America.

(c) In the event of a national emergency, such as war, hostilities or situations where war or hostilities is imminent, the application of this Article shall be limited in accordance with emergency measures taken by the Government of the Republic of Korea in consultation with the military authorities of the US.

5. (a) Should the Republic of Korea adopt measures allocating labor, the United States Armed Forces shall be accorded allocation privileges no less favorable than those enjoyed by the Armed Forces of the Republic of Korea.

(b) In the event of a national emergency, such as war, hostilities, or situations where war or hostilities is imminent, employees who have acquired skills essential to the mission of the United States Armed Forces shall, upon request of the United States armed forces and through mutual agreement, be deferred from Republic of Korea military service or other compulsory service.

34-13   0058

The United States Armed Forces shall furnish in advance to the Republic of Korea lists of those employees deemed essential.

6. Members of the civilian component shall not be subject to Korean laws or regulations with respect to their terms and condition of employment.

AGREED MINUTES

1. It is understood that the Government of the Republic of Korea shall be reimbursed for direct costs incurred in providing assistance requested pursuant to paragraph 2.

2. The undertaking of the United States Government to conform to Korean labor laws, customs, and practices, does not imply any waiver by the United States Government of its immunities under international law. The United States Government may terminate employment at any time the continuation of such employment is inconsistent with the military requirements of the United States Armed Forces.

3. Employers will withhold from the pay of their employees, and pay over to the Government of the Republic of Korea withholdings required by the income tax legislation of the Republic of Korea.

4. When employers cannot conform with provisions of labor legislations of the Republic of Korea applicable under Paragraph 3 on account of the military requirements of the United States Armed Forces, the matter shall be referred, in advance whenever possible, to the Joint Committee for mutual agreement.

34-14   0059

5. A union or other employee group shall be recognized unless its objectives are inimical to the <u>common</u> interests of the United States <u>and the Republic of Korea</u>. Memberships or non-memberships in such groups shall not be factor in employment or other actions affecting employees.

(Underlining indicates modifications from the U.S. draft tabled at 80th session)

Understandings

Re Paragraph 1(a)

The persons (invited contractors) shall be those who are operating in Korea under contract with the United States armed forces at the time of coming into force of this Agreement and such other persons who thereafter come into Korea shall be subject the determination by the Joint Committee.

Re Paragraph 1(b)

The reference of the member of Korean Service Corps to exclude from this Article shall not imply in any way that the Government of the Republic of Korea has concedes to affecting their rights and protection which are normally accorded to Korean laborers under the relevant provisions of labor legislation of the Republic of Korea.

Re Paragraph 4(a)

The "recognized employee organization" referred to in the sub-paragraph means a labor union or other employee group, except that which is not recognized pursuant to the provisions of Agreed Minute #5. (This understanding stands only when the Korean draft is accepted by the U.S. side.)

Re Agreed Minute #2

The termination of employment referred to in the second sentence shall be referred, in advance whenever possible, to the Joint Committee for mutual agreement, except in case of such termination as may be legally made in accordance with the relevant provisions of labor legislation of the Republic of Korea.

0061

3ω-16

UNDERSTANDING

It is understood that the deviation from Korean labor legislation may not be referred to the Joint Committee in the case when
such referral would seriously hamper military operations. and

It is understood that the "appropriate action" referred to in Agreed
Minute #4 can only be ~~made~~ *taken* upon mutual agreement by both Governments.

0062

Agreed Minute #4

X   When employers cannot conform with provisions of labor legislation

of the Republic of Korea applicable under this Article on account of

the military requirements of the United States armed forces, the

matter shall be ~~reported~~ *referred*, in advance whenever possible, to the Joint

Committee for consideration and appropriate action. In the event

mutual agreement cannot be reached in the Joint Committee regarding

appropriate action, the issue may be made the subject of review

through discussions between appropriate officials of the Government

of the Republic of Korea and the diplomatic mission of the United

States of America.

미국 개수정안 (6월 18일)

승총 (양해사항 有)

0063

再修正案 (6月18日提案)

AGREED MINUTE

4. When employers cannot conform with provisions of labor
legislation of the Republic of Korea applicable under Paragraph 3
on account of the military requirements of the United States
Armed Forces, the matter shall be referred to the Joint Committee
for mutual agreement. In the event that an agreement cannot be
reached on the matter in the Joint Committee, it may be made the
subject of review for appropriate action through consultation between
the appropriate authorities of both Governments.

X UNDERSTANDING

It is understood that the deviation from Korean labor legislation
may not be referred to the Joint Committee in the case when such
referral would seriously hamper military operations.

17-4   0064

3. To the extent not inconsistent with the provisions of this Article or the military requirements of the United States Armed Forces, the conditions of employment, compensation, and labor-management relations established by the United States Armed Forces for their employees shall conform with provisions of labor legislation of the Republic of Korea.

Agreed Minute

4. When employers cannot conform with provisions of labor legislation of the Republic of Korea applicable under Paragraph 3 on account of the military requirements of the United States Armed Forces, the matter shall be referred to the Joint Committee for mutual agreement whenever possible.

Understanding

"The deviation from Korean labor legislation shall be referred to the Joint Committee for mutual agreement whenever possible, X except in the case when such referral would seriously hamper military operations."

(Discussed at informal meeting on June 17, 1965. and temporarily agreed.)

(비측 원제안)
---- the matter shall be reported, in advance whenever possible to the Joint Committee for its consideration and appropriate action

17-5   0065

ARTICLE XXV   LABOR

1. In this Article the expression:

(a) "employer" refers to the United States Armed Forces
(including nonappropriated fund ~~activities~~ *organizations*) and the persons referred
to in the first paragraph of Article (XVIII).

(b) "employee" refers to any civilian (other than a member of
the civilian component) employed by an employer, except (1) a member
of the Korean Service Corps and (2) a domestic employed by an individual
member of the United States Armed Forces, civilian component or dependent
thereof. Such civilian personnel shall be nationals of the Republic of
Korea.

2. Employers may recruit, employ and administer their personnel.
Recruitment services of the Government of the Republic of Korea will
be utilized insofar as is practicable. In case employers accomplish
direct recruitment of employees, employers will provide such relevant
information as may be required for labor administration to the Office
of Labor Affairs of the Republic of Korea.

3. To the extent not inconsistent with the provisions of this
Article or the military requirements of the United States Armed Forces,
the conditions of employment, compensation, and labor-management
relations established by the United States Armed Forces for their
employees shall conform with provisions of labor legislation of the
Republic of Korea.

4. (a) In consideration of provision for collective acction in
labor legislation of the Republic *of* Korea, any dispute between employers
and employees or any recognized employee organization, which cannot be
settled through grievance or labor relations procedures of the United

/7-6

0066

States Armed Forces, shall be settled as follows:

(1) The dispute shall be referred to the Office of Labor Affairs of the Republic of Korea for conciliation.

(2) In the event that the dispute is not settled by the procedure described in (1) above, the matter will be referred to the Joint Committee, which may refer the matter to a special committee designated by the Joint Committee, for further conciliation efforts.

(3) In the event that the dispute is not settled by the procedure outlined above, the Joint Committee will resolve the dispute, assuring that expeditious procedures are followed. The decisions of the Joint Committee shall be binding.

(4) Failure of any recognized employee organization or employee to bide by the decision of the Joint Committee on any dispute, or engaging in practices disruptive of nromal work requirements during settlement procedures, shall be considered just cause for the withdrawal of recognition of that organization and the discharge of that employee.

(5) Neither employee organizations nor employees shall engage in any practice disruptive of normal work requirements unless a period of at least 70 days has elapsed after the dispute is referred to the Joint Committee, as stipulated in subparagraph (2) above.

(b) The Joint Committee, taking into consideration the role of the employees of the United States Armed Forces in the defense of the Republic of Korea and pertinent provisions of legislation of the Republic of Korea, shall determine those categories of essential employees who shall not exercise the right of further collective action in the event a labor dispute is not resolved by the foregoing procedures.

19-7   0067

In the event an agreement cannot be reached on this question in the Joint Committee, it may be made the subject of review through discussions between appropriate officials of the Government of the Republic of Korea and the diplomatice mission of the United States of America.

(c) In the event of a national emergency, such as war, hostilities, or situations where war or hostilities may be imminent, the application of this Article shall be limited in accordance with emergency measures taken by the Government of the Republic of Korea in consultation with the military Authorities of the United States of America.

5. (a) Should the Republic of Korea adopt measures allocating labor, the United States Armed Forces shall be accorded allocation privileges no less favorable than those enjoyed by the Armed Forces of the Republic of Korea.

(b) In the event of a national emergency, such as war, hostilities, or situations where war or hostilities may be imminent, employees who have acquired skills essential to the mission of the United States Armed Forces, shall, upon request of the United States Armed Forces, be deferred, through mutual consulation, from Republic of Korea military service or other compulsory service. The United States Armed Forces shall furnish in advance to the Republic of Korea lists of those employees deemed essential.

6. Members of the civilian component shall not be subject to Korean laws or regulations with respect to their terms and condition of employment.

AGREED MINUTES

1. It is understood that the Government of the Republic of Korea shall be reimbursed for direct costs incurred in providing assistance requested pursuant to Paragraph 2. /ɔ-8

0068

2. The undertaking of the United States Government to conform to of the Republic of Korea the labor legislation does not imply any waiver by the United States Government of its immunities under international law. The United States Government may terminate employment at any time the continuation of such employment is inconsistent with the military requirements of the United States Armed Forces.

3. Employers will withhold from the pay of their employees, and pay over to the Government of the Republic of Korea withholdings required by the income tax legislation of the Republic of Korea.

4. When employers cannot conform with provisions of labor legislation of the Republic of Korea applicable under Paragraph 3 on account of the military requirements of the United States Armed Forces, the matter shall be referred, in advance whenever possible, to the Joint Committee for mutual agreement.

5. A union or other employee group shall be recognized unless its objectives are inimical to the common interests of the United States and the Republic of Korea. Membership or non-membership in such group shall not be a factor in employment or other actions affecting employees.

0069

労務條項

17-10   0070

第25條　勞務

1. 本條에 있어서:
  가. "雇傭主"란 合衆國軍隊(非歲出資金諸機関 包含) 및 第18條第1項에 規定된者를 말한다.
  나. "雇用人"이란(1) 韓國勞務勤務団의 構成員과 合衆國軍隊의 構成員, 軍屬 或은 그 家族이 個人이 雇傭한 家事使用人을 除外한 雇傭主가 雇傭을 (軍隊의 構成員이 아닌) 民間人을 말한다. 그러한 民間人은 大韓民國의 國籍을 가진 者라야 한다.

2. 雇傭主는 그들의 人事를 募集, 雇用 管理 할수있다. 大韓民國政府의 募集事務機関은 實際로 可能한限 利用된다. 雇傭主가 雇用人을 直接 募集을 할 境遇 雇傭主는 勞動行政上 必要한 關係情報를 大韓民國勞動庁에 提供한다.

3. 本條의 規定 및 合衆國軍隊의 軍事上 必要에 相反되기 않는限 雇用의 條件, 補償 및 勞使関係는 大韓民國의 勞動法令의 合衆國軍隊가 그들의 雇用人을 爲하여 設定한 諸規定 에 準하여야 한다.

13-11.　　0071

4. 水 大韓民國 勞動法을中 團體行動에 關한 規定을 ~~尊重~~ 不拘
하여 雇用主와 雇用人 或은 承認된 雇用人團体名의
~~如何한 爭議勞等등~~ 各個團号防의 不平處理 或은 勞動關係節次에
依하여 解決되지 않는 境遇에는

다음과 같이 解決되어 水한다.

(1) ~~緩爭~~ 爭議는 大韓民國 勞動廳에 調整을 爲하여 回附되어야
한다.

(2) ~~爭議가~~ 爭議가 前 記(1) 節次에 依하여 解決되지 않을 境遇
그事件은 合同委員会에 回附되며 그때 合同委員会
는 그가 指定한 特別 委員会에 再調整을 爲하여 同事件을 回附할
수있다.

(3) 爭議가 上記節次에 依하여 解決되지 않을 境遇
合同委員会는 ~~참 爭議를~~ 迅速한 節次가 되따르록 確
認하여 解決한다. 合同委員会의 多數決定은
拘束力을 갖는다.

(4) ~~如何한~~ 承認된 雇用人團体 或 雇用人이 爭議에 關한 合同
委員会의 決에 不服하거나 或은 解決節次期間中
正常業務要件을 確保하는 行爲는 그 團体의 ~~承認권~~
~~撤回하며~~ 그 雇用人와 解雇의 完全 原因으로 看做된다.

(5) 雇用人 團体 或은 雇用人은 爭議가 上記(2)項
에 規定된대로 合同委員会에 回附된後 적어도
70日의 期間이 経過하지 않는限 正常業務

17-12   0072

要件을 붙히는 行為를 하여서는 아니된다.

나. 合同委員會는 合衆國軍隊 雇傭人의 大韓民國
防衛에 있어서의 ~~義務~~ 大韓民國法令 ~~失喪된~~ 의 關聯
~~團體~~ 規定을 考慮하여 前記節次에 依하여
解決되지 않을 경우 團體行動權을
行使하지 못할 緊要한 雇傭人의 範疇를 決定한다.

合同委員會에서 이 問題에 關하여 合意에 到達할
수 ~~었~~없을 境遇 그 問題는 大韓民國政府의
關係官과 合衆國外交使節 間의 討議를
通하여 ~~審查~~ 討議의 對象이 될수 있다.

다. 戰爭, 敵對行爲 或은 戰爭이나 敵對行爲가 切迫한 狀態
와 같은 國家非常時의 境遇에 本條의 適用은 合衆國
軍當局과의 協議下에 大韓民國政府가 取하는
非常措置에 따라 制限된다.

5. 가. 大韓民國이 勞動을 規定하는 措置를 取할 境遇
合衆國軍隊는 大韓民國 國民이 享有하는것 보다
不利하지 않는 配定特權이 賦與되어야 한다.

나. 戰爭, 敵對行爲 或은 戰爭이나 敵對行爲가 切迫한
狀態와 같은 國家非常時의 境遇에 合衆國軍隊
의 ~~任務~~이 緊要한 技術을 習得한 雇傭人은
~~維持任務~~

13-13   0073

合衆口 軍隊의 要請으로 相互協議下에 大韓民口
兵役 或은 其他 强制服務로부터 延期되어야한다.
合衆口 軍隊는 必要하다고 생각되는 그러한 雇用人의
名單을 事前에 大韓民口에 提供하여야한다.

6. 軍屬 構成員은 그들 任用과 雇用條件에 關聯
하여 韓口의 法律 或은 諸規程에 服하지이니 한다.

合意議事錄

1. 大韓民口政府가 야고 次에 따라 要請을 받은
援助를 提供함에 所要 支授經費에 對하여
賠償 弁償 것 아야한다을 諒解 한다.

2. 大韓民國勞動法令에 準據한다는 合衆國政府의
約束은 合衆口政府는 國際法上의 免除를
抛棄 것 味하지이니한다.

合衆口政府는 雇用의 繼續이 合口
軍隊의 軍事上必要에 相反하는 때는 언제든지
그와같은 雇用을 停止시킬수 있다.

3. 雇用하니 合衆口軍隊의 軍事上 必要 때문에
第3項에 大韓民口 勞動法令이 準據치못
수없을 때 그 內容을 可能한 限 事前에 合同
委員會에 相互合意를 爲하여 國阵되어야한다.

17 14

5. 組合 或은 其他 雇傭人 團體은 ●의 目的이
合義□고 大韓民□의 利益에 背反 되지않는 限
規□로 되여야 한다. 그러한 團體의 會員 或은
非會員 ~~의~~ 雇傭 ~~에 ~~無關하여 要~~ 或은 雇傭人에게
影響을 주는 ~~差別 待遇와 要件 이 있어되 이었어~~
~~其의~~ ~~要因이 되여서는~~ ~~것~~ 이니 된다.

한·미국 간의 상호방위조약 제4조에 의한 시설과 구역 및 한국에서의 미국군대의 지위에 관한 협정(SOFA)   375
전59권. 1966.7.9 서울에서 서명 : 1967.2.9 발효(조약 232호) (V.35 체결 교섭 및 준비, 1965.5-12월)

외무부 의견　　　　　　　　1965. 7. 5.

　　당부에서는 별첨과 같은 귀부 의견에 따라 미국측과 접촉하여 군계약자 본인에 한하여서 만 형사재판권조항의 관계규정을 적용할 것을 제의하였으나 미국측은 미국 시민인 고용인과 그들의 가족에게도 어떠한 제규정이 적용되어야 한다는 것이 본국정부의 입장이라하며, 또한 본협정의 조속한 체결을 위하여 현재 양국간에 남은 유일한 미해결점임을 고려하여 원안 대로 재가하여 주시기 바랍니다.

法務部 意見

　当部意見은 다음과 같습니다

軍招請契約者에 対한 刑事
裁判權에 関하여는 招請
契約者 本人에 限해서만 該,
解하여도 無妨한것으로 思
料 됩니다

0076

기 안 자	미 주 국 이 근 팔	전 화 번 호		공 보	필 요	불 필 요

	과 장	국 장	차 관	장 관		

협 조 서 명	법무부: 검찰과장	검찰국장	차 관	장 관	보 존 년 한	
기 안 년 월 일	1965. 6. 26.	시 행 년 월 일		통 제 관	정 서	기 장
분 류 기 호 문 서 번 호	외구미 722.2—					

경 유 수 신 참 조		건 의	발 신		

제 목	주둔군지위협정 체결 교섭에 임할 우리측 입장

　　1.　주둔군지위협정 체결 교섭 실무자회의에서 한·미 양국간의 의견차이로 말미하마 상금 해결을 보지 못 하고 있는 군요청계약자에 대한 형사재판권 행사문제에 관하여 당부에서는 우리 나라의 재판권 행사를 확보하는 한편 미국측 요구를 감안하여 다음과 같은 해결방안을 수립코저 하오니 재가하여 주시기 바랍니다.

　　2.　군요청계약자에 대한 형사재판권 행사 문제가 하기 방안대로 해결된다면 형사재판권조항을 비롯하여 기타 협정 전반에 걸친 모든 문제에 완전 합의를 보게 될 것 임을 첨언합니다.

　　군요청계약자에 대한 형사재판권 행사문제에 관한 해결방안

1.　한·미 양국 입장:

　가.　한국측: (1) 한국당국은 한국 내에서 발생한 범죄로서 한국 법에 의하여 처벌할 수 있는 범죄에 관하여 군요청계약자, 그의 고용인, 및 그들의 가족에

공통서식 1—2 (갑)　　　　　　　　　　　　　　　　　　　　(16절지)

0077

대하여 재판권을 행사하는 제1차적 권리를
가진다.

(2) 만약 한국당국이 그러한 재판권을 행사하지
않기로 결정하는 경우에는 조속히 미군당국에
통고하여야 한다. 미군당국은 통고 접수 후
미국법에 의하여 부여된 바에 따라 재판권을
행사한다.

나. 미군속: (1) 군초청계약자, 그의 고용인, 및 그들의 가족은
미군속 및 그들의 가족에 관한 형사재판권
조항의 관계규정에 복하여야 한다.

2. 해결방안: (1) 한국당국은 한국내에서 발생한 범죄로서 한국
법령에 의하여 처벌할 수 있는 범죄에 관하여
군초청계약자, 그의 고용인, 및 그들의 가족에 대하여
전속적 재판권을 행사하는 권리를 가진다.

(2) 상기 경우에 한국 방어에 있어서의 그들의 역할을
고려하여 형사재판권조항중 제5항의 재판전
피의자의 신병구금, 제7항의 재판후 수형자의
신병구금, 및 제9항과 그 합의의사록에 열거된
피의자의 권리에 관한 각 규정이 적용된다.

(3) 만약 한국당국이 재판권을 행사하지 않기로
결정하는 경우에는 조속히 미군당국에 통고
하여야 한다. 미군당국은 통고 접수 후 미국법에
의하여 부여된 바에 따라 재판권을 행사한다.

끝.

0078

기 안 지

<table>
<tr><td rowspan="2">기 안 자</td><td colspan="2">미주과
황영재</td><td>전 화
번 호</td><td colspan="2">공 보</td><td>필 요</td><td>불 필 요</td></tr>
<tr><td>과장
6/7</td><td>국장</td><td>국 장</td><td colspan="2">차 관</td><td colspan="2">장 관</td></tr>
<tr><td rowspan="4" colspan="2">협조자
서명
기안
년월일
분류기호
문서번호</td><td>법무부:
법무과장</td><td>법무국장</td><td>법무차관</td><td>법무장관</td><td colspan="2">보 존
년 한</td></tr>
<tr><td>1965. 7. 6.</td><td>시행
년월일</td><td colspan="2">통제판</td><td>정 서</td><td>기 장</td></tr>
<tr><td colspan="5">외구미722.2</td><td></td><td></td></tr>
</table>

<table>
<tr><td>경수참</td><td>유신조</td><td colspan="2">건 의</td><td colspan="3">발 신</td></tr>
</table>

제 목 민사청구권 조항에 대한 우리측 입장

제 81 차 주둔군지위협정 체결교섭 실무자회의에서 우리측이

제안한 민사청구권 조항의 적용시기에 대하여 (합의 의사록 1(나)항),

미국측은 별첨과 같은 양해사항을 제안하였는바, 본협정체결교섭을

조속히 완료하기 위하여 미국측의 제안을 수락할것을 건의 하오니

재가하여 주시기 바랍니다.

유첨: 한미양측의 입장 1부, 끝

3 ― 1

0079

별 첨 : <u>서울지역을 제외한 기타지역에 있어서의 주요 민사 청구권</u>

<u>조항의 적용시기에 대한 한.미 양측의 입장 :(합의 의사록 1(나)항)</u>

1. 한국측 입장 :

"제 5항, 제 6항, 제 7항 및 제 8항의 규정은 실행 가능한 가장

빠른 시일에, 합동위원회가 결정하는 바에 따라, 대한민국의

기타 지역에 그 적용을 확대한다."

"The provisions of paragraphs five, six, seven and
eight will be extended, at the earliest date
practicable, to other areas of the Republic of Korea
as determined by the Joint Committee."

2. 미국측 입장 :

아래와 같은 "양해사항" 을 회의록에 채택할 조건으로 한국안을

수락한다.

(양해 사항)

" 합의 의사록 1(나) 항에 관하여, 한국의 기타 지역에 대한

제 5항, 제6항, 제 7항 및 제 8항의 규정의 적용은 한국의

청구관계기관의 상기 규정을 시행할수 있는 능력에 근거를 둔다. "

With regard to Agreed Minute #1(b), the
extension of the provisions of Paragraphs five, six,
seven, and eight to other areas of Korea will be
based upon the capability of the Korean claims service
to emplement those provisions.   끝.

3 - 2   0080

DRAFT OF MINUTES - 82nd SOFA Session 2 July 1965

Claims Article XXIII

1. At the 81st negotiating session, the Korean negotiators tabled a revised draft of the Claims Article, including modifications of Paragraph 5 (e) (iii) and Paragraph A2 of the Agreed Minutes, as well as a change in the understanding on Paragraph 12 relating to the Korean Service Corps. The United States negotiators are pleased to accept this revised Claims Article, subject to ROK acceptance of an agreed understanding for the Agreed Joint Summary.

2. With regard to Agreed Minute A2, we agree with the Korean negotiators that claims settlement authority for all areas of the Republic of Korea should be transferred to the Korean Claims Service at the earliest date practicable, as determined by the Joint Committee. We believe the record makes clear that the extension of these claims responsibilities to areas beyond Seoul Special City will depend upon the development of the ROK Claims Service. Our primary concern in this matter is to insure prompt and equitable settlements for Korean claimants against the USFK. Therefore, we accept ROK draft of this Article as tabled, contingent upon US-ROK agreement on the following understanding in the Agreed Joint Summary:

> "With regard to Agreed Minute No. 1(b), the extension of the provisions of Paragraphs five, six, seven , and eight to other areas of Korea will be based upon the capability of the Korean claims service to implement those provisions."

3. We trust that we are now in full agreement on the Claims Article.

3-3

0081

Claims Article:

The Korean negotiators accept the US proposal regarding the Claims Article in order to reach full agreement at the present session.

We also believe, as stated by the US negotiators just now, that our primary concern in this matter is to insure prompt and equitable settlements of the claims for damages caused by USFK. ~~for Korean claimants.~~ Therefore, extension of these claims responsibility to the areas beyond Seoul Special City should be made at the earliest date practicable, as determined by the Joint Committee. The Korean negotiators firmly believe that ~~the~~ decision of the Joint Committee to effectuate this Article through ~~out~~ ~~the entire area of~~ the Republic of Korea should be made as soon as the Korean claims service ~~completes the preparation necessary to discharge~~ *is well prepared to hear* its responsibilities under this Article.

With this fact in mind, the Korean negotiators ~~are~~ accept~~ing~~ the following understanding in the Agreed Joint Summary as proposed by the US negotiators:

"With regard to Agreed Minute 1(b), the extension of the provisions of Paragraphs five, six, seven, and eight to other areas of the Republic of Korea will be based upon the capability of the Korean claims service to implement those provisions."

Claims Article:

The Korean negotiators accept the US proposal regarding
the Claims Article in order to reach full agreement at
the present session.

We also believe, as stated by the US negotiators just
now, that our primary concern in this matter is to
insure prompt and equitable settlements of the claims
for damages caused by USFK. Therefore, extension of
those claims responsibility to the areas beyond Seoul
Special City should be made at the earliest date practicable,
as determined by the Joint Committee. The Korean
negotiators firmly believe that decision of the Joint
Committee to effectuate this Article throughout the Republic
of Korea should be made as soon as the Korean claims
service is well prepared to bear its responsibilities under
this Article.

With this fact in mind, the Korean negotiators accept
the following understanding in the Agreed Joint Summary
as proposed by the US negotiators:

"With regard to Agreed Minute 1(b), the extension of the

provisions of Paragraphs five, six, seven, and eight to

other areas of the Republic of Korea will be based upon

the capability of the Korean claims service to implement

these provisions."

0083

민사 청구권 조항에 대한 양해 사항

합의 의사록 1 (b) 항에 관하여, 한국의 기타 지역에 대한
제 5 항, 제 6 항, 제 7 항 및 제 8 항의 규정의 적용은
동 규정을 시행할수 있는 한국 청구관계 기관의 능력에
근거를 둔다.

  With regard to Agreed Minute #1(b), the
extension of the provisions of Paragraphs five,
six, seven, and eight to other areas of Korea
will be based upon the capability of the Korean
claims service to implement those provisions.

0084

Claims Article

With regard to Agreed Minute #1(b), the extension of the provisions of Paragraphs five, six, seven, and eight to other areas of Korea will be based upon the capability of the Korean claims service to implement those provisions.

0085

<u>Claims Article</u>

With regard to Agreed Minute #1(b), the extension of the provisions of Paragraphs five, six, seven, and eight to other areas of Korea will be based upon the (demonstrated) capability of the Korean claims service. (to implement those provisions.)

0086

별 첨 : <u>서울지역을 제외한 기타지역에 있어서의 주요 민사 청구권</u>
<u>조항의 적용시기에 대한 한.미 양측의 입장 :(합의 의사록 1(나)항)</u>

1. 한국측 입장 :

"제 5항, 제 6항, 제 7항 및 제 8항의 규정은 실행 가능한 가장
빠른 시일에, 합동위원회가 결정하는 바에 따라, 대한민국의
기타 지역에 그 적용을 확대한다."

"The provisions of paragraphs five, six, seven and
eight will be extended, at the earliest date
practicable, to other areas of the Republic of Korea
as determined by the Joint Committee."

2. 미국측 입장 :

아래와 같은 "양해사항"을 회의록에 채택할 조건으로 한국안을
수락한다.

(양해 사항)

"합의 의사록 1(나) 항에 관하여, 한국의 기타 지역에 대한
제 5항, 제6항, 제 7항 및 제 8항의 규정의 적용은 한국의
청구권기기관의 상기 규정을 시행할수 있는 능력에 근거를 둔다."

With regard to Agreed Minute #1(b), the
extension of the provisions of Paragraphs five, six,
seven, and eight to other areas of Korea will be
based upon the capability of the Korean claims service
to emplement those provisions.

단. 0087

非公式 合意案	韓國側 改正案	美國側 代案
第〇3條 諸求權		
合意議事錄	1. 協定發効와 同時에 全國에서 發効한다	1. 協定發効日로 부터 特別地域에서는 61個月後, 其他地域에서는 1年6個月이 發効한다
2. 非公務中 民間人에게 가진 損害의 경우 米軍代表方式에 의한 規定은 서울特別市에서는 協定發効後 6個月後에, 其他地域에서는 全國을 통하여 發効한다 發効可能한限 군지 VAA로 迅速히 發効한다		

388 주한미군지위협정(SOFA) 서명 및 발효 13

보건사회부 의견에 대한 건의

1965. 7. 8.

시정전문이제도록

노무조항에 대한 별지 보건사회부 의견에 대하여 아래와 같이
해결할 것을 건의 합니다.

1. 제 3항과 합의 의사록 제 4항에 관하여

미측안을 원안대로 수락하되 아래와 같은 운영상의 지침을
추가 함으로써 해석상의 미비점을 배제한다.

가. 합의 의사록 제 4항의 군사상 필요에 의한 합동위원회
에의 회부는 제3항 단서의 "군사상 필요에 상반하는 "
경우에도 적용된다.

나. 군사상 필요로 사전 합의가 불가능하였던 것은 반드시
사후에 합동위원회에 회부하여 검토하며 필요시 합동
위원회의 결정에 따라 교정조치(矯正措置)
를 취한다.

2. 제 1항 (b)에 관하여

KSC 와 가사 사용인은 1964. 6. 7일자합의 결재 원안
대로 해결한다.   끝.

의무부장관   차관   구미국장   미주과장

0089

보건사회부장관   차관   노동청장   차장   노정국장

공통서식 1-2 (갑)   11-1   (16절지)

기 안 지

기 안 자	미주과 김기조		전 화 번 호		공 보		필 요	불필요
미주과장	구미국장	외무부차관	외무부장관	노동청장	보사부차관	보사부장관		
		전결						5-24
		부 재 중						
협 조 자 서 명	노정과장	노정국장	노동청차장		보 존 년 한			
기 안 년 월 일	1965. 6. 21.	시 행 년 월 일		통 제 판	정 서	기 장		
분 류 기 호 문 서 번 호	외구미 722.2							

意 見 書

노정국장 허명훈

(1) 勞務條項中

1. 의(b)를 다음과 같이 修正할것

   勞務者라함은 使用者에 依하여 雇傭된 民間人(軍屬係外)을 말하며 이러한民間人은 大韓民國의 國民이어야한다

(理由)

1. K.S.C도 一般勤勞者로서 法上 勞動權을 享有하며 現也勞組까지 結成 活動하고있는바 이를 一般勤勞者와 分離하여 取扱하여 그 勞動權을 剝奪함은 不可함

2. 家事使用人은 勞動基準法의 適用에서는 除外되고 있으나 其他 勞動權은 認定받고있으므로 8軍關係家事使用人만을 例外取扱 할 何等의 理由가 없음

(2) 3項中「美國軍隊의 軍事的 必要에 及하지않는限」을「別途로 相互合意되지 않는限」으로 할것

0030

(理由)

美國側案과 韓國側案이 大同小異한것이라면 우리側原案대로 主張하는것이 妥当 함, 右部意見으로서는 合意要件을 原案에 明示하고 合意許次를 合意錄에 記載하였으니 蛇足이라고봄

따라서 合意錄 4次中「美國軍의 軍事的 要請 때문에」는 削除되어야 맞이 妥当함

유 첨 : 1. 제 81 차 고섭회의에서 제안한 우티측 수정안

2. 제 82 차 회의에 제시할 수정안

3. 미측 수정안에 대한 해겹방안

4. 노무조항 전문.   끝.

노동무사 재부류(1966.12.31.)   0091

공동서식 1-2 (갑)   (16절지)

11-1

기 안 지

제 목	미주둔군 지위협정 노무조항의 타결방안

　　　　1965. 6. 7 합의결재를 토대로 동 입자로 개최되었던 제 81 차

심무자 교섭회의에서 미측이 제시한 안에 대하여 우티측은 별첨(1)과

같이 수정안을 제시하였던바 미측은 우티안을 전부 수락하되 제 3 항과

합의 의사록 제 4 항을 별첨 (2) 와 같이 수정할것을 제안하고 있는바

이를 차기 제 82 차 심무자 회의에서 별첨 (3) 과 같은 방안으로

해결함으로서 노무조항 전체에 대하여 별첨 (4) 와 같이 타결할것을 건의

합니다.

유 첨 : 1. 제 81 차 교섭회의에서 제안한 우티측 수정안

　　　　 2. 제 82 차 회의에 제시할 수정안

　　　　 3. 미측 수정안에 대한 해결방안

　　　　 4. 노무조항 전문.　　　　끝.

　　　　　　　분동무서류 재부류(1966. 12. 31.)　　　　0091

LABOR ARTICLE

(Underlining indicates modifications from
the U.S. draft tabled at 80th session)

1. (b).... Such civilian personnel shall be nationals
of the Republic of Korea.

3. To the extent not inconsistent with the provisions
of this Article or except as may otherwise be mutually
agreed, the conditions of employment, compensation,
and labor-management relations established by the
United States Armed Forces for their employees
shall conform with provisions of labor legislation
of the Republic of Korea.

4. (a)(5)...... to the Joint Committee, as stipulated
in subparagraph (2) above.

5. (b)......... be deferred through mutual consultation
from Republic of Korea.......

Agreed Minutes

4. When employers cannot conform with provisions of
labor legislation of the Republic of Korea applicable
under Paragraph 3 on account of the military requirements
of the United States Armed Forces, the matter shall be
referred, in advance whenever possible, to the Joint
Committee for mutual agreement.

0092

//-2

5. A union or other employee group shall be recognized
unless its objectives are inimical to the <u>common</u>
interests of the United States <u>and the Republic of Korea</u>.
Membership or non-membership in such group shall not be
a facter in employment or other actions affecting
employees.

0093

//-3

LABOR ARTICLE

(Underlining indicates modifications from
the Korean revised draft tabled at 81st session)

3. To the extent not inconsistent with the provisions
of this Article or the military requirements of the
United States Armed Forces, the conditions of employment,
compensation, and labor-management relations established
by the United States Armed Forces for their employees
shall conform with provisions of labor legislation
of the Republic of Korea.

Agreed Minute

4. When employers cannot conform with provisions
of labor legislation of the Republic of Korea applicable
under this Article on account of the military requirements
of the United States armed forces, the matter shall be
referred, in advance whenever possible, to the Joint
Committee for consideration and appropriate action.
In the event mutual agreement cannot be reached in the
Joint Committee regarding appropriate action, the issue
may be made the subject of review through discussions
between appropriate officials of the Government of the
Republic of Korea and the diplomatic mission of the
United States of America.

0094

11-4

미측 수정안에 대합 우티측 해결방안

1. 미측 제안에 대한 섭명

   가. 미측은 우티측 수정안 제 3 항 중 "별도로 상호 합의 되지
   않는한" 이탄 구점이 합의 의사록 제 4 항 "미국군의 군사상
   필요로" 타는 구점과 일치하지 아니합으로 3 항에도 동일한
   "미군사 상의 필요에 **상반**하지 않는한" 으로 수정하여야
   한다는 주장임. 그외에 있어서는 우티측 제 3 항 수정안
   을 수락하겠다함.

   나. 합의 의사록 제 4 항에 있어서 우티측은 불가능한때를
   제외 하고는 사전 상호 합의제를 주장한데 대하여 미측은
   합의에 도달하지 못할 경우의 대책을 고력하여 합동위원회
   에서 심의하여 척접한 조치를 마련하는 제도가 타당하며
   그더한 적접한 조치에 대하여 합동위원회에서 합의에
   도달하지 못할 경우 외교경로를 통하여 해결합수 있어야
   한다고 주장함.

2. 우티측 해결 방안

   가. 이상의 미측 주장은 타당성이 있으며 우티측에서 이미
   합의 하였거나 우티측에서 기대하는 바와 상당히 접근한
   수정안이탁 사료됨으로 미측 수정안 제 3 항을 수락하고

   나. 첫째재 "가능한 한 사전에" 탄 미군이 군사 작전상
   합동 위원회에의 회부가 불가능한때에 한정하고 둘째재

11-5

0095

소위 "적절한 조치" 란 상호 합의가 이루어진 연후에만
취합수 있다는 조건을 부치면 우리측의 목적을 관철합수
있는 것으로 사료됨으로 다음과 같은 양해 사항을 부친다는
조건하에 합의 의사록 제4 항에 대한 미측 수정안을 수락
합것을 건의함.

UNDERSTANDING

It is understood that the deviation from Korean
labor legislation may not be referred to the Joint
Committee in the case when such referral would
seriously hamper military operations and that the
"appropriate action" referred to in Agreed Minute
#4 can only be taken upon mutual agreement by both
Governments.

11-6   0096

법 첩 (4)

ARTICLE XXV   LABOR

1. In this Article the expression:

(a) "employer" refers to the United States
Armed Forces (including non-appropriated fund organizations)
and the persons referred to in the first paragraph of
Article (XVIII).

(b) "employee" refers to any civilian (other
than a member of the civilian component) employed by an
employer, except (1) a member of the Korean Service
Corps and (2) a domestic employed by an individual
member of the United States Armed Forces, civilian component
or dependent thereof. Such civilian personnel shall be
nationals of the Republic of Korea.

2. Employers may recruit, employ and administer their
personnel. Recruitment services of the Government of the
Republic of Korea will be utilized insofar as is practicable.
In case employers accomplish direct recruitment of employees,
employers will provide such relevant information as may
be required for labor administration to the Office
of Labor Affairs of the Republic of Korea.

3. To the extent not inconsistent with the provisions
of this Article or the military requirements of the
United States Armed Forces, the conditions of employment,
compensation, and labor-management relations established
by the United States Armed Forces for their employees

0097

11-7

shall conform with provisions of labor legislation of the
Republic of Korea.

4. (a) In consideration of provision for collective
action in labor legislation of the Republic of Korea,
any dispute between employers and employees or any
recognized employee organization, which cannot be
settled through grievance or labor relations procedures of
the United States Armed Forces, shall be settled as follows:

(1) The dispute shall be referred to the Office
of Labor Affairs of the Republic of Korea for conciliation.

(2) In the event that the dispute is not settled by
the procedure described in (1) above, the matter will
be referred to the Joint Committee, which may refer the
matter to a special committee designated by the Joint
Committee, for further conciliation efforts.

(3) In the event that the dispute is not settled by
the procedure outlined above, the Joint Committee will
resolve the dispute, assuring that expeditious procedures
are followed. The decisions of the Joint Committee
shall be binding.

(4) Failure of any recognized employee organization
or employee to bide by the decision of the Joint Committee
on any dispute, or engaging in practices disruptive of normal
work requirements during settlement procedures, shall
be considered just cause for the withdrawal of recognition

0098

11—8

of that organization and the discharge of that employee.

(5) Neither employee organizations nor employees shall engage in any practice disruptive of normal work requirements unless a period of at least 70 days has elapsed after the dispute is referred to the Joint Committee, as stipulated in subparagraph (2) above.

(b) The Joint Committee, taking into consideration the role of the employees of the United States Armed Forces in the defense of the Republic of Korea and pertinent provisions of legislation of the Republic of Korea, shall determine those categories of essential employees who shall not exercise the right of further collective action in the event a labor dispute is not resolved by the foregoing procedures.
In the event an agreement cannot be reached on this question in the Joint Committee, it may be made the subject of review through discussions between appropriate officials of the Government of the Republic of Korea and the diplomatic mission of the United States of America.

(c) In the event of a national emergency, such as war, hostilities, or situations where war or hostilities may be imminent, the application of this Article shall be limited in accordance with emergency measures taken by the Government of the Republic of Korea in consultation with the military Authorities of the United States.

5. (a) Should the Republic of Korea adopt measures

0099

11—9

allocating labor, the United States Armed Forces shall
be accorded allocation privileges no less favorable
than those enjoyed by the Armed Forces of the Republic
of Korea.

(b) In the event of a national emergency, such as war,
hostilities, or situations where war or hostilities may
be imminent, employees who have acquired skills
essential to the mission of the United States Armed
Forces, shall, upon request of the United States Armed
Forces, be deferred through mutual consulation from
Republic of Korea military service or other compulsory
service. The United States Armed Forces shall furnish
in advance to the Republic of Korea lists of those
employees deemed essential.

6. Members of the civilian component shall not be
subject to Korean laws or regulations with respect to
their terms and condition of employment.

AGREED MINUTES

1. It is understood that the Government of the
Republic of Korea shall be reimbursed for direct costs
incurred in providing assistance requested pursuant to
Paragraph 2.

2. The undertaking of the United States Government
to conform to the labor legislation of the Republic
of Korea does not imply any waiver by the United States
Government of its immunities under international law.
The United States Government may terminate employment at

0100

11-10

any time the continuation of such employment is
inconsistent with the military requirements of the
United States Armed Forces.

3. Employers will withhold from the pay of their
employees, and pay over to the Government of the Republic
of Korea withholdings required by the income tax
legislation of the Republic of Korea.

4. When employers cannot conform with provisions
of labor legislation of the Republic of Korea applicable
under this Article on account of the military
requirements of the United States armed forces, the
matter shall be referred, in advance whenever possible,
to the Joint Committee for consideration and appropriate action.
In the event mutual agreement cannot be reached in the
Joint Committee regarding appropriate action, the
issue may be made the subject of review through
discussions between appropriate officials of the
Government of the Republic of Korea and the diplomatic
mission of the United States of America.

5. A union or other employee group shall be
recognized unless its objectives are inimical to the
common interests of the United States and the Republic
of Korea. Membership or non-membership in such group
shall not be a factor in employment or other actions
affecting employees.

끝

0101

관리	恭恭
번호	2045

韓美間駐屯軍地位協定中 重要條項에 関한 解説

┌─────────────────────────────┐
│ 普通文書로再分類 : 協定批准同意後 │
└─────────────────────────────┘

外 務 部

1965年 8 月

0102

目　　次

0103

刑事裁判權條項

I. 刑事裁判權條項 概要

1. 相互尊重의 原則에 立脚한 裁判權 回復

今般 우리나라가 美國과 駐屯軍 地位協定을 締結함으로써 過去 大田協定下에서 駐韓美軍이 排他的 裁判權을 行使하여 왔던 狀態를 止揚하고 本 刑事裁判權條項에 依據 韓·美兩國이 接受國 또는 派遣國으로써 各己 相互尊重의 原則下에서 裁判權을 行使하게 되었다.

2. 韓·美兩國間의 裁判權 行使

即「나토」協定, 美·日協定을 包含한 各國協定의 先例에 따라 美合眾國은 公務執行中 犯罪 또는 美國 軍隊內部의 犯罪에 對하여 第1次的 裁判權을 가지며

-1-

大韓民國은 其他의 모든 犯罪에 対하여 第1次的

裁判权을 行使하게 되었다.

3 第1次的 裁判权의 拋棄와 撤回

   또한 大韓民國은 独逸補充協定의 拋棄條項의 形態

를 받아들여 大韓民國이 가지는 第1次的权利를 一

括的으로 美國에 拋棄하되 이러한 拋棄는 個個의

事件이 発生하였을 境遇 大韓民國의 司法上의 利益

으로 말미아마 大韓民國 法廷에서 裁判하는것이 必

要하다고 決定하는 境遇에는 大韓民國이 权利拋棄를

撤回할수 있는 权利를 가지는 것을 條件으로 하였으

며 또한 权利拋棄의 撤回를 둘러싸고 韓·美両國間

에 意見差異가 있을 때에도 大韓民國이 最終的인

決定权을 갖게 되었다.

-2-

0105

4. 被疑者의 拘禁과 权利

　　그 밖에도. 本條項은 大韓民國의 法廷에서 裁判을
받는 美軍關係者의 权利를 規定하고 있는데 이러한
权利는 韓國憲法과 關係法律이 保障하고 있는 权利
는 勿論 美合衆國憲法과 訴訟制度에서 美國市民에게
保障된 基本权을 비롯하여 合衆國政府代表를 모든
訴訟節次에 參與시킬수 있는 权利를 包含하고 있다

　　또한 大韓民國의 安全에 關한 罪를 犯한者는 大韓
民國이 拘禁하며 其他 裁判前被疑者는 合衆國 軍当
局이 拘禁하는 것으로 되었다

5. 独逸 補充協定과의 共通点

　　이와같이 우리나라가 第1次的 裁判权의 抛棄를
비롯하여 被疑者의 拘禁, 搜査上의 協助等 여러面에

~3~

0106

서 独逸補充協定의 形態를 받아들이게 되었는데 이

것은 우리나라가 独逸國의 境遇와 같이 國土両斷으

로 因하여 共産軍과 對峙하고 있기 때문에 國土防衛

를 爲하여서는 駐屯軍이 恒時 臨戰態勢를 갖출수

있도록 接受國이 可能한限 모든 便宜를 提供하여야

한다는 共通点을 지니고 있다는 事實로부터 緣由한

것이다.

Ⅱ. 重要問題別 內容

本條項에 規定된 重要規定의 內容을 問題別로 考察

하여 보면 다음과 같다.

裁判权行使에 對한 例가

우리나라의 裁判权行使는 戒嚴令宣布의 境遇 및

-4-

0107

韓國의 領域과 犯罪에 關하여 다음과 같은 例外的
規定을 두었다

가. 戒嚴令宣布와 裁判權行使

(1) 內 容

우리나라가 戒嚴令을 宣布하였을 때에는 그
宣布地区內에서는 刑事裁判权條項의 效力이 停止
되며 그 地域內에서 戒嚴令이 解除될때 까지
美軍当局이 專属的裁判权을 行使한다

(2) 解 說

(가) 戒嚴令은 戰時, 事變等 國家非常事態時에 宣布
되며 逮捕, 拘禁, 搜索 및 裁判等 訴訟節次
全般에 걸쳐 國民의 自由와 权利를 制限하게
됨으로 이런때에는 美軍當局이 專属的인 裁判

~5~

0108

權을 行使하는 것으로 規定하였다.

(나) 各國 協定에 이러한 先例는 없지만 美國이
協定을 맺고있는 各國에는 戒嚴令制度가 없거나
또는 制度自体는 있어도 実地 宣布한 일이
없다는 事実을 考慮하여 이를 成文化한 것이
다.

나. 韓國領域外 犯罪

(1) 内 容

우리나라의 裁判权은 美軍人, 軍属 및 그들의
家族이 우리나라 領域外에서 犯한 犯罪에는 미
치지 아니한다.

(2) 解 説

(가) 各國 協定에 先例가 없으나 実地 運営上

- 6 -

0109

接受國이 이러한 事件을 取扱한 例가 없으며,

(나) 또한 우리나라 防衛를 爲하여 駐屯하는 美軍이 國外에서 우리 刑法第5條에 規定된 重要한 犯罪를 犯한 者를 構成員, 軍屬 또는 그들의 家族으로 從軍시킬 理도 万無할 것임으로 우리나라의 裁判权이 미치지 아니하는 것으로 하였다.

2. 專屬的裁判权의 抛棄要請

(1) 内 容

우리나라가 가지는 專屬的 裁判权을 特定事件에 있어서 美軍当局이 合同委員會에서 抛棄할것을 要請하면 韓國当局은 好意的考慮를 할것을 規定하고 있다.

~ 7 ~

0110

(2) 解說

(가) 비록 美國法令에 處罰規定은 없다 할지라도 美國軍隊의 行政的, 또는 懲戒的制裁로서도 充分히 그 目的을 達成할수 있는 輕微한 犯罪의 境遇를 予想하여 法的根據를 마련한데 不過하다.

(나) 要請이 있을때 好意的考慮를 하고 안하고는 韓國当局의 才量에 달려 있으며 國家安危에 關한 重要犯罪는 비록 要請을 할 境遇에도 抛棄할수 없음은 当然하다.

3. 公務執行中 犯罪

(1) 内容

美軍当局은 美軍人, 또는 軍屬이 一定한 公務를 執行하는 동안 作爲 또는 不作爲로 因하여 犯罪를

~8~

0111

犯하였을 境遇 第1次的 裁判权을 行使한다

(2) 解 説

(가) 公務執行証明書 発行权者

美國軍人, 또는 軍属이 公務執行中 行爲로 因한 犯罪로 말미아마 우리나라 捜査当局에 依하여 立件되었을 때에는 美國軍隊의 関係当局이 그 嫌疑받는 犯罪가 公務遂行中 行한 行爲에 基因한 것이라는 証明書를 発行하게 되어 있으며 이와 같은 証明書는 그 事件에 対한 裁判权 行使当局을 決定하기 爲한 充分한 証據가 된다

(나) 韓國当局의 異議提起와 再検討

美軍当局이 発行한 証明書의 内容에 対한 反証이 있을 때에는 韓國検察総長은 異議를 提起

~9~

0112

할수 있으며 이때에는 韓國政府 關係当局과 駐

韓美國外交使節은 반드시 再檢討하여야 한다.

(다) 國際的 先例

　　美·日協定 第17條의 合意議事錄 第3(가)(2)項,

独逸補充協定 第18條, 「웨스트·인디즈」協定 第

9條 11項等은 다같이 派遣軍의 指揮官 또는

關係当局이 公務執行証明書를 發行하는 것으로

되어 있으며 其他 「나토」協定의 当事國인 英國,

불란서, 「이태리」, 토의기等 各國도 또한 同一하다.

(라) 公務의 定義

(ㄱ) 어떤 犯罪가 公務執行中 行하여진 것이라고

　　証明하는 權限이 美國当局에 있을 境遇에도

　　公務라는 것이 무엇인가를 明確히 規定할 必要가

~/°~

0113

가 있다. 그래서 本 協定에서는 "公務라는

것은 美國軍隊 軍人, 軍屬이 公務를 執行하는

期間中 行한 모든 行爲를 包含하는 것이 아니

라는 점을 明白히 하는 同時에 그 個人이

執行하고 있는 公務의 機能으로서 行할것이

要求되는 行爲에만 適用된다고 限定하였다.

(ㄴ) 이와 같이 公務의 內容을 限定한 國際的

先例는 어느나라 協定에서도 찾아볼수 없다

이 規定은 実地 運営上 公務執行中 犯罪與否

를 決定하기 爲한 重要한 判斷의 基準이 될

것이다.

4. 우리나라의 第1次的 裁判权의 抛棄

(1) 內 容

~//~

0114

우리 나라 協定은 独逸補充協定에 規定된 抛棄制度를 採択하여 우리 나라가 行使하기로 되어 있는 第1次的 裁判权을 一旦 美國을 爲하여 一括的으로 抛棄한後 個個事件이 発生하였을때에 우리나라가 裁判权을 行使하는것이 重要하다고 認定할 때에는 抛棄하였던 第1次的 裁判权을 徹回하여 裁判할수 있는것으로 하였다.

(2) 解 説

(가) 友邦 美國의 軍隊가 우리 나라의 要請에 따라 이땅에 駐屯하여 우리나라 軍隊와 더불어 共同으로 國土를 防衛함에 있어서 恒時 臨戦態勢를 갖추어야 한다는 그들의 軍事上의 特殊使命을 考慮하여 独逸의 境遇와 같은 抛棄制度를 採択

~ 12~

0115

하게 된 것이다.

(나) 그러나 우리나라의 安全에 關한 犯罪, 殺人에 關한 犯罪, 强姦, 强盜罪를 비롯하여 우리나라가 裁判하는것이 重要하다고 認定할 때에는 抛棄하였던 裁判權을 撤回하여 裁判할수 있다.

(다) 또한 우리나라가 抛棄를 撤回하였을 境遇에 韓·美兩國間의 意見差異가 있을때에도 우리나라가 裁判權을 行使하기로 決定할 때에는 그러한 決定은 最終的이며 確定的인 것으로된 것은 独逸補充協定에서는 볼수 없는 有利한 規定인 것이다.

(라) 「나토」協定, 美·日協定, 희랍協定, 「비델란드協定, 独逸補充協定等 各國協定은 條文上의 表現差異에도 不拘하고 實地運營에 있어서는 이들 各國들은

~/3~

0116

다같이 美軍關係總犯罪件數의 80% 乃至 100% 에 達하는 많은 事件을 抛棄하고 있는 것이 実情이다.

(마) 우리나라도 韓·美両國間의 特別한 友好関係와 國際社會의 一員이라는 뜻에서 이와 같은 各國 의 一般的인 先例에 따른 것이다.

5. 被疑者의 裁判前拘禁

(1) 内 容

우리나라가 裁判權을 가지는 事件에 関聯된 美 軍人, 軍属 또는 家族이 逮捕되었을 때에는 被疑 者에 対한 모든 裁判節次가 다 끝나고 法院의 判決이 確定될때 까지 美軍当局이 被疑者를 拘禁 한다. 그러나 韓國의 安全에 関한 犯罪를 行한

~14~

한·미국 간의 상호방위조약 제4조에 의한 시설과 구역 및 한국에서의 미국군대의 지위에 관한 협정(SOFA) 417
전59권. 1966.7.9 서울에서 서명 : 1967.2.9 발효(조약 232호) (V.35 체결 교섭 및 준비, 1965.5-12월)

被疑者는 韓國当局이 拘禁한다.

(2) 解　説

(가) 各國의 協定의 先例를 보면 接受國이나 또는
派遣國 軍当局이 犯人을 逮捕하였을 때에는 一
般的으로 派遣國 軍当局이 拘禁하게 되어 있다.
本項의 規定과 같은 先例는 独逸補充協定第22條
에서 볼수 있으며 希臘協定 第3條, 「네델란드」
協定, 「니카라구아」協定 第7條4項等도 亦是 모든
裁判節次가 끝날때까지 派遣國 軍当局이 被疑者
를 拘禁하는 것으로 되어 있다.

(나) 그러나 우리나라 当局이 捜査나 裁判을 할수
있게 하기 爲하여 美軍当局은 모든 適切한 便
宜를 提供하여야 함은 勿論, 証據의 湮滅 또는

~15~

0118

犯人의 逃走等을 防止하기 爲하여 必要한 措置
를 取하게 되어 있다

6. 刑의 執行

(1) 內 容

美國当局이 韓國法院이 言渡한 自由刑을 服役中
에 있는 美軍人, 軍屬 또는 그들의 家族의 拘禁
을 引渡하여 달라고 要請할 때에는 韓國当局이
이러한 美國当局의 要請에 対하여 好意的인 考慮
를 할것을 規定하고 있다

(2) 解 說

(가) 이와 같은 規定은 美國軍隊의 特殊한 軍事上
의 使命과 또한 우리나라 拘禁施設의 現実이
欧美 各國의 拘禁施設의 水準에 到達되지 못하고

- 16 -

0119

있는 点等을 考慮에 넣어 特殊한 境遇 美側要請

이 있을것을 考慮한 것이다

(나) 그러나 이 規定은 어디까지나 好意的인 考慮

를 할것을 規定하고 있는데 不過한 것이며 仍

仍의 境遇 美國当局의 要求를 받아들이고 안

들이고는 전혀 韓國当局의 決定에 달려 있는

것이다.

(다) 韓國当局이 美國当局의 要請을 받아들여 受刑

者의 拘禁을 美國当局에 引渡하였을 때에는 美國

当局은 残余刑期를 美國의 拘禁施設에서 継續

執行하여야 하며

(라) 이러한 때에는 美國当局은 受刑者의 服役動向

에 関한 情報를 定規的으로 韓國当局에 提供하

~17~

0120

여야 할뿐더러 韓國政府代表는 隨時로 이들의
服役狀況을 視察 確認할 權利를 가진다.

7. 被疑者 또는 被告人의 權利

(1) 內 容

第9項은 우리나라 裁判권에 服하는 被疑者 또는
被告人이 訴訟節次에 있어서 享有하는 權利를 列
擧하고 있다.

(2) 解 說

(가) 이와 같은 權利들은 우리나라 憲法과 關係國
內法이 被疑者 또는 被告人의 利益을 爲하여
保障하고 있는 여러 權利를 再確認한것일 뿐만
아니라

~18~

0121

(사) 其他 各國의 先例 또는 美國憲法이 美國市民
에게 認定한 基本權들을 規定한 것이다

~19~

0122

請 求 權 條 項

I 槪 要

　請求權條項은 美・日協定이나「나토」諸國間의 協定과 事實上 同一하게 規定되었다 따라서 一般被害者는 韓國法에서 保障된 節次에 따라 駐韓美軍의 行爲에 依한 損害賠償을 받을수 있는 것이다 그 重要 內容을 보면 大略 다음과 같다

1. 公務執行中 兩國政府의 軍隊財産과 其他 政府財産 에 對한 損害

　가 韓・美兩國軍隊가 公務執行中의 行爲로 그들 軍 隊의 어느 一方이 使用하는 財産에 損害가 發生 하였을 때에는 請求權을 相互 抛棄하고,

　나 그 損害가 其他의 政府財産에 發生하였을 때에

0123

는 $1,400 以下의 損害는 相互 抛棄하며, $1,400
을 超過하는 損害에 對하여는 韓·美兩國이 合意에
依하여 選定하는 1名의 韓國人 仲裁人으로 하여금
損害賠償責任과 損害賠償金을 決定하여 解決도록 되
었다. 이때에 賠償金은 兩國政府가 다음과 같이 分
担한다

　(1) 損害의 責任이 美國側에게만 있을때

　　　　　韓國 25%, 美國 75%

　(2) 損害의 責任이 不明確하거나 또는 共同責任이

　　　있을때

　　　　　韓國 50%, 美國 50%

2. 公務執行中 美國軍隊가 韓國政府가 아닌 第三者에
對하여 損害를 加하였을때

-21-

0124

가 損害賠償節次

　　駐韓美軍이　主로　韓國國民이라고　볼수　있는　第
三者에　損害를　加하였을　때에는　韓國政府가　韓國
法에　依하여　解決하게　된다　이때에　駐韓美軍의
行爲를　韓國軍의　行爲로　看做하여　韓國政府가　損
害賠償에　對한　責任을　갖게되는　것이다　따라서
被害者는　國家賠償法에　依하여　國家賠償審議委員會
에　損害賠償請求를　提起하거나　또는　韓國政府를
相對로　民事訴訟을　提起하게　되며, 이때에　決定된
賠償金은　于先　韓國政府가　被害者에게　支拂하게
된다

나 韓·美兩國政府間의　關係

　　以上과　같은　節次에　따라　韓國政府가　被害者에게

-22-

0125

支拂한 賠償金은 上記 / (나)의 境遇와 같은 比率로서 兩國政府가 分担하게 된다.

또한 韓國政府는 損害賠償請求가 國家賠償法에 따라 解決하게 될때에는 그 損害에 対한 賠償責任과 賠償金額에 対하여 美國当局과 相互 合意下에 決定하여야 하는 것이다. 그러나 이것은 어디까지나 賠償金을 負担하게 되는 韓國政府와 美國政府間의 対内的인 関係로서 被害者에 対하여는 何等의 影響이 없는 것이며, 따라서 被害者는 韓國法에 依하여 民事訴訟을 提起할수 있음은 勿論이다.

3. 非公務中의 美國軍隊의 損害行爲

非公務中의 美軍에 依한 모든 損害에 対하여는

~23~

0126

韓國政府가 損害賠償金을 査定하여 美國当局에 通告

하면 美國当局은 그 賠償金의 支拂與否를 決定하여

被害者에게 直接 損害賠償을 할수 있으나 被害者가

이에 滿足하지 않을 때에는 加害者인 美軍(初人)을

相対로 韓國의 民事訴訟을 提起하므로서 損害賠償問

題의 解決을 模索하게 된다.

4. 重要條項의 適用時期

上記第2 및 3項을 包含한 主要請求权條項의 適用

時期는 다음과 같다.

가. 서울地域 ; 協定発效 6個月後.

나. 其他地域 ; 合同委員會의 決定에 따라 実行可能

한 가상 빠른 時日内,

~24~

0127

Ⅱ. 重要問題別內容

1. 公務執行中 第三者에 对한 損害

가. 內容

公務執行中 第3者에 对한 損害의 境遇 請求權은 美‧日 協定이나 「나토」 諸國間의 協定 內容과 같이 接受國인 우리나라의 軍隊가 損害를 加하였을 때에 適用하는 우리나라 法令에 依하여 解決하게되어 있으나, 請求權者가 우리나라의 國家 賠償法에 따라 損害賠償을 請求할때에, 國家 賠償審議 委員會는 損害賠償 責任과 賠償金額을 決定함에 있어 美国 当局과 相互 合意하게 되어 있다. (그러나 請求權者가 우리나라法에 依한 民事訴訟을 提起할때에 아무런 影響을

~25~

받지 아니함은 前述한바와 같다)

나. 解說

國家 賠償審議 委員会의 損害賠償請求에 처한
裁定은 1951年에 制定된 國家賠償法과 1962
年에 制定된 同 節次法에 따라, 國家 또는 公
共団体에 처한 損害賠償請求를 迅速하고 圓滿히
解決하기 爲한 하나의 簡易節次인 것이다.

同 委員会는 法務次官이 委員長이 되고, 法務部
의 各 局長, 判事 1名, 辯護士 1名과 損害賠
償 請求와 関聯된 関保部處의 代表 1名이 委
員으로 構成되어 있으며, 同 委員会는 請求事件
을 審議하고 賠償金을 査定하여 法務長官의 裁
可를 어어 賠償金을 決定하고, 이 決定된 賠償

~26~

0129

金을 請求权者에게 通知하여 請求权者가 滿足할

때에는 그 賠償金을 支拂하게 되는 것이다

　따라서 請求权者는 國際賠償審議委員会의 決定에

不滿이 있을때에는 民事訴訟을 提起할수 있는

것이다

　本條에서 우리가 美国当局과 相互 合意하여

損害賠償金을 決定하게 된것은 (1) 美軍에 依한

事故로 發生하는 請求权의 關係部處는 美軍当局

으로 看做할수 있으며, (2) 美軍当局의 代表를

우리나라의 國家賠償審議委員会의 委員으로 委囑

할수 없으며, (3) 国家賠償制度는 어디까지나 請·

求权者의 同意를 要하는 하나의 簡易節次에 不

過하다는 諸般事情을 參酌한 것이다.

~21~

0130

2. 重要請求权條項의 適用時期

　가. 內容

　　　請求权條項의 第5項(公務執行中 第三者에 처한 損害), 第6項(非公務中의 損害), 第7項 (車輛의 無許可使用으로 일어나는 損害) 및 第8項(公務執行與否와 車輛使用의 許可有無에 처한 紛爭의 解決)을, 서울 特別市 地域에서는 協定發効 6個月后에, 그리고 其他地域에 있어서는 合同委員会의 合意에 依하여 各各 適用토록 하였다.

　나. 解說

　　　이는 両国의 関係当局이 本條의 規定을 適用하는데 必要한 準備를 爲한 期間으로서 마련된

~38~

한·미국 간의 상호방위조약 제4조에 의한 시설과 구역 및 한국에서의 미국군대의 지위에 관한 협정(SOFA) 전59권. 1966.7.9 서울에서 서명 : 1967.2.9 발효(조약 232호) (V.35 체결 교섭 및 준비, 1965.5-12월)

것이다.

서울特別市에서 일어나는 事故로 因한 請求는 協定発効日로부터 6個月后에 効力을 가지도록 한 것은 우리나라에서는 처음인 이 새로운 制度의 採択을 爲한 豫算措置나 이 制度의 効率的인 運営을 爲한 事前 研究가 必要하기 때문인 것이다.

그러나 現在 서울特別市에는 国家賠償審議委員会의 運営을 뒷받침하여 주는 機構가 直接 位置하고 있어 本條에 依한 請求行政을 取扱할수 있는 必要한 準備를 하는데 다른 地域보다 比較的容易할것을 予想하여 協定発効 6個月后에 自動的으로 本條를 適用토록 한 것이다.

-29-

0132

其他 地域에 처하여는 韓國当局이 適切한 準備를 하면 即時 合同委員会에서 그 適用時期를 決定하게 될 것이다.

日本의 境遇를 보면, 地方의 請求事務를 取扱하는 機關으로서 各 地方에 位置한 防衛施設局이 있는 것이다. 우리나라는 現在 이와 類似한 機構가 全然없을 뿐만 아니라, 이런 地方 機構에 配置할 人員도 確保하고 있지 못한 것이다.

따라서 이러한 準備가 完了될때 까지는 本條의 一部規定을 適用할수 없는 것이다. 이러한 不可避한 準備가 完了될때 까지는 美軍当局이 請求에 처한 責任을 지게되는 것이다.

~30~

勞 務 條 項

I. 槪 要

勞務條項은 美國軍隊가 韓國人 雇傭員을 直接雇傭하는 制度를 持續하되 募集에 있어서 可能한限 韓國政府의 募集裁關을 利用한다고 規定하고 있다.

이 條項은 雇傭條件, 補償 및 勞使關係에 있어서 韓國勞動關係 法令을 遵守함을 原則으로 하였으며 軍事上必要로 韓國法令을 遵守치못할 境遇에는 可能한限 事前에 合同委員会에 回附하여 解決方案을 講究하기로 되어 있다. 雇傭主인 美軍은 韓國所得稅法令에 依據하여 雇傭員의 賃金中에서 源泉課稅額을 控除하여 韓國政府에 納付하기로 되어 있다.

~31~

0134

本條項에 依하여 雇傭主와 雇傭員間의 爭議는 于
先 不平處理와 勞動關係節次에 依하여 解決하되 解
決되지 않을 境遇에는 다음과 같은 세段階로 解決
하기로 되어 있다.

첫째, 勞動方에 回附하여 調整하고,

둘째, 合同委員會에 回附하고 그는 特別分科委員會
에 調整을 依賴하며,

셋째, 合同委員會가 直接解決한다.

이 合同委員會의 決定은 拘束力을 가지되 第2段階
인 合同委員會에 回附後 ㄱㅇ日의 期間이 経過된
后에도 勞動爭議가 解決되지 않을 境遇에는 雇傭員
이나 雇傭員団体(勞動組合)는 正常業務를 妨害하는
行爲(罷業을 包含한 団体行動权의 行使)를 할수

~32~

0135

있도록 되어 있다. 그리고 団体行動权은 原則的으로

모든 雇傭員이 亨有하지만 合同委員会는 韓国의 国

防上 또는 韓国의 関係法令의 規定을 参酌하여 団

体行動权을 行事하여서는 안될 緊要한 雇傭員의 範

囲를 決定하기로 되어 있다.

끝으로 雇傭員団体 即 勞動組合은 韓国法令에 依

하여 組織되면 当然히 雇傭主에 依하여 承認된다.

그러나 그러한 勞動組合의 目的이 韓・美共同利益에

背反할 境遇에는 承認되지 않기로 되어 있다.

Ⅱ. 重要問題別 内容

1. 雇傭員의 直接 雇傭制度

가. 内 容

美軍, 非歲出資金機関, 招請契約者인 雇傭主는

-33-

0136

韓國人 雇傭員을 直接募集하고 雇傭한다.

나. 解說

(1) 雇傭主가 雇傭員을 直接雇傭함은 우리法令이나 다른 모든 나라에서 通用되는 一般原則이다.

(2) 日本이나 独逸에서 間接雇傭制를 採用하고 있는바 이는 戰后 敗戰国으로서 労務者를 戰爭賠償의 一環으로 提供하였던 歷史的 緣由로 確立된 制度이며 敗戰国이 아닌 我国은 解放后부터 直接雇傭制를 採択, 伝統化된 것이다.

(3) 이러한 直接雇傭制下에서 政府는 第三者의 立場에서 公正하게 雇傭員의 利益을 追求하는데 介入함으로서 成果를 올릴수 있다.

(4) 間接雇傭制下에서는 雇傭員団体〈労動組合〉의

~34~

0137

団体交涉权과 団体行動权의 行使에 있어서 그

相对가 雇傭主가 아닌 雇傭員들의 自国政府가

된다. 이 境遇. 萬若 我国에서 그러한 制度를

採用하게 된다면 雇傭員들은 国軍의 雇傭員과

同一한 取扱과 待遇를 받게 될것이다. 그들은

大体로 労動運動에 從事할수 없게되어 있음으로

本條項에 依한 間接雇傭制下의 団体行動权을 確

保할수 없었을 것이다. 日本이나 独逸에서는 그

軍隊의 雇傭員들이 団体行動权을 갖고 있음으로

美軍雇傭員에도 同一한 適用을 하는데 支障이

없었다.

(5) 本協定에서 原則的으로. 直接雇傭制를 採択하였

지만 雇傭主는 可能한限 韓国政府의 募集機関을

~35~

通하여 雇傭員을 募集하기로 하였으며 그 境遇

募集에 所要된 直接経費를 韓国政府에게 辨償하

기로 하였다.

2. 雇傭員의 適用範圍

가. 內 容

雇傭員은 美国軍隊, 招請契約者의 非韓国人 雇

傭員, 韓国労務団 (KSC) 団員 및 家事使用人을

除外한 雇傭主가 雇傭한 모든 韓国国籍을 가진

民間人으로 한다.

나. 解 説

(1) 이中에 問題가 또는 韓国労務団 団員의 除外

는 政府가 그들을 6.25動乱中에는 戦時動員法

에 依하여 美軍에게 提供하였고 그后는 自由募

-36~

集에 依하여 提供하여 왔음으로 그 雇傭方法이

美軍의 다른 一般雇傭員과 相異하였다.

(2) 따라서 韓國勞務団의 地位는 從來나른 美軍雇

傭員과 同一하지 않았으며 그들의 地位에 關하

여는 別途로 交涉하기로 되어 있다.

(3) 이들의 地位協定을 締結함에 있어서 政府는

過去에도 物議를 일으킨바를 充分히 參酌하여

그들의 基本权을 確保하는 同時에 最大限의 利

益을 追求하도록 美國当局과 交涉에 臨할 作定이

다.

3. 韓國勞動法令의 遵守

가. 內 容.

雇傭主는 雇傭의 條件, 補償 및 勞使関係에 있어

~37~

서 美軍의 軍事上必要에 背馳되지 않는限 韓国
의 勞動関係法令을 遵守한다.

나. 解 説

(1) 여기서 勞動條件, 補償 및 勞使関係란 모든 雇
傭主와 雇傭間의 関係를 意味하여 그를 韓国法
令에 다르기로 한 原則은 当然한 規定이나 美
軍의 軍事上必要에 背馳되는 境遇 韓国勞動法令
을 遵守하지 않을수 있는 余地를 마련한것이
問題가 된다.

그러나 이와 같은 軍事上必要에 따라 韓国法
令을 遵守하지 못하는 것은 美軍의 軍事上의
任務와 戦時等과 같은 非常時에 韓国法令을 그
대로 지키지 못할 것임으로 마련한 規定이다.

-38-

0141

(2) 다른 協定에도 이와 恰似한 規定이 있는바 例
컨대 日本의 境遇에는 "別途 相互合意하는 限
度內에서" 란 規定으로 合意만하면 어떠한 境遇
에도 (軍事上 必要時만 限定하지 않고) 接受国의
法令을 遵守하지 않으며 「리비아」 協定에는
"一般的으로……遵守한다"는 規定으로 遵守限界
를 雇傭主인 美軍에게 一般的으로 決定할수있는
裁量을 주었다.

(3) 우리協定에는 軍事上必要時 韓国法令을 遵守하
지 못할 境遇를 認定하였지만 合意議事錄第4項
에서 軍事上必要로 韓国法을 遵守치 못할時는 可
能한限 事前에 合同委員会에 回附하여 適切한
措置를 講究하고 適切한 措置에 肉하여 合同委

~89~

0142

員会에서 合意되지않을 境遇에는 外交經路를 通하여 再檢討하기로 하였다.

時間的 余裕가 없어 合同委員会에 事前에 回附하지 못한것은 事后에라도 回附하여야 함은 当然한 일이다. 事后에 回附한 것中에서 適当한 理由없이 韓国法令을 遵守하지 않은것에 對하여 韓国側은 異議를 提起할수 있으며 그러한 境遇의 損害에 對하여 矯正措置를 要求할수 있게되어 있다.

4. 爭議調整節次

가 內 容

雇傭主와 雇傭員間의 爭議는 (1)勞動片, (2)合同委員会와 그의 特別分科委員会, (3)合同委員会에

- 40-

0143

回附하여 調整하되, 第2段階인 合同委員会에 回
附된后 70日이 経過하여도 爭議가 解決되지
않을 境遇 雇傭員은 団体行動权을 行使할수 있
다.

나. 解 說

(1) 이 境遇 調整期間이 너무길기 때문에 雇傭員의
団体行動权行使를 너무長期間 束縛한다는 異論이
있을 것이나, 韓国의 労働爭議法에 依하여도 調
整期間에 20日(一般事業) 或은 30日(公益事
業) 仲裁期間에 20日, 그리고 緊急調整時 30日
間 都合 70日 혹은 80日間은 爭議行爲를
할수 있도록 冷却期間으로서 規定되어 있음으로
韓国法令의 規定과 거의 비슷하다. 다만 労働方

-41-

0144

에 回附된 날로부터 冷却期間을 起算하지 않은

것이 問題가 되나 이는 勞動方에서 10日以上

調整을 할 境遇에만 韓國法과 差異가 생기게

되지만 韓國雇傭員의 權益을 擁護할 勞動方이

10日以上 問題를 掌握하고 있지 않을수 있음

으로 問題가 되지 않는다.

5. 團体行動权의 行使

가. 內 容

團体行動权은 原則的으로 모든 雇傭員이 亨有

하되 合同委員会는 團体行動权을 行使하지 못할

緊要한 雇傭員의 範囲를 決定한다.

나. 解 說

(1) 一部 緊要한 雇傭員의 團体行動权行使를 合同

- 42 -

0145

委員会가 制限한다는 것이 問題가되나 이는美軍

이 韓国의 防衛를 爲하여 駐屯하므로 그 軍務

遂行上 莫大한 支障을 招来할 特定雇傭員의 団

体行動权의 行狀를制限하자는 것이며 韓国法令에도 ~~勞動組合法 第8條 1.2項~~

(單純한 勞務에 從事하는者는 勞動運動을 할수

있으나) 그들中에서 重要한 機密事務, 庶務, 人事

物品出納, 経理 또는 勞務者의 監督事務에 從事

하는者는 勞動運動을 爲한 集団的行動을 하지못

하게 되어있다.

(2) 美軍의 單務遂行上 不可缺한者란 高度의 技術

을가진 熟練技術者等으로서 戦時等 危急時 臨战

態勢에 支障이 있는 団体行動权의 行使만을 制

限하자는 것이며 一般的인 雇傭員의 权利를 制

限하자는 것이 아니다.

-43-

기 안 지

기안자	미주과 황영재	전화 번호			공보	필 요	불 필 요

	과 장	국 장		차 관	장 관

협 조 성 명							보 존 년 한

기 안 년 월 일	65. 8. 26.	시 행 년 월 일				정 사	기 장

분류기호
문서번호 외구미-7222

경 유 수 신 참 조	대통령 비서실장	발 신	장 관

제 목   한·미간 주둔군 지위협정 체결 문제.

1. 그간 한·미간의 실무자 교섭을 통하여 주한 미군에 대한

군대지위 협정 체결교섭은 현재 협정 전문에 사실상 합의를 봄으로써

체결교섭은 일단 끝났 것으로 볼수 있으나 지난 8월 10일 수정된

미·비 기지협정은 한미 협정과는 차이가 있는 내용으로 되었읍니다.

2. 따라서 미비기지협정 개정을 계기로 이미 교섭이 사실상

완결된 한미 협정에 대한 문제점을 별첨과 같이 검토 보고 합니다.

유 첨 : 미·비 기지협정 개정에 따르는 한·미 행정협정 교섭

재검토 1부.   끝.

보통문서로 재분류(1966.12.31)

형사 재판권에 관한 미·비 기지협정 개정에
따르는 한·미 행정협정 교섭의 문제점.

1. 미·비 기지협정의 수정내용과 한미 합의 내용의 차이점:

   가. 제 1차적 관할권의 포기:

   (1) 한·미 합의 내용

   (가) 한국은 1차적 재판권을 미국에 일단 포기하고,

   (나) 한국은 사건에 따라 재판권 행사가 불가피하다고 결정할
       경우 포기한 재판권을 미국당국이 통고한 날로 부터 21일내에
       철회할수 있다.

   (다) 포기철회에 관하여 한·미 양국 정부간의 의견이 대립될때에는
       외교분야를 통하여 그 해결을 모색할수 있으나, 한국당국의
       철회에 관한 결정은 최종적이다.

   (2) 미·비 협정의 수정 내용

   (가) 비율빈 당국이 재판권을 행사함이 중요하다고 결정하는 경우
       를 제외하고는 미국당국의 요청이 있으면 1차 재판권을
       미군당국에 포기,

   (나) 포기요청은 범죄 발생 통고후 <u>10일</u> 내에 서면으로 하여야 한다.

   (다) 상기 요청한 날로 부터 <u>15일</u>내에 재판권 행사에 대한 통고가
       없으면 포기한 것으로 간주.

   나. 재판권 행사 대상자에 관한 범위:

   (1) 한·미 합의내용

   합중국의 재판권에 복하는 자를, 합중국 군대의구성원, 군속 및
   가족으로 규정함.

   (2) 미·비 협정 수정내용

   합중국의 재판권에 복하는 자를, 합중국 군법에 복하는 모든자
   (군속 또는 가족은 포함하지 않음 로 규정함.

- 1 -

0148

다. 기타 차이점:

수정된 미.비 협정에는 우리가 이미 미국과 합의한 아래와 같은 규정이
없음.

(1) 계엄령이 선포된 지역에서는 한국당국은 재판권을 행사할수 없다.

(2) 한국 영토밖에서 범한 범죄에 대하여는 한국당국은 재판권을 행사
할수 없다.

(3) 한국의 전속적 재판권에 대한 미국의 포기요청에 대하여 한국당국은
호의적인 고려를 한다.

2. 운영면으로 본 실질적인 차이:

한.미 합의 내용과 개정된 미.비 기지협정의 재판관할권 조항에 있어서
가장 중요한 내용이라 할수 있는 1차 재판권의 포기에 관한 규정을 보면
미.비 기지협정은 미군의 포기요청에 대하여 비율빈이 포기여부에 대한
완전한 재량권을 행사할수 있다는 점에서 체제상 우리보다 상당히 유리한
방향으로 규정되었으나, 한.미 합의내용도 미측에 우리의 1차 재판권을
일단 포기는 하나 포기의 철회에 관한 완전한 재량권이 확보되고 있다는
점에서 볼때 궁극적으로는 재판권할권을 우리의 재량과 결정에 따라
행사 할수 있으며 실질적인 효과면에서는 커다란 차이가 없을 것임.

3. 미.비 기지협정의 수정내용이 한.미 합의내용과의 차이에서 야기될 문제:

상술한바와 같이 실제 운영상의 차이는 그렇게 크지 않을 것이나 미.비
기지협정의 내용이 비율빈 측의 1차 재판권을 우리처럼 일단 미측에 포기
하지 않고 재판권 행사에 있어서의 자주성을 보유하고 있다는 점에 비추어,
한.미 합의내용이 한국의 1차 재판권을 일단 미국측에 포기해두고,
포기의 철회로서 재판권을 행사하게 되어 있다는 것은 명분과 체면에 치중
하는 일부 우리 국민들 눈에는 비율빈 보다 체제상 불리한 협정이라고
보이게될 우려가 있음.

0149

- 2 -

4. 미·비 기지협정의 개정교섭의 배경:

가. 1947년에 체결된 미·비 기지협정은 그간 형사 재판권을 위요하고 많은 문제를 일으켜 오던중, 지난 8월 10일에 동 협정의 형사 재판권 조항만을 개정하게 되었다.

나. 형사 재판권 조항에 대한 개정을 하게된 직접적인 계기는 1964년 11월 "클라크" 미공군기지 사격장에서 일어난 미공군 *Cole* 사병에 의한 비율빈 소년의 살인 사건을 계기한 비율빈 국민의 대미감정의 급격한 악화와 그후의 계속적이며 대대적인 반미 시위등으로 말미아마 비율빈 정부나 미국 정부는 동 협정을 빠른 시일내에 수정하지 않을수 없는 불가피한 입장에 놓이게 되었던 점에 있다 할 것이다.

다. 또한 비율빈은 오는 10월에 대통령 선거가 있으며 집권당은 기지협정 개정문제를 대통령 선거에 관련된 가장 큰 정치적 문제로 취급하여 미국측과의 교섭에 임한 결과 재판 관할권 조항만을 다른 조항과 분리 취급 합의하여 부분적인 수정에 성공한 것이다.

5. 한·미 협정교섭 (특히 형사 재판권) 의 배경:

가. 한국은 형사 재판권 조항 교섭에서 당초부터 비율빈이 이번에 수정에 성공한바와 같은 체제의 내용을 주장해 왔으나, 미측은 서독 보충협정 체제보다 못한 내용을 주장하여 완강한 반대를 되풀이 해 왔던 것임. 따라서, 행정협정 교섭의 핵심을 이루는 이 문제 해결의 지연으로 말미아마 협정 교섭 전체가 부진 상태를 면하지 못하였던 것이다.

나. 이와 같은 교섭의 부진상태를 타개하기 위하여 대통령의 방미를 계기로 한미 상방은 서독 보충협정과 같은 체제에 따라 해결키로 한것임. (미국이 노무조항에서 노동자의 기본권을 인정하는 대신 서독 보충협정의 포기조항을 수락하였음.)

6. 한·중·비 각국의 교섭현황:

가. 한국 : 대통령 방미를 계기로 가장 문제가 되었던 형사 재판권 조항 및

0150

- 3 -

노무조항에 관한 원칙문제가 해결되므로서 협정 전반에 걸쳐 일괄

타결이 진첩되어 교섭 실무자 간에는 지난 6월 중순에 이미 협정의

전 조항에 대하여 사실상 완전 합의를 보아 현재 다만 공식적인

최종 실무자 회의를 거쳐 서명할 시기를 검토 중임.

나. 비율빈 : 10여년에 걸친 교섭을 한후 지난 8월 10일에 형사 재판권

조항만을 수정하였으며, 기타 조항에 관하여는 앞으로도 교섭

을 계속하여 수정하지 않으면 안될 것임.

다. 중 국 : 자유중국 역시 10여년에 걸친 교섭을 하여 왔으며, 지난

7월 30일에는 협정 조문에 완전 합의를 보아 양교섭 당사국이

협정 조인에 필요한 절차를 끝내고 즉시 서명하게 되었다는

요지의 공동 성명이 발표 되었으나 아직 서명을 하지 않고

있으며, 합의된 협정 내용을 탐지중이나 현재로서는 알수 없음.

7. 결 론 :

가. 미·비 기지협정과 우리가 미국측과 합의한 내용을 비교하여 볼때,

우리가 합의한 내용은 형사 재판권 조항에 있어 비율빈이 이미 수정

한 내용보다 조문의 체제상 불리하게 되었다고 해석될수 있는 요소를

내포하고 있다. 따라서 국내의 일부층에서의 비판이 예견된다.

나. 그러나 대통령의 방미를 계기로 교섭이 진전되어 사실상 지난 6월

중순에는 협정 전 조항에 대하여 완전 합의를 본바 있는 협정을 재교섭

하고져 하는 경우에는 다음과 같은 문제가 야기될 것이 예상됨.

(1) 재교섭의 경우 협정의 내용을 우리측의 희망대로 수정할수 있어야 한다.

(2) 현재까지의 교섭 경위를 보아 우리측에게 유리하게 수정하고져

재교섭을 요청 하더라도 미측이 이에 응할 것이라는 기대를

가지기는 극히 곤난하다.

(3) 따라서 협정의 체결은 무기한 지연 또는 침체될 것으로 예견됨.

(4) 이러한 사태가 발생하면 행정협정 뿐만 아니라 앞으로 한·미

간의 외교교섭에 상당한 영향을 끼칠 것으로 예상됨.

0151

(5) 따라서 현 단계로서 생각할수 있는 최선의 방법으로는 행정협정 체결을 당분간 현 상태로 두고 한·미 관계와 기타 국내의 제반 사정을 전망할수 있는 시간적 여유를 가지는 것이 필요하다고 봄. (중·미 협정이 8월 중에는 서명될 것이라함.)

0152

기 안 지

기안자	미주과 이근팜	전화 번호			공보	필요	불필요
	과 장	국 장			차 관	장 관	
협조자명						보존 년한	
기안 년월일	1965. 9. 6.	시행 년월일		통 제 판		정서	기장
분류기호 문서번호	의구미						
경유 수신 참조	대 통 령 비 서 실 장			발신		장 관	
제 목	한·미간 주둔군 지위협정 체결교섭						

1. 주한 미군에 관한 군대 지위협정 체결교섭은 그간 한·미간의 실무자 교섭을 통하여 현재 협정 전문에 사실상 합의를 봄으로서써 현안 이던 교섭은 일단 끝났읍니다.

2. 한편, 미·비 양국이 개정을 교섭하여 오던 미·비 기지협정중 형사 재판권 조항이 지난 8월 10일 수정 조인되었으며, 미·중 양국이 10여년간 교섭하여 오던 미·중간 주둔군 지위협정도 8월 31일 "타이페이" 에서 정식으로 조인된바 있읍니다.

3. 따라서 미·비 기지협정 개정과 미·중 주둔군 지위협정의 체결을 계기로 이미 교섭이 사실상 완결된 한·미간 협정안에 관련된 제반 문제점을 별첨과 같이 검토 보고 합니다.

유 첨 : 1. 한·미간 협정 체결교섭의 문제점 1부.

2. 각국 협정의 형사 재판권 조항 대비표 1부.   끝.

공통서식 1-2 (갑)   보통군사호 재판규 (1964. 12. 31)   (16절지)

중·미협정 체결과 미·비 기지협정 중 형사 재판권에
관한 개정에 따르는 한·미 협정 체결교섭의 문제점.

1. 미·중 협정 및 미·비 기지협정중 수정된 형사 재판권과 한·미간에 합의된
   내용과의 차이점:

가. 형사 재판권

   (1) 제 1 차적 재판권의 포기:

      (가) 한·미 합의 내용

         1. 한국은 제 1 차적 재판권을 미국을 위하여 포기한다.

         2. 한국은 특정 사건에 있어서 재판권 행사가 불가피하다고
            결정할 경우 미국당국이 통고한 날로 부터 21일 이내에
            포기한 재판권을 철회할수 있다.

         3. 한국이 권리 포기를 철회한 경우 한·미 양국 관계당국 간에
            양해가 성립되지 않을 때에는 미국 정부는 한국 정부에 이의
            를 제기할수 있다.

         4. 한국 정부는 양국정부의 이의을 충분히 고려하여 외교분야에
            있어서의 그의 권한을 행사하여 의견차이를 해결한다.

         5. 한국 정부가 의견 차이를 해결함에 있어서 한국이 재판권을
            행사함이 불가피하다고 결정하는 경우 권리 포기의 철회는
            최종적이며 확정적이다.

      (나) 미·중 협정의 내용

         미·중 협정은 독일 보충협정의 포기조항의 형태를 그대로 채택
         하고 있음. 즉, 상기한 한·미 협정안의 내용중 1, 2, 3 및 4항의
         규정과 동일함.

      (다) 미·비 협정의 수정내용

         1. 비율빈 당국이 재판권을 행사함이 중요하다고 결정하는

0154

- 1 -

경우를 제외하고는 미국정부의 요청이 있으면 제 1 차적
재판권을 미국당국에 포기한다.

2. 포기요청은 범죄 발생 통고후 10일 내에 서면으로 하여야 한다.

3. 상기 요청한 날로 부터 15일 내에 재판권 행사에 대한 통고가
없으면 포기한 것으로 간주한다.

(2) 재판권 행사 대상자의 범위:

(가) 한·미 합의 내용

합중국 군대의 구성원, 군속 및 그들의 가족.

(나) 미·중 협정의 내용

합중국 군법에 복하는 모든자.

(합중국 법령이 달리 규정하지 않는한 군속 및 가족을 포함함.)

(다) 미·비 협정의 내용

합중국 군법에 복하는 모든자.

(군속 및 가족은 포함하지 않음. 단, 합중국 정부는 합중국
법령에 변경이 있을 경우 비율빈 국 정부에 통고함.)

(3) 재판전 피의자의 구금:

(가) 한·미 합의 내용

모든 재판 절차가 종결되고 한국 당국이 요청할때 가지 합중국
군 당국이 피의자를 구금한다.

(나) 미·중 협정의 내용
한·미 협정의 내용과 동일.

(다) 미·비 협정의 내용
한·미 협정의 내용과 동일.

- 2 -

한·미국 간의 상호방위조약 제4조에 의한 시설과 구역 및 한국에서의 미국군대의 지위에 관한 협정(SOFA)
전59권. 1966.7.9 서울에서 서명 : 1967.2.9 발효(조약 232호) (V.35 체결 교섭 및 준비, 1965.5-12월) 455

(4) 기타 차이점:

(가) 미·중 협정 및 미·비 협정에는 한·미 간에 합의된 아래와 같은 규정이 없음.

1. 계엄령이 선포된 지역에서는 형사 재판권 조항의 적용이 정지되고 합중국 군 당국이 전속적 재판권을 행사한다.

2. 한국의 전속적 재판권에 대한 합중국의 포기요청에 대하여 한국당국은 호의적인 고려를 한다.

(주) 한·미간에 합의된 다음과 같은 규정이 미·중 협정에도 있음.
"한국 영역밖 에서 행한 범죄에 대하여서는 한국 당국의 재판권이 미치지 아니한다."

나. 노 무

(1) 노동 조건

(가) 한·미 합의 내용

본조의 규정과 미군의 군사상 필요에 배치되지 않는한 노동 조건, 보상 및 노사관계는 한국 노동법령의 제 규정을 따라야 한다.

(나) 미·중 협정의 내용

노무조달은 유사한 상황하에서 중국 정부 기관에게 적용되는 것보다 일반적으로 불리하지 아니한 조건으로 행한다.

(2) 노동쟁의의 해결

(가) 한·미 합의 내용

1. 노동쟁의는 순차적으로 (ㄱ) 노동청, (ㄴ) 합동위원회 분과위원회 (ㄷ) 합동위원회에 회부 조정한다.

2. 제2 단계에 회부된후 70일이 경과하여도 해결되지 않을 경우 고용원은 단체 행동권을 행사할수 있다.

(나) 미·중 협정의 내용

1. 노동쟁의는 조정을 위하여 합동위원회에 제출할수 있다.

다. <u>청 구 권</u>

(1) 공무 집행중 제 3 자에 대한 손해.

(가) 한·미 합의 내용

<u>1.</u> 한국 정부가 한국법에 따라 해결.

<u>2.</u> 국가 배상법에 따라 해결할 때에는 배상책임과 배상금에 관하여 합중국 당국과 합의한다.

(나) 미·중 협정의 내용

합중국 법의 관계 규정에 의거 해결한다.

(2) 비공무중의 손해

(가) 한·미 합의 내용

<u>1.</u> 한국당국이 청구를 심사, 배상금을 사정하여 합중국 당국에 통보한다.

<u>2.</u> 합중국 당국은 보상금의 지불여부와 그 금액을 결정.

<u>3.</u> 피해자가 만족할 때에는 보상금을 합중국 당국이 지불하고 한국당국에 그 결과를 통보 한다.

<u>4.</u> 피해자가 불만시 한국의 민사소송에 의하여 해결한다.

(나) 미·중 협정의 내용

합중국 정부는 합중국 관계당국이 결정하는 바에 따라 배상금을 지불한다.

2. 운영면으로 본 실질적인 차이:

가. 한·미 합의내용과 미·중 협정:

미·중 협정의 제 1 차적 재판권의 포기에 관한 규정은 독일 보충협정의 포기조항의 규정을 문자 그대로 채택한 것으로서 한·미 간에 합의된 포기 조항과 대체적으로 동일하나 다만 한국 당국이 포기를 철회하였을 때에 한·미 양국간에 양해가 성립되지 않을 경우 한국 정부가 의견차이를 해결함에 있어서 한국이 재판권을 행사함이 불가피하다고 결정하는 경우에는

- 4 -

한·미국 간의 상호방위조약 제4조에 의한 시설과 구역 및 한국에서의 미국군대의 지위에 관한 협정(SOFA)
전59권. 1966.7.9 서울에서 서명 : 1967.2.9 발효(조약 232호) (V.35 체결 교섭 및 준비, 1965.5-12월) 457

권리포기의 철회는 최종적이며 확정적이다는 규정에 해당하는 부분이
결여되어 있음으로 협정의 체제상은 물론 실지 운영상으로도 우리나라의
포기조항의 규정보다는 불리한 것임.

나. 한.미 합의내용과 미.비 협정

한.미간에 합의된 내용과 개정된 미.비 협정의 형사 재판권 조항에 있어서
가장 중요한 내용이라 할수 있는 제 1 차 재판권의 포기에 관한 규정을 보면
미.비 기지협정은 미군의 포기요청에 대하여 비율빈 국이 포기여부에 대한
완전한 재량권을 행사할수 있다는 점에서 체제상 우리보다 상당히 유리한
방향으로 규정되었으나, 한.미 간의 합의 내용도 독일 보충협정의 포기조항의
형태를 우리에게 유리하도록 일부 수정 채택한 것으로서 한국이 제 1 차적
재판권을 미국에 일괄적으로 포기하나 포기의 철회에 관한 완전한 재량권
을 확보하고 있다는 점에서 볼때 궁극적으로는 우리의 재량과 결정에 따라
재판권을 행사 할수 있으며 따라서 실질적인 효과면에서는 커다란 차이가
없을 것임.

3. 미.비 기지협정의 수정내용과 미.중 협정이 한.미 간에 합의된 내용과의 차이
에서 야기될 문제:

가. 미.비 기지협정의 내용이 상술한바와 같이 실제 운영상의 차이는 그렇게
크지 않을 것이나 비율빈 국이 제 1 차적 재판권을 사전에 미국당국에 포기
하지 않고 재판권 행사에 있어서의 자주성을 보유하고 있다는 점에 비추어,
한.미 간의 합의 내용이 한국의 제 1 차적 재판권을 일괄적으로 미국측에
포기해두고, 포기의 철회로서 재판권을 행사하게 되어 있다는 점은 명분과
체면에 치중하는 일부 우리나라 국민들에게는 미.비 협정보다 체제상
불리한 협정이라고 보이게될 우려가 있음.

나. 그러나 한편, 우리나라가 권리 포기의 철회의 효과면에서 최종적이며 확정적
인 결정권을 확보한 점은 미.중 협정의 포기조항에 비하여 보다 유리하며
국민들도 이러한 점을 납득할수 있을 것임.

4. 한.미 협정 체결교섭 (특히 형사 재판권) 의 배경:

가. 한국은 형사 재판권 조~~항~~구성~~해서~~~~럼~~된 미.일 협정과 같은 내용을

주장하여 왔으나 미측은 도리혀 독일 보충협정보다 불리한 내용을 주장
하여 완강한 반대를 되풀이 해 왔던 것임.

따라서, 협정 체결교섭의 핵심을 이루는 이 문제 해결의 지연으로
말미아마 협정 교섭 전체가 부진 상태를 면하지 못하였던 것임.

　　나. 이와 같은 교섭의 부진상태를 타개하기 위하여 대통령의 방미를 계기로
미국이 노무조항에서 노무자의 기본권인 쟁의권을 한국에 인정하는 대신,
한국이 독일 보충협정의 포기조항을 원칙적으로 수락하기로 합의 하였음.

　　다. 이와 같은 양국 지도자간의 합의에 입각하여 협정 체결교섭 전반에 걸쳐
일괄 타결이 급속도로 진첩되어 교섭 실무자 간에는 지난 6월 중순경
까지는 이미 협정의 전 조항에 대하여 사실상 완전 합의를 보아 현재
다만 공식적인 최종 실무자 회의를 거쳐정식으로 조인할 시기를 검토중에
있음.

5. 미·중 협정의 체결교섭의 배경:

　　가. 근 11년간이나 교섭을 진행하여 오던 미·중 양국은 1965년 8월 31일
"타이페이" 에서 20개 조항으로 되어 있는 미·중간 주둔군 지위협정에 조인
하였음.

　　나. 중국은 교섭에 임함에 있어서 미·일간 협정의 형태를 목표로 노력을 하여
왔으나 미국측이 서독과 체결한 보충협정의 형태를 완강히 주장하여 양측
의 의견이 상반되어 교섭의 타결이 지연되어 오던중 수차에 걸친 미군의
총격 사건에 자극되고 또한 한·미, 중·미간 협정 체결교섭이 성숙하여
짐에 따라 이에 보조를 마추어 금번 교섭을 타결하게된 것임.

　　다. 중국 정부는 주둔군 지위협정의 체결 자체를 중요시하는 것보다 일단
유사시에 대만이 위협을 받았을 때에 미국과 공동 보조를 취하고져 하는
보다 고차적인 국가 이익을 고려에 넣어 금번 협정을 체결하게된 것이라함.

6. 미·비 기지협정의 개정교섭의 배경:

　　가. 1947년에 체결된 미·비 기지협정은 그간 형사 재판권을 위요하고 많은

- 6 -

0159

한·미국 간의 상호방위조약 제4조에 의한 시설과 구역 및 한국에서의 미국군대의 지위에 관한 협정(SOFA)
전59권. 1966.7.9 서울에서 서명 : 1967.2.9 발효(조약 232호) (V.35 체결 교섭 및 준비, 1965.5-12월) 459

문제를 일으켜 오던중, 지난 8월 10일에 동 협정의 형사 재판권 조항만을 개정하게 되었음.

나. 미.비 기지협정의 형사 재판권 조항에 대한 개정을 하게된 원인은 동 조항이 비율빈 국에 불리한 요소를 내포하고 있었다는 사실에 있었지만 그 직접적인 계기는 1964년 11월 25일 Clark 미공군기지 사격장에서 일어난 미공군의 Cole 사병에 의한 비율빈 소년의 살인 사건과 1965년 1월 15일 Subic 미 해군 기지에서 미해병대의 Edwards 및 Thomas 두 사병에 의한 비율빈 어부 살인 사건의 발생을 계기로 한 비율빈 국민의 대미 감정의 급격한 악화와 그후의 계속적이며 대대적인 반미 시위등으로 말미아마 비율빈 정부나 미국 정부는 동 협정을 빠른 시일내에 수정하지 않을수 없는 불가피한 입장에 놓이게 되었던 점에 있다 할 것임.

다. 또한 비율빈은 오는 10월에 대통령 선거가 있으며 집권당은 기지협정 개정문제를 대통령 선거에 관련된 가장 큰 정치적 문제로 취급하여 미국측 과의 교섭에 임한 결과 재판권 조항만을 다른 조항과 불리 취급, 부분적인 수정에 성공한 것임.

라. 비율빈 국은 형사 재판권 조항을 제외한 기타 조항에 관하여서는 앞으로도 교섭을 계속하여 수정할 의향이며, 이에는 상당한 시일을 요할 것임.

7. 결   론

가. 미.비 기지협정 및 미.중 협정과 우리가 합의한 내용을 비교하여 볼때, 한.미간의 합의 내용은 형사 재판권, 노무, 청구권등 중요 조항에 있어서 미.중 협정보다 상당히 유리하게 되어 있으나, 형사 재판권 조항은 우리가 협정 체결교섭 시초부터 목표로 하였던 미.일 협정은 물론, 비율빈 국이 이미 수정한 내용보다 조문의 체제상 불리하게 되었다고 해석될수 있는 요소를 내포하고 있음. 따라서 한.미 협정이 체결되면, 이러한 점에 대한 국내의 일부 층으로 부터의 비판이 예견됨.

나. 그러나 대통령의 방미를 계기로 교섭이 진전되어 사실상 지난 6월 중순

0160

까지에는 협정의 전 조항에 대하여 완전 합의를 본바 있는 내용을 우리정부가 재 교섭 하고져 하는 경우에는 다음과 같은 문제가 야기될 것이 예상됨.

(1) 재교섭의 경우 한·미 양국 대통령 간에 원칙적으로 합의된바 있는 형사 재판권의 포기조항을 비롯하여 협정의 중요내용을 우리측의 희망대로 수정할수 있어야 함.

(2) 그러나 현재 까지의 교섭 경위로 보아 우리가 현재 합의된 내용 보다 우리측에게 유리하게 수정하고져 재교섭을 요청 하더라도 미국측이 이에 응할 것이라는 기대를 가지기는 극히 곤난함.

(3) 더욱이 우리나라가 비율빈 국이 국민의 격렬한 반미 시위의 결과 수정에 성공한 형사 재판권 조항과 동등하게 협정안을 수정할 것을 미측에 제기하는 경우에도 우리나라가 교섭 당초 부터 미·일 협정의 형태를 확보코져 꾸준히 노력하였으나 미국측의 완강한 반대로 여의치 못하였던 교섭 경위에 비추어 미·일 협정의 내용과 동등한 미·비 협정의 형사 재판권 조항의 수준을 확보할 가능성이 희박하며 또한 미국측의 종전 태도에서 협정안의 수정 가능성을 입증할만한 아무런 변동의 징조도 찾아 볼수 없음.

(4) 특히 한·미 간의 합의 내용이 지난 8월 31일 조인된 미·중 협정의 내용보다 전반적으로 유리하다는 것이 판명된 이상 우리측의 재교섭 제의 이유의 타당성이 희박하여 졌으며 미국으로서도 만약에 우리측 요구에 응하게 된다면 중국으로 부터의 반발도 예견하지 않을수 없으며 이러한 일련의 사태는 미국으로 하여금 우리측의 재교섭제의 를 수락하기 곤난하게 만들 것임.

(5) 따라서 우리측이 재교섭을 제의하는 경우 협정의 체결은 무기한 지연 또는 침체될 것으로 예견됨.

(6) 이러한 사태가 발생하면 행정협정 뿐만 아니라 앞으로 한·미간의 외교 교섭에 상당한 영향을 끼칠 염려가 있음.

(7) 그러므로 현 단계에서 생각할수 있는 최선의 방법으로서는 한·미 간에

한·미국 간의 상호방위조약 제4조에 의한 시설과 구역 및 한국에서의 미국군대의 지위에 관한 협정(SOFA)
전59권. 1966.7.9 서울에서 서명 : 1967.2.9 발효(조약 232호) (V.35 체결 교섭 및 준비, 1965.5~12월) 461

이미 합의된 협정안 대로 ~~조인을~~ 하되, 다만 협정 조인 및 국회의
동의 요청 시기 결정을 당분간 보류함으로서 국내의 제반 사정을 전망
할수 있는 시간적 여유를 가지는 것이 필요하다고 봄.

보~~호~~ 재분류(1966. 12. 31.)

2. 준비

0163

1965. 6. 21

韓美間 駐屯軍地位協定의 締結에 즈음하여:

1. 協定締結의 經緯

    6.25動亂이 勃發하자 유엔決議 決議에 따라 (32라대운용량 비버에게 정거함 1965. 6. 23. 라장)
友邦 美國軍隊가 유엔軍의 一員으로서 參戰하게 되자
美國軍隊의 地位에關하여 1950年 7月12日 大田에
서 切迫한 戰時라는 與件下에서 暫定的條件으로 韓. 美間
兩國間에 公翰交換形式으로 締結된 所謂 大田協定에 依據
美駐屯軍에 對한 排他的인 裁判權을 美軍當局에 移讓하
지 된것은 周知의 事實이다.   그러나 休戰이 成立
된後 10餘年이란 長久한 歲月이 經過하도록 歷代政權
이 妥結을 짓지못해해 오던 協定을 現政府가 새로서
妥結함으로써 우리나라가 거두게 된 實益을 살펴보면
大略 다음과 같은 몇가지를 들을수 있을 것이다.

    1. 첫째로 : 우리나라가 共産侵略으로 부터
國土를 防衛하기 爲하여 友邦美國軍隊를 맞아드리긴

— 1 —

0164

하였지만 所謂 大田協定이라는 것은 急迫한 戰時下에서

부드기 締結된 協定이며 이러한 協定이 休戰後 10年

이 지나도록 包括的인 軍隊地位協定으로 代替되지 못하

였다는 事實은 우리나라의 主權行使가 그만큼 制約을

받아왔다는 것을 말하는것인데 現政府가 비로서 美國軍

隊의 地位에 關한 全般的이며 包括的인 協定을 締結하

게 됨으로서 우리나라가 外國軍隊의 地位에 關한 한

制約되었던 主權行使가 完全히 回復하게 될 것이다.

2. 實體로 : 이協定의 締結은 韓·美兩國間에

오래동안 懸案問題로 끌어오던 交涉을 圓滿이 友好的이

며 協助的인 精神에 立脚하여 解決하였다는 것은 韓·

美兩國間의 傳統的인 友好·協力精神의 再闡明이라 할수

있는 同時에 우리나라의 外交的 成果라고 할수있다.

3. 月面로 : 歷代政權이 오랜歲月을 두고

締結을 試圖하였음에도 不拘하고 成功으로 이끌지

못하였던 協定이 오늘날 締結된 것은 美國이 우리나라

가 國內的으로는 政治的인 安定을 이룩하고 經濟的으로

-2-

한·미국 간의 상호방위조약 제4조에 의한 시설과 구역 및 한국에서의 미국군대의 지위에 관한 협정(SOFA) 전59권. 1966.7.9 서울에서 서명 : 1967.2.9 발효(조약 232호) (V.35 체결 교섭 및 준비, 1965.5-12월)

發展의 터전을 마련하게된 事實과 아울러 對外的으로 우리나라가 屈東 나아가서는 國際的 舞臺에서 擔當하고 있는 役割의 重要性을 認定한 結果라 아니할수 없는 것이다.

2. 交涉 經緯

休戰이 成立된 後 大田協定을 代替하는 새로운 駐屯軍地位協定을 締結하여야 한다는 國民의 輿論에 따라 1953年 8月 7日 韓·美 相互 防衛條約 假調印時에 韓·美 兩國은 이승만·델레스 共同聲明書에서 相互 防衛條約 發効 即時 美國軍隊地位協定 締結을 交涉하기로 合意한바 있었으며 그에따라 散發的인 交涉이 있기는 하였으나 別다른 成果를 거두지 못하였던 것이다.

韓·美兩國間에 本格的인 交涉이 始作된 것은 1962年 9月 20日 兩國間에 第1次 實務者級 交涉會談가 開催된 때라 할수있으며, 그後 1965年

— 3 —

0166

5月 미국에서 開催된 JOHNSON 美國大統領과의 會談에서 協定의 重要 未解決問題에 對한 原則的인 合意를 봄으로서 難案이던 交涉은 急進展을 보여 1965年 6月까지 80餘回에 達하는 交涉會議 끝에 마침내 온國民의 念願이던 交涉에 매듭을 짓게 된 것이다.

3. 協定의 內容

本 協定은 美國軍隊가 우리나라에 入國한때부터 出國할때에 이르기 까지 일어날수 있는 모든問題를 總網羅한 방대한 것으로서 協定의 各條項에 規程된 內容을 通하여 우리가 얻은 成果中 가장 重要한 成果는 大略 다음과 같다.

1. 刑事裁判管轄權條項:

過去 美軍關係者에 依하여 發生하는 各種 犯罪에 對하여 美軍當局이 大田協定下에서 排他的인 裁判權을 行使한 結果로서 論議되었던 國民의 鬱憤내지는

—4—

0167

輿論의 비등으로 한미아마 兩·美間의 敦篤한 友好關係
에 기열이 잘 順應가 일지도 않았으나 이제 兩國間에
相互 尊重의 原則에 立脚한 駐屯軍地位協定이 締結됨으
로써 이러한 誤解와 不信으로 因하여 惹起되던 問題를
事前에 除去함으로써 韓·美間의 旣存 親善關係를 더욱
두텁게 하는데 크게 이바지 하게 될 것이다.   우리는
刑事裁判管轄權條項下에서 重要犯罪에 對하여 우리나라가
裁判權을 行使함이 特히 重要하다고 決定하는 境遇에는
우리가 裁判權을 行使할수 있는 契機가 마련된 것이다.

    2. 民事請求權條項:

        지금까지 駐韓美軍이 우리나라 領土內에서

違法한 行爲로 個人의 人命이나 財産에 미친 모든 損

害에對한 賠償은 오직 美軍當局이 그들의 國內法에

依하여 一方的으로 解決하여온 것이다.   따라서

被害者들은 가혹 억울한 일이 있는 境遇일지라도 公平

한 處遇를 依賴할수 있는 길이 事實上 封鎖되어 있었

던 것인데 금번 本協定 締結로 한미아마 被害者는

— 5 —

0168

韓國法令에 規定된 바에 따라 民事訴訟을 提起할수 있게

되었으며 英國軍隊의 構成員은 原則的으로 韓國의 民事裁

判으로 부터 免除되는 일이 없게 되었다.

　　3.　勞務關連事項 :

　　　　英軍當局이 韓國人 雇傭함에 있어서 戰時및

비에 準하는 特別한 境遇를 除外하고는 韓國의 勞動關係

法令에 規定된 雇傭條件을 遵守하게 되었다.　　따러어

英軍에 從事하는 雇傭人에게 憲法과 勞動關係法令에서 保

障된 勤勞者의 基本權인 團結權 團體交涉權 및 團體行動

權이 明文上 保障된 것이다.

4.　結　言

　　끝으로 上述한 바와 같은 成果에도 不拘하고

一部 國民들中에는 英國이 다른나라와 締結한 協定에 比

하여 期待하였던 바와 다소 거리가 있음을 指摘하는 분

들이 있을지 모르지만 이것은 나라에 따라 事情이

—5—

0169

다룬기 띠문이며 우리나라의 境遇에는 8.15解放과
더불어 맺어지고 6.25事態이란 試鍊과 또한 美軍이
韓·美間 相互防衛條約에 立脚하여 우리나라에 駐屯하며
休戰線을 두고 恒時 戰時態勢를 가추고 共產軍과 對峙
하고 있다는 事實에 비추어볼때 間國의 期待가 어긋나
지 않는 協定이라는 것을 首肯할수 있을 것으로 確信
하는 바이다.

앞으로 우리들에게 남은 問題는 本協定을 어떻게 補
足할수 있게 運營하느냐 하는것 뿐이며 韓·美間의 傳
統的인 友好關係에 立脚하여 政府의 關係當局은 勿論
國民여러분에서도 이協定의 根本精神을 理解하고 充足한
만한 成果를 거두기 爲하여 積極 協助있으시기 바라마
지 않는 바이다.

-9-

0170

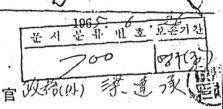

大統領指示事項
確認報告書

대비경(일)

報告番號 (65) 第　　　號

1965. 6

문서분류번호 보존기간

七〇〇　　　명기 3

大統領 閣下

報告官 政務(마) 梁達承

指示事項　韓美行政協定 締結 交涉

大統領 閣下께서　　　月　　　日　　　에게 指示하신 上記 事項에 對하여 다음과 같이 그 施行狀況을 確認 報告 하나이다.

1. 現況

前番의 報告時와 같으며, 美軍의 招請契約者의 處遇가 問題로임.

- 韓國側의 主張 : 美軍의 軍屬이나 家族과 같이 取扱 않겠다.

- 美國側의 主張 : 韓國側의 排他的 裁判管轄權은 認定하되, 그들의 일의 重要性을 考慮하여, Pre-trial custody, Confinement, trial safeguard 는 現行政協定 規定대로하다.

2. 展望

韓國側이 讓步하여 7月1日 이나 2日 에 安을 合意 된것을 發表하고 未末週 (7月 8日~9日) 에는

大統領秘書室

17432

0171

한·미국 간의 상호방위조약 제4조에 의한 시설과 구역 및 한국에서의 미국군대의 지위에 관한 협정(SOFA)
전59권. 1966.7.9 서울에서 서명 : 1967.2.9 발효(조약 232호) (V.35 체결 교섭 및 준비, 1965.5-12월)　471

正式 調印 된 주定임.

　한가지 問題点은 法務長官이 擴征中에 있어
7月3日 歸國 주定인바, 駐日代表部 経由 連報로
同意를 얻도록 한것임.

한•미 간 주둔군 지위협정의 체결에 즈음하여 발표할
대통령 담화문 (초안)

오늘 12년간 한•미 양국의 현안 문제로 해결을 보지 못한
한•미간 주둔군지위에 관한 협정이 정식으로 체결됨에 대하여
본인은 국민 여러분과 더불어 기쁨을 금하지 못하겠습니다.

돌이켜 보건대 8•15 해방과 더불어 우방 미국 군대가 일본국
에 대한 무장 해제와 군정 실시를 위하여 1945년 9월 9일 우리나라에
진주하였으며 그후 우리나라의 독립과 더불어 임단 접수 이었던
것은 국민 여러분의 주지의 사실입니다.

그러나 1950년 6•25일 북괴의 불법 남침이 발발하자 미국
군대는 우리 인접부장 이사회의 결의에 따라 우방군의 일원으로서
참전하였으며 이에 따라 우리나라는 미국 군대의 지위에 관하여
1950년 7월 12일 대전에서 정부와 전시라는 여건으로 잠정적으로
미국 군대에 대한 배타적인 재판권 행사를 미군 당국이 부여하는
대전협정을 체결한 것입니다.

그러나 1953년 7월 27일 휴전이 성립되고 1953년 10월 1일
한•미 양국간에 상호 방위조약이 체결되고 이 조약에 따라 우리나라는
미 주둔군의 지위에 관한 협정을 체결할 것을 미국 정부에 요구
한바 있으며 1953년 8월 7일 한•미 상호 방위조약 가조인시에
발표한 이승만•덜레스 공동 성명에서 상호 방위조약 맺은 즉시
미국 군대 지위협정의 체결을 교섭하기로 합의한 이래 오늘까지
꾸준한 교섭의 노력으로 그 결실을 보기된 것입니다.

우리정부가 이번에 역대 정부가 결심을 보지못한 정부와
국민의 관심사의 아니었던 미 주둔군 지위협정은 성공미에 해결
하게된 의의를 상격보면.

첫째로, 우리나라가 공산 침략으로 부터 국토를 방위하기
위하여 우방 미국 군대를 맞아 주둔이 있어서 체결한 소위 주둔협정

한·미국 간의 상호방위조약 제4조에 의한 시설과 구역 및 한국에서의 미국군대의 지위에 관한 협정(SOFA)
전59권. 1966.7.9 서울에서 서명 : 1967.2.9 발효(조약 232호) (V.35 체결 교섭 및 준비, 1965.5-12월)

이라는 것은 긴급한 현시하에서 미군이기 배타적 재판권의 행사를
허용한 것이며 기타 미군을 위시한 유엔 사령부와 체결된 마야협정,
또는 여타 개별적 경제관계 협정이 휴전후 10여 년이 지나도록
프랑키인 군대 지위협정으로 대체되지 못하였다는 사실은 우리나라의
주권 행사가 그만큼 제약을 받아 왔다는 것을 말하는 것인데
본 협정에 이르러서 미국 군대의 지위에 관한 전반적이며 프랑적인
협정을 체결하게 됨으로써 우리나라가 미국 군대의 지위에 관한 한
제약되었던 주권행사를 완전히 회복하게 될 것입니다.

둘째로, 이 협정의 체결은 한·미 양국간에 오랫동안 현안문제로
끌어오던 교섭을 양국이 우호적이며 협조적인 정신에 입각하여
해결하였으므로 이는 한·미 양국간의 전통적인 우호, 협력 정신의
재 천명이다 말할 수 있는 동시에 우리나라의 외교적 성과라고 말할 수
있습니다.

세째로, 역대 정부가 오랜기간을 두고 교섭을 시도 하였음에도
불구하고 성공으로 이끌지 못하였던 협정이 오늘날 체결된 것은
미국이 우리나라가 군립에 의해서 국내적으로 정치적인 안정을 이룩하고
입법, 행정, 사법등 각 부문에 걸쳐 현저한 발전을 이룩하였다는
사실을 미국 정부가 인정한 결과다 아니할수 없습니다.

우리는 6.25 동란을 통해 수많은 미군이 우리나라에서 그
생명을 바쳤으며 지금도 휴전선을 두고 항시 긴서 태세를 갖추고
공산군과 대치하고 있다는 엄연한 사실에 비추어 볼때 이 협정이
우애정등의 원칙하에서 맺어진 협정이다는 것을 국민 여러분이
수긍할수 있을 것으로 확신하는 바이며 이 협정 체결로 한·미
양국의 우호 관계가 일층 돈독히 되기를 염원 합니다.

끝으로 한·미 양국간의 전통적인 우호관계에 입각하여

정부의 관기당국은 물론 국민 어떠분께서도 이 협정의 근본정신
을 잘 이해하고 만족할 만한 성과를 걷우기 위하여 각국 협조

있기를 바라는 바입니다.

0175

한·미 간 군대 지위 협정 (행정 협정)과
헌법과의 관계에서 발생하는 논의 점

1. 우리나라 헌법상의 헌법과 조약의 효력 문제
2. 2 중 국적자와 헌법상의 기본권
3. 일정한 고용원에 대한 단체 행동권의 제약

1965.   7. ?   29.

방 교 국   조 약 과

0176

1. 우리나라 헌법상의 헌법과 조약의 효력 문제

1. 우리나라 헌법 제 5 조는 "(1) 이 헌법에 의하여 체결, 공포된 조약과 일반적으로 승인된 국제 법규는 국내법과 같은 효력을 가진다" 라고 규정하고 있는바, 본 조에 규정된 국내법이 국내에 시행되고 있는 모든 법 — 즉, 법률 뿐만 아니라 헌법 까지도 포함하는지 일응 논의가 있음. 다만, 현재의 대부분의 학설은 헌법 우위설을 취하고 있기는 하나 현재로서는 대법원의 유권적 해석을 내린바는 없음.

국내법이 헌법 까지도 포함 한다면 우리나라 헌법은 헌법과 조약의 효력 관계에 있어서 동위설을 취한 것이며, 그렇다면 후법 우선의 원칙이 적용됨.

그렇다면 금번 체결, 공포될 행정 협정도 헌법과 저촉되는 면에서는 행정 협정이 우선 하므로, 위헌의 문제가 발생할 여지가 없음.

2. 국제 사회의 발달에 따라 국제법과 국내법의 효력관계에 관한 국제 법상의 일반적인 통설은 일원론(一元論)중에서 특히 국제 법

0177

- 2 -

우위설 또는 동 위설을 주장하고 있음. 특히 대다수 국가

(예, 불란서, 서독 일본) 이 이러한 태도임이 주목됨.

3. 특히, 본 행정 협정은 다른 일반 조약과는 상이한 특수성이 있는바, 일국의 군대를 타국에 주둔 시킴에 따라서 발생하는, 파견국과 접수국의 대인고권(対人 高权) 및 영토고권(領土 高权) 의 충돌을 조정하려고 한 협정인 것이라는 점을 유념하여야 할것임.

4. 이와 관련하여 독일 기본법 제 24 조 제 1 항과 제 2 항은 주목되는 바임.

"   Article   24

    (1) The Federation may, by legislation, transfer soverign powers to inter-governmental institutions.

    (2) For the maintenance of peace, the Federation may enter a system of mutual collective security; in doing so it will consent to such limitations upon its rights of sovereignty as will bring about and secure a peaceful and lasting order in Europe and among the nations of the world.

    (3) ...   ".

0178

二重國籍者에 対한 裁判権 問題

協定 第22條 第4項은, 大韓民國 國民 또는 大韓民國에 通常
居住하고 있는 者라 하드라도 合衆國 軍隊 構成員에 対하여는
合衆國 軍当局이 本 協定上의 裁判権을 가진다 라고 規定하고 있는바,
이에 關하여 우리나라 憲法 第24條 第1項 (裁判請求権)에 違反하여
違憲이라는 見解가 있으나. 違憲이 아니라고 生覚함.

〈理由〉

① 비록 大韓民國 國民이라 하드라도, 그들의 同意에 따라 合衆國에
対한 忠誠을 宣誓하고 同國 軍隊人이 되는때에는, 그들은 同軍隊를
規律하는 軍事 裁判権 및 懲戒権에 服従할 義務를 受諾한
것이며 이는 反面 이와 抵触되는 우리 憲法上의 裁判 請求権을 이미
抛棄한 것이라고 解釈되어, 本 協定은 다만 이러한 抛棄事実을
確認한 것에 不過하다고 生覚함.

② 設使 이러한 者에 対한 裁判権의 行使의 問題에 있어서는,
本 協定의 達造 여하에 따라서는 우리側이 裁判権을 行使할 수 있다고
生覚함.

야, (가) 専属的 裁判権에 있어서는 매양으로 問題되지 않으며,
(나) 우리나라가 第1次的 裁判権을 가지는 경우, 合衆国 軍当局의
抛棄要請이 있다 하드라도, 우리나라가 裁判権을 行使함이
特히 重要하다고 決定하면. 이러한 者들이 正当한 裁判権
行使가 可能함 (合衆諸事録 第3項 (나)에 관련어)
合衆國 当局이 第1次的 裁判権을 가지는 경우라 하드라도
우리 側이 그 取利抛棄가 特히 重要하다고 認定할데에
取利抛棄를 要請할 수 있음 (第22條 第3項 (나)).

③ 二重國籍者에 対한 派遣國 軍当局의 裁判権을 認定한 國際的
先例가 許多하다. 即,「나토」協定 第7條 第4項, 美日協定 第17條
第4項,「오스트랄렬」協定 第8條 第4項,「웨스트·인디지」協定 第9條
第4項 等이다. ─── 美中協定 第14條 第4項. 美比協定 第13條 第4項

0173

2. 2 중 국적자와 헌법상의 기본권

행정협정 (안) 제 22 조 제 4 항에는 " 본조의 전기 제 규정은 합종국 당국이 대한민국의 국민인자 또는 대한민국에 통상적으로 거주하고 있는 자에 대하여 재판권을 행사할 권리를 가진다는 것을 뜻하지 아니한다. 다만, 그들이 합종국 군대의 구성원인 경우에는 그러하지 아니하다". 라고 규정하고 있는바, 본 협정의 발효와 동시에, 우리나라는 대한민국 국민이거나 대한민국에 통상적으로 거주하지 않는 합종국 군대의 구성원에 대하여는 형사 재판권을 행사 하지 못한다는 것이며, 이는 반면 이러한 자가 우리나라 헌법 제 24 조 제 2 항에 규정된바, "헌법과 법령에 정한 법관에 의하여 법률에 의한 재판을 받을 권리" (재판 청구권)가 박탈됨으로 위헌이라는 견해가 있음.

그러나, 위헌이 아니라는 이유로서는,

1. 상기한 자들이 미국 군대에 자원 입대하였을때에 미국의 법령에 복종할 의무를 수락한 것이며, 이는 동시에 대한민국의 헌법 상의 권리를

0130

포기하거나, 행사하지 아니할 의사를 나타낸 것이며, 이러한 사실을 본

협정으로서 확인한것에 불과하며, 또한 우리나라 헌법상의 기본 태도는

자유 민주주의를 채택하고 있으므로, 이러한 자의 그러한 의사를 존중

하여 그러한 재판 청구권의 포기나 불행사를 용인함이 오히려 헌법의

태도에 부합 할것임.

2. 우리나라 국민이 특별 권력 관계인 군 복무관계에 서게되면,
특수한 규율이 적용되는 범위 내에서 헌법상의 기본권 보장을 받지
못하며, 미국 국민이 군에 복무하면 자국 헌법의 기본권마저 제한됨
다함은 동일한 현상일 것임.

그런데, 본제의 2 중 국적자의 경우에만 유독히 미군 특수규율이

적용되는 한도내에서도 우리나라 헌법상의 기본권이 보장되어야 함은

법의 일반 원리에 오히려 반함.
또는 각국의 선례를 하면,
3. 군대 지위협정 (행정협정)을 체결하고 운영하는 제 국가 —!

일본, 서독, 이태리, 토이기 에서는 위헌이 논의 된바, 없었을 뿐만

0181

아니라 사실에 있어서 그러한 경우가 하나도 발생하지 않았다ㅁ 함.
(물론 이론개는 各各 현실개 존재개개청청 (개々등) 가비 출력 존개개

4. 법도 사실을 기초로 하여 실행 가능한 사안에 대하여 준수 되어야

한다는 규범적 성격을 부여하여야 할 것이므로, 이러한 여건에 대한

사실면도 무시할 수 없음.

첫재, 2 중 국적자인 합중국 군대의 구성원이 어느 법죄로 인하여

미 군법 회의에 의한 재판이나 징계를 받는 경우에 이러한

자의 미국 법령 준수의 선서에도 불구하고 대한민국 법원에

의한 재판을 받겠다고 요구 할것인지의 문제,

둘재, 2 중 국적자인 합중국 군대 구성원은 미 군대에 복무한다

하드라도 우티나타 헌법상의 권티 뿐만 아니타 의무도 이행

하여야 합이 당연할 것인바, 예컨대 병역 의무를 필하지

않은 병역 기피자토서 처단 할 수 있을지의 문제,

이러한 우티나타 헌법상의 의무를 이행하지 못한다고 하여 기본권을

0182

- 6 -

부인하여도 무방하다는 해석이나, 론의는 없겠지만 이와 같은 2 중

국적자의 우리나라 헌법에 대한 지위는 불 완전한 것이므로, 미국의

대인 고권 특히 그 특별 권력과 충돌한 면에서 까지 우리나라 헌법

상의 기본권을 부여하여야 한다함은 법이 추구하는 일반 원리에 오히려

보손되리라 생각됨.

0183

3. 일정한 고용원에 대한 단체 행동권의 제약

1. 행정협정(안) 제 17 조 제 4 항 (나)에는 "합동 위원회는, 합중국 군대의 고용원의 대한민국 방위에 있어서의 역할과 대한민국 법령의 관계 규정을 고려하여, 노동 쟁의가 전기 절차에 의하여 해결되지 아니 하는 경우에는, 더 이상 단체 행동권을 행사 하여서는 아니될 긴요한 고용원의 제 범주를 결정한다"라고 규정하고 있음.

2. 헌법 제 29 조 제 1 항에서 규정한 근로의 권리 (근로 3 권인 단결권, 단체 교섭권 및 단체 행동권)는 질서 유지 (秩序維持)나 공공복리(公共福利)에 영향을 미칠 경우에는 법률로서 제한할 수 있는 기본권이므로, 헌법 제 32 조 제 2 항에 따라 질서 유지나 공공복리를 노동권의 본질적 내용을 훼손하지 않는 범위내에서 법률과 동일한 효력을 가지는 본 행정 협정으로서 제한할 수 있을 것임.)

따라서, 상기 행정 협정 (안) 제 17 조 제 4 항 (나)의 규정은 합헌 이라고 하겠음.

0184

3. 이점에 관하여, 상기 행정 협정의 규정은 위헌이라고 하는 견해가 있는바, 이는 헌법 제 32 조 제 2 항의 적용을 받을 수 있는 경우만 행위를 기준으로 하여서만 법률로서 제한 가능한 것이며, 우리나라 국민의 일부를 범주 (範疇)로서 한정하여 기본권을 제한할 수 없다는 것임.

그러나, 공공복리나, 질서유지를 위하여서는 비단 행위를 기준으로 하여 제한할 수 있을 뿐만 아니라, 공공 복리나 질서 유지를 위하여 최소한도로 요구되는 일정한 범위의 국민에 대하여 범주를 정하여 법률로써 제한 가능하리라고 생각되며, 이는 현행 법령에서 그 예를 발견할 수 있음.

예컨대, 근로 기준법 제 50 조는 사회부의 취직 인허증이 없는 한 근로자로서 취업할 수 없다고 하였으며, 동법 제 70 조는 일정한 질병에 걸린 자에게는 취업을 하지 못하도록 규정하고 있음.

0185

특히, 행정 협정 (안)의 상기 규정은 우리나라 국토 방위 상의

역할을 고려한 만큼 우리나라 국가 자체의 안위에 관한 사항이며

또한 최상 위의 질서 유지라 할 것임. 따라서 이러한 국가 안위에

관한 질서 유지를 위하여 이 질서 유지에 영향을 미칠만한 최소

한도로 필요하고 긴요한 고용원에 대하여 근로 3권 중 단결권 및

단체 교섭권은 인정하고 다만 단체 행동권만은 행사하지 못하도록

합동 위원회가 결정함은 우리나라 헌법 제 29 조 제 1 항 및 제 32 조

제 2 항에 위반 한다고 생각되지 아니함.

0186

o 퇴임권 o 改定을.
  o 法律으로 支配를 하다. 위원 아니다.
  o 승낙을 (의회)
  o 청장 ㅣ 노동대 ㅣ ... 채용.
    노동법을 적용의 줄이 ㅣ

법 제 처

법제일741-3⁰   (74)9800－9809(구) 4319   1965. 7. 31

수 신 : 외무부장관

제 목 : 한·미 군대지위협정 (행정협정)

　　　귀부에서 65. 7.7. 외방조 741－1102으로 심의 요청하신 위의건안은 그 내
용을 검토한바동 협정은 외국군대의 지위에관한 조약일뿐만 아니라·국가에 재정적 부
담을 과하는 사항및 입법사항이 포함되어 있으므로 동 협정의 체결에는 헌법 제56조
제1항에 의하여 국회의 동의를 요함을 회시합니다. 끝

예고문   보동문서도 재분류(본협정체결시)

　　　　　법 제 처 장   서   일

0188

한·미간 주둔군 지위협정에 관한
발 표 문

1965. 8. 13.

한·미 양국 교섭 실무자들은 1965년 8월 13일 개최된 제 82 차
교섭회의에서 한·미간 주둔군 지위협정에 관하여 합의 안의를 보았다.
동 회의에서는 형사 재판권, 노무조항, 민사 청구권등 각 종의 조항을
비롯하여 지금까지 미 해결로 남아 있던 모든 문제에 관하여
최종적 합의가 이루어 졌다.

대한민국 이동원 외무부 장관과 "원스톤. 지. 부라운" 주한
미국 대사는 김정 또는 작성이 완료되는 대로 서울에서 협정문
에 서명하게 된 것이다. 이 협정은 대한민국 정부와 주한 미합중국
군대간의 모든 업무를 망라한 것이며 서문을 비롯하여 31개 조항으로
되어 있다.

이 새로운 협정은 대한민국 정부가 협력하에 되다 이 협정을
승인 이었다는 사실을 합중국 정부에 통고한 날로 부터 3 개월 후에
발효할 것이다. 또한 이 협정은 1950년 7월 12일 자로 재간된
대전협정과 주한 미합중국 군대에 관한 한 1952년 5월 24일 대한민국
과 통합 사령부간의 경제 조정에 관한 협정을 대기하고 대처할 것이다.

0189

<u>Press Release on US-ROK Agreement on SOFA</u>

The Korean and American negotiators reached full
agreement on the US-ROK Status of Forces Agreement
at the 82nd negotiating session on August 13, 1965.
Final agreement was reached on the wording of three
key articles, Criminal Jurisdiction, Labor, and Claims,
as well as on all other previously unresolved articles.

The ROK Foreign Minister, Mr. Tong Won Lee,
and the American Ambassador, Mr. Winthrop G. Brown,
will sign the document in Seoul as soon as the formal
texts have been prepared. The Agreement includes
a Preamble and 31 articles covering all aspects of relations
between the Government of the Republic of Korea and the
United States military forces in Korea.

The new Agreement will enter into force three
months after the date the Korean Government notifies
the U.S. Government that it has approved the Agreement
in accordance with its legal procedures. The Status
of Forces Agreement will supercede and replace Taejon
Agreement of July 12, 1950 and Agreement on Economic
Coordination of May 24, 1952 between Unfied Command and
the Republic of Korea, as related to U.S. armed forces
in Korea.

0190

협 조 전	응신기일

분류기호 : 외기획-	제 목 : 한미행협 P. R.

수신 : 구미국장   발신일자 : 1965. 8. 24. (협조제의)

기획 관리 실장   (발신명의) 백 인 한   대 구희원

(제1의견)

국가안전보장회의 사무국의 요청이 있으니 한미행정협정체결

추진 현황의 P. R. 사항을 구체적으로 1965. 8. 26. 가지 통보

해주시기 바랍니다. 끝.

(제2의견)

공통서식 1-23   (16절지)

0191

협 조 전	응신기일

분류기호 외구미 1156	제목 한·미 주둔군 지위협정 선전

수신 기획관리실장	발신일자 65. 8. 25. (협조제의)

구 미 국 장   (발신명의)   장   상   문

1. 1965. 8. 24. 외기획 응신임.   (제1의견)

2. 한·미간 주둔군 지위협정은 상금 체결교섭이 진행중에 있음으로

   그 내용은 공표하여서는 아니됨을 알려 드립니다.   끝.

   분 단게가 나는것

                                                              (제2의견)

수신: 각 심국과장   1965. 10. 6.

제목: 국회 외무위원회에 보고할 자료.

    10월 12일 (화요일) 국회 본회의 산회후에 외무위원회가
개최케 되었는바 이에 대비하여 각 심국과는 다음 재목에
관한 자료를 작성하여 10월 8일 오전중으로 기획관리실장에게
필히 제출하여 주시기 바람.

                       다   음

1. 국제정세보고.

    가. 인도 - 파키스탄 관계.

    나. 인도네시아 쿠데타.

    다. 싱가폴의 마레이샤 연방으로 부터의 이탈 문제.

    (상기 나 및 다 에 대하여는 신중을 기할 것)

2. 한미행정협정 체결 교섭 중간 보고.

3. 일본 비준국회에 대한 중간 보고.

4. 아.아.회의에 관한 정세변화.

5. 제20차 유엔총회 대책.

6. 국정감사 수검 태세.

추각. 상각 자료를 유인물로 작성위계이니 구체적으로 작성하
        시기 바람.

                            차 관 문덕주

                            0193

미주둔군지위협정 체결 교섭
(규정감사 자료)

1965.10.8.

1. 방 침

우리측은 접수국의 이익을 최대한으로 보장하기 위하여 미국이
각국과 체결한 "나도"협정 및 미·일협정등의 선례를 기준으로 하여
한·미 양국이 주권평등의 원칙에 입각하여 상호 만족할 수 있는
협정을 ~~빠른시일내에~~ *가까운장래에* 체결하기 위하여 교섭을 추진함.

2. 처리 현황

가. 1962 년 9 월 20 일 제 1 차 실무자회의를 재개한 이래 한·미 양측은
   잠정적으로 결정한 29 개중요 조항에 관한 토의를 시작, 노력한
   결과, 1964 년 9 월 9 일 까지 62 차에 달하는 실무자회의를
   개최하여 20 개조항에 완전 합의를 본바 있음.

나. 1964 년 10 월 이후 우리측은 현안인 교섭의 조속한 타결을 위하여
   실무자회의를 계속 추진하는 한편 주한미국대사와의 회담, "번디"
   차관보와의 회담, 이동원 장관의 방미등 미국정부 고위층과의 접촉을
   통하여 우리측 입장에 대한 미국정부의 이해와 협조를 촉구하였음.

다. 그러나 협정의 핵심인 형사재판권, 노무, 청구권등 제 중요 미해결
   조항을 위요한 한·미양측의 의견차의로 말미아마 양측은 별다른
   진전을 보지 못 하고 있던중 1965 년 5 월 중순 박대통령의 방미를
   계기로 한·미 양국 대통령은 형사재판권, 노무 등 조항을 비롯한 협정
   전반에 대한 조기 타결 원칙에 합의를 보기에 이르렀음.

3. 성과 요약

가. 한·미 양측은 한·미 양국 대통령의 조기 타결 원칙에 입각하여
   실무자급 회의를 적극 추진한 결과 1965 년 6 월 7 일 개최된
   제 81 차 회의까지 협정의 전문과 31 개조항중 전문 및 25 개
   조항에 완전 합의를 보게 되었음.

나. 그러나 81 차 회의에서도 해결을 보지 못한 형사재판권, 노무,
   청구권, 초청계약자, 시설과 구역, 협정의 효력 발생등 각 조항에

C101

관하여 우리측은 미측과 예의 접촉을 계속하여 대체적인 합의를 보았음. (별첨 진도표 참조)

4. 앞으로의 전망

가. 한.미양측은 제 81 차 회의 이후 비공식 접촉을 통하여 대체적으로 합의를 본바 있는 중요 미결 조항에 대하여 앞으로 개최될 완전없는것 하고 아주 가까운 고성천쓴 제 82 차 회의에서 공식적으로 이를 확정할 것이며,

나. 합의된 내용에 따라 협정의 조문 정리가 끝 나는 대로 국내법 가까운장래에 절차에 의거 년내에 서명한 후 국회에 동의를 요청할 것임.

쓰것임

라. 애로 및 건의사항

현재 한국이 휴전상태 하에 있다는 특수성과 현행법령 및 제도의 빈번한 개정, 및 국내 제반 실정이 교섭상 우리의 입장을 약화 하는 요인이 되고 있음.

미주둔군 지위협정 체결교섭

(1964년도 국정감사 시 지적사항에 관한 65년도 추가 국정감사 자료)

1. 64년도 국정감사 지적사항

미주둔군 지위협정의 조속한 체결을 위하여 확고한 계획과 신념을 가지고 책임있게 회답을 추진할 것.

2. 1965. 9. 30. 현재까지 조치사항

우리측은 한·미간 실무자회의 및 고위층 회담 개최를 통하여 협정의 체결 교섭을 조속한 시일내에 타결로자 적극 노력함.

가. 한·미간 실무자 회의 개최

(1) 1964년 9월 11일 개최된 제 63차 실무자 회의 이래 1965년 6월 7일 개최된 제 81차 실무자 회의 까지 19회에 달하는 한·미간 실무자 회의를 개최하여 협정의 전문 및 31개 조항중 전문 및 25개 조항에 완건 합의를 보았음.

(2) 그러나 협정의 핵심인 형사 재판권, 청구권, 노무등 중요조항을 비롯한 6개 조항에 관하여는 완건한 합의에 도달하지 못하였으므로 그후 한·미 양측은 계속 공식 또는 비공식 교섭을 거듭한 결과 현재 이들 미합의 조항에 관하여 대체적인 합의를 보게 되었음.

나. 한·미간 고위회담을 통한 교섭 추진

실무자급 교섭회의 의 정기적 개최와 아울러 우리측은 주한 미국대사 및 주미대사를 통한 교섭, 한·미간의 고위층 회담 개최등을 통하여 우리측 입장에 대한 미국정부의 이해와 협조를 촉구한바 있으며 그중 중요 사항은 아래와 같음.

0196

(1) 1964년 10월 3일 이동원 외무부 장관은 방한중인 미국 무성의 "우이미암 번디" 극동 담당 차관보와 회답하고 우미정부의 입장에 대한 미국정부의 성의를 촉구하였으며 양인은 한·미한의 주둔군 지위협정 체결교섭을 조속한 시일내에 타결할 것에 합의함.

(2) 1965년 3월 중순에 이동원 외무부 장관은 방미하여 "떠스크" 미국무장관과 회답하고 현안인 협정의 체결에 관한 우미정부의 입장을 강조하였으며 "떠스크" 장관은 한국 정부의 입장을 충분히 고려할 것과 가능한 한 조속한 시일내에 최종적인 합의에 도달하기 위하여 교섭을 촉진할 것에 합의함.

(3) 1965년 5월 18일 방미중에 있던 박 대통령은 존슨 미국 대통령과 협정의 교섭은 도달한 현안 문제에 관하여 도의한 결과 형사 재판권, 노무등 중요문제에 관하여 원칙적인 합의에 도달하였으며 가까운 장래에 완전 합의에 도달하게될 것임을 확인하였음.

0197

통일교의

뉴욕 타임스 에머슨 샤핀 기자와의 단독회견 질문서

1. 통일문제:

   유엔에 있어서의 한국문제 자동상정을 재고하는 경우
   어떠한 방법으로 한국통일에 대한 노력을 할것인가.

2. 한일협정에 대한 일본의회의 비준전망에 대하여 어떠케
   생각하는가.
   만일 비준이 된다면 한일협정이 아세아에 어떠한 영향이
   있을 것으로 보는가.

   Ⓑ 이 中軍狀果 에 要 日�→ (Samention에 Ⓐ)

3. 해외에서의 북괴의 활동에 대한 대비책은 무엇인가

◁ 4. 한미 주둔군 지위 협정의 조인은 언제쯤으로 보는가.

Ⓐ 家에 揚에 사務
   要 企 報官에 多 ?   23 回거니지

"뉴욕타임스", "에머슨.샤핀" 기자와의

장관 단독 기자회견 자료.

(한미 주둔군 지위협정 관기) 65.10.23. 공보관실에

발송.

(문) 4. 한미 주둔군 지위협정의 조인은 언제쯤으로 보는가?

(답) 한미 주둔군 지위협정은 아시다 싶이 정치적 고려와 기술적인 제문제
가 수반되고 해결되어야만 체결되는 것으로 생각합니다.

한.미 양국은 다같이 조속한 시일내에 주둔군 지위협정이 체결되는 것이
한미간의 우호관기를 보다더 공고히 하는데 공헌 할것이라는
정치적 고려에서 본 협정 체결교섭은 추진하여 왔으며 그간 상방의
성의있는 교섭으로 완결단계에 들어오게 된 것입니다.

그러나 우리정부로서는 미국이 각국과 체결한 협정의 선레와
주한 미군의 사명 및 역활의 중요성을 감안하여 국회와 국민의 이해
와 지념을 받을수 있는 내용의 협정이 되도록 최종적 교섭을 진행
하고 있으며 단시일내에 완건한 타개를 될것으로 확신하는 바입니다.

지금까지 시일이 걸리는 이면에는 또한 먼저 말한 기술적인 제문제
가 있기 때문입니다. 우리 협정이 완결되면 협정의 전 조문이
약 6만자에 달할 것으로 추측되는 방대한 것이 됩니다.

한국이 맺은 어떠한 협정보다 방대한 것이 됩니다. 이렇게 많은
조문은 거의 모든 분야를 망라하는 법률용어도 표현 하는데는
시일이 걸립니다. 조문의 내용에 대한 원칙은 한.미 양측이 거의
합의 하였읍니다.

0199

중요조항인 형사 재판권, 민사 청구권, 노무등 에서의 수개점 만
해결되면 완전한 합의가 이루어 집니다. 그래서 본협정의 조인은
머지않은 장래에 실현될수 있다고 봅니다.   끝.

0200

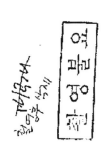

0201

「뉴욕·타임스」記者와 会見資料

4. 韓美駐屯軍地位協定의 調印은 언제쯤으로 보는가?

答

駐屯軍地位協定은 아시다싶이 ~~어떠한 境遇에 있어서든지~~ 政治的考慮와 法律上의 諸問題가 ~~發生時에~~

隨伴되고 解決되어야만 締結되는 것으로 생각합니다.

~~우리의 境遇 對外的인 政治的考慮는 美國의~~

~~四國과 같이, 早速한 時日內에~~

~~우리와 駐屯軍地位協定을 締結하려는 입장國家는~~

~~美國의 ...~~

... 여기에 있어 온 國民이 本協定의 무엇을 ...

그러나 우리 政府로서는 美國이 ...國과 締結한 ...

協定을 希求하고 있다는 見地에서 早速한 締結이 ...要求되나 萬若에 國民의 期待에 어긋나는 ...에 ...駐屯美軍의 ...

協定을 締結하면 國會에서 特히 野黨에서

非難이 激甚할 것을 予想할수 있습니다.

이 ...에 慎重을 ...으로 國會와 國民의 ...

이러한 非難을 받지 않을 協定 即 우리에

...利한 協定을 締結하기 위하여 ...

... 期하기에 時日이 걸려 있으며 앞으로도

... ... 短時日內에 ... ...

502 주한미군지위협정(SOFA) 서명 및 발효 13

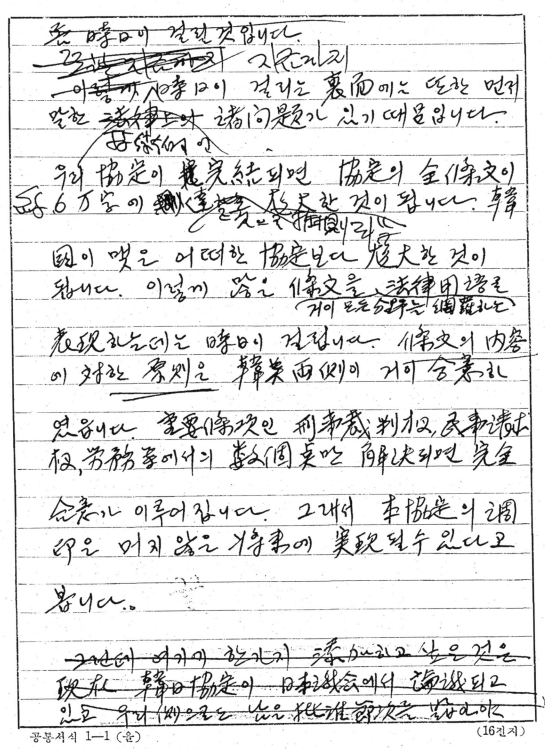

꽤 時日이 걸린것입니다.
~~22 월에 차선까지~~ 지난까지
~~이동까~~ 時日이 걸리는 裏面에는 또한 먼저
말한 ~~諸事項~~ 諸問題가 있기 때문입니다.
~~旁 系統에 서~~

우리 協定이 完結되면 協定의 全條文이
~~6万字~~ 의 ~~個人達成을~~ 尨大한 것이 됩니다. 韓
~~것으로 插圖以라~~

國이 맺은 어떠한 協定보다 尨大한 것이
됩니다. 이렇게 많은 條文을 法律用語로
거의 모든 分野를 綱羅하는

表現하는데는 時日이 걸립니다. 條文의 內容
에 對한 原則은 韓美両側이 거의 合意하

였읍니다. 重要條項인 刑事裁判权, 民事請求
权, 勞務等에서의 數個处만 解決되면 完全

合意가 이루어집니다. 그래서 本協定의 調
印은 머지 않은 將來에 實現될수 있다고

봅니다.

~~그런데 여기에 한가지 追加하고 싶은 것은~~
~~現在 韓日協定이 日本議会에서 論議되고~~
~~있고 우리側으로는 많은 批准節次을 밟어야~~

한·미국 간의 상호방위조약 제4조에 의한 시설과 구역 및 한국에서의 미국군대의 지위에 관한 협정(SOFA)　503
전59권. 1966.7.9 서울에서 서명 : 1967.2.9 발효(조약 232호) (V.35 체결 교섭 및 준비, 1965.5-12월)

A. As you may aware, our preoccupation to the conclusion of
the status of Forces Agreement between Korea and the United
States has been the political consideration we have to taken
into account and the technical problems we have encountered to
settle down. We have been negotiating the Agreement under
political consideration that friendship and amical relationship
between Korea and the United States will be greatly enhanced
by early conclusion of the Agreement. Thanks to sincerity
and endeavor of negotiating teams of both countries, the
Agreement has come to the final stage, Our Government has been
trying to conclude such an Agreement as our National Assembly
and the people can understand and support. Of course, we
have taken into accout of the precedented Agreements which the
United States has so far concluded with other countries and
of the important role of the United States armed forces in their
defense mission in Korea. The signing of the Agreement has been
delayed due to the technical problems, as I mentioned earlier.
When the Agreement is finalized, the whole articles will
comprise 60,000 words in Korean version and 30,000 words in English
version, Therefore, this Agreement is the most enormous
one than any other Agreement Korea has ever concluded.
It ought to take time to polish out so many articles in legal
terms in almost every field. Both sides have reached agreement
on principles in almost all articles. If in the articles some points
with respect to criminal jurisdiction, claims and labor
are settled down, full accords will be made in all articles.
Therefore, I would say that the signing of the SOFA is foreseeable
in near future.

0204

한·미간 주둔군 지위협정 체결교섭.
(제 3 공화국 수립 이티 업격자료)

1965. 11. 17.

1. 협정체결의 필요성.

가. 주한미군은 6. 25 동난의 발발과 더불어 유엔군의 일원으로 참전한
이래 1950년 7월 12일 한·미간에 체결된 쏘위 대전협정과 1952년 5월 24일
체결된 합동 사령부와의 경제조정에 관한 협정 (쏘위 "마이야" 협정) 에
의하여 배타적인 형사 재판권 행사를 비롯한 광범위한 특권과 면제를
향유하여 왔던 것이다.

나. 그러나 상기 제 협정은 모두 긴박한 사태하에서 전쟁 목적수행을 위하여
체결된 것이었으며 그후 미국 군대가 한·미 상호 방위조약에 의거
체재후 계속 우리나라에 주둔하게 됨에 따라 이와 같은 협정들이 상호 주권존중
의 원칙에 입각한 새로운 협정에 의하여 대치되어야 함은 너무나
당연한 일이다.

2. 제 3 공화국 수립 이전의 현황

가. 한·미 양국은 1953년 8월 7일 한·미 상호 방위조약 가조인시 이승만
"덜레스" 공동성명을 통하여 동조약 유효직후 미국군대의 지위를 규제할
새로운 협정의 체결을 교섭하기로 합의 하였으며, 그후 우리나라의 역대 정부
는 미국 정부에 대하여 협정 체결을 위한 교섭을 시작할 것을 요구하여
왔던 것이다.

나. 미국정부는 이와 같은 우리나라의 요망에 호응하여 민주당이 집권한 후인
1961년 4월 17일 제 1 차 한·미간 교섭회의를 개최하였으나 5. 16 군사혁명
으로 일단 중단되고 말았다.

다. 그후 미국군대의 총격사건, "린치" 사건등을 비롯한 각종 사건의 접중으로
말미아마 자극된 국민의 여론을 뒷받침한 정부의 교섭재개요구를 미국측에
수락, 마침내 1962년 9월 20일 제 1 차 한·미간 실무자급 교섭회의를
개최한 이래 제 3 공화국 정부 수립직전인 1963년 12월 5일 개최된
제 36 차 회의에 이르기까지 협정의 전문과 31개 조항중 전문 및 11개
조항에 합의를 보았다.

0205

3. 제 3.공화국 수립 이후의 업적

가. 제 3 공화국 수립 직후인 1964년 1월 29일 "러스크" 미국무장관의
방한을 맞이하여 박 대통령은 "러스크" 미국무장관과 더불어 일면의
회합을 갖고 양국간의 중요 문제를 검토하는 자리에서 다년간 현안문제로
남아온 미주둔군 지위협정 체결교섭을 조속한 시일내에 타결할 것을 요망
하는 우리 정부의 입장을 강조하고 이에 대한 미국 정부의 각별한 이해와
적극적인 협조를 요청하였으며,

나. 1964년 8월 17일 이동원 외무부 장관은 "부라운" 특사 주한미국대사와
한.미간의 공동관심사 전반에 관하여 논의한후 양인은 현안인 협정을
가능한 한 조속한 시일내에 체결하기 위하여 노력을 경주할 것을 다짐한바
있으며, 1964년 10월 3일 미국무성의 "번디" 극동담당 차관보의 내한을
계기로 이동원 장관과 "번디" 차관보는 이러한 조기타결 원칙을 재확인하였다.

다. 또한 이동원 외무부 장관은 박 대통령의 1965년 5월의 방미에 앞서
1965년 3월 중순에 도미하여 미국정부의 지도자들과 여러 현안문제에 관하여
회담을 가진후 1965년 3월 17일 이동원 외무부 장관은 "러스크" 미국무장관은
서울에서 진행되고 있는 한.미 양국간의 교섭을 검토한 결과 양국 정부가
가능한 한 빠른 시일내에 최종적 합의에 도달할수 있도록 교섭을 촉진하는데
의견의 일치를 보았다.

라. 이와 같이 우.미정부는 일면 실무자급 회의를 거듭하여 각 조항별 토의를
계속하는 한편, 기회있을때 마다 미국정부 지도자들과의 고위회담 개최를
통하여 협정의 조속한 체결을 위한 미국정부의 성의를 촉구하여 온 결과
박 대통령의 방미견인 1965년 5월 12일 까지 79 회에 달하는 실무차급 회의
끝에 전문과 31개 조항중 전문 및 19개 조항에 완전합의를 보았다.
그러나 협정의 핵심이라고 할수 있는 형사 재판권, 청구권, 노무등 중요
조항을 위요하고 한.미 쌍방의 의견차이로 말미아마 진전을 보지 못하던중
1965년 5월 18일 박 대통령의 방미를 기하여 "와싱톤" 에서 개최된
한.미 양국 지도자간의 회의에서 협정의 중요 미해결 문제에 대한 원칙적인 합의
를 보았던 것이다.

0207   0206

65-5-92

0208

마. 한·미 양측은 이와같은 양국 대통령간에 합의를 본 협정의 조기타결원칙에 입각하여 실무자급 회의를 적극 추진한 결과   상태에 있던 교섭은 급진전을 보이게 되어 1965년 6월 7일 개최된 제 81차 회의까지에는 협정의 전문과 25개 조항에 합의를 보았다.

바. 그러나 제 81차 회의에서도 해결을 보지 못한 형사재판권, 청구권, 노무등을 비롯한 6개 조항에 관하여는 그후 우리측은 미국측과 접촉을 계속하여 교섭의 조기타결에 노력한 보람있어 현재 한·미 양국은 협정 전반에 의하여 대체적인 합의에 도달하는데 성공하였다.

4. 결 론

한·미 양국은 지금까지의 합의 내용을 기초로 한 조문정비가 끝나는 대로 가까운 장래에 협정에 서명하게될 것이며 동 협정이 비준등의 절차를 거쳐 발효하게 되면 미군당국에 배타적인 형사재판권을 인정하였던 대전협정은 물론, 미국군대에 광범위한 특권과 면제를 허용하였던 소위 "마이야" 협정을 포기하고 이에 대치하게될 것이다.

따라서, 그렇게 되면 주한미국군대의 구성원, 군속 및 그들의 가족은 미군의 군사상의 사명 수행에 불가사한 필요성이 있을 경우를 제외하고는 원칙적으로 우리나라의 법령에 의하여 규제될 것이다.

0209

85-5-18(3)

0210

協 調 電

응신기일 1965.11.23: 14:00 까지

1965. 11. 23. 상오 11:00시접수

분류기호 외기획-115

제 목 국회예결위원회에서의 정책질의시
국무총리 답변사항 작성제출

수신 구미국장(미주과장)

발신일자 1965.11.23.   (협조제의)

기 획 관 미 심   장발신명의)
백 인 환
백 인 환

(제1의건)
　명일 국회에 국무총리 께서 출석하시며 예상되는 질문
사항에 대한 답변자료를 작성제출 할것을 총리 비서실에서 요청하여왔으니
다음 사항에 대한 책임있는 답변을 작성해 보내주시기바랍니다.

　　"답 변 사 항"

　한미행정협정체결이 늦어지는 이유는 무엇인가? 앞으로의 전망은
이떤가 ?
　　　　　　　　　　　　　　　　끝.

(제2의건)

공통서식 1-23　　　　　　　　0211　　　(16절지)

한·미간 주둔군 지위협정 체결교섭

1965. 11. 23.

1. 협정의 체결이 지연되는 이유

(1) 한·미 양국이 1962년 9월 20일 제 1 차 교섭회의를 개최함으로써 본격적으로 협정 체결을 위한 교섭을 개시한 이래 1965년 6월 7일 개최된 제 81차 회의에 이르는 동안 전문과 31개 조항으로 구성되어 있는 협정중 전문과 25개 조항에 합의를 보았음.

(2) 주지하시는 바와 같이 현안인 협정의 조기 타결원칙은 정부의 기본방침의 하나로 되어 왔으나 한·미 상호 방위조약에 의거 한국군과 더불어 국토의 공동방위 사명을 수행하고 있는 미군의 지위를 규제하게될 협정의 내용이 원칙적 또는 기술적인 복잡한 문제를 내포하고 있기 때문에 완전합의에 도달하기 위하여서는 상당한 시일을 요할 뿐만 아니라 한·미간의 의견 차이로 말미암아 그간 수차에 걸친 병론상태를 면할수 없었으며 81차 회의까지도 형사 재판권, 노무, 청구권, 초청계약자, 시설과 구역 및 협정의 효력발생등 6개 조항에 관하여서는 상호 만족할만한 해결을 보지 못하였던바 다행이도 우리측은 계속 미국측과 접촉하여 조기타결에 노력한 보람있어 현재 협정 전반에 걸쳐 대체적인 합의를 보는데 까지 교섭을 이끌어 왔음.

0212

2. 앞으로의 전망

  앞으로의 남은 교섭과정은 대체적인 합의에 도달한 몇몇 중요조항에
대한 완전합의를 공식회의를 통하여 장차 쌍방이 확인하고 또한
그 합의내용을 기초로한 조문정리를 끝내는 작업이라고 하겠으며
한·미 양국은 이러한 남어지 교섭과정과 작업을 가까운 장래에 끝내고
협정에 서명하게될 것이며 그 시기는 내년초가 될 것으로 봄.   끝.

0213

기 안 지

<table>
<tr><td rowspan="2">기 안 자</td><td colspan="2">미주과
이근팔</td><td>전화
번호</td><td></td><td colspan="2">공 보</td><td>필 요</td><td>불필요</td></tr>
<tr><td colspan="2" rowspan="3"></td></tr>
<tr><td colspan="2">과 장</td><td>국 장</td><td>차 관</td><td colspan="2">장 관</td></tr>
<tr><td colspan="6"></td></tr>
</table>

협 조	자 명				보 존 년 한	
기 안 년 월 일	1965. 12. 22.	시 행 년 월 일		통 제 관	정 서	기 장
분 류 기 호 문 서 번 호	외구미 722.2					
경 수 참	유 신 조	건 의		발 신		

제 목   주둔군 지위협정 체결교섭에 관한 좌담회 개최

한·미간 주둔군 지위협정의 체결을 앞두고 동 협정의 체결 및

비준 동의 시기를 중심으로 한 국민의 대 정부 여론의 선도를 위한

P.R. 활동의 일환으로 당부에서는 그간 동 교섭의 추이와 결과에

대하여 특별한 관심을 표명하여 온 저명한 대학교수 및 변호사를 초청

하여 지금까지 한·미간 교섭회의에서 원칙적인 합의를 본 협정안을

중심으로 다음과 같이 좌담회 및 이에 따른 만찬회를 개최하고저 하

오니 이를 재가하여 주시기 바랍니다.

가. 좌담회 개최

　　1. 일 시 : 1965년 12월 29일 (수요일) 하오 4시.

　　2. 장 소 : 외무부 제 1 회의실

　　3. 초청자의 범위 : 지금까지 신문 또는 잡지상에 협정에

　　　　　　　　　　관한 논설을 발표한 교수 및 기타 사계의

　　　　　　　　　　저명교수와 변호사로서 그 명단은 다음과 같음.

공통서식 1-2 (갑)　　　　　　　　　　　　　　　(16절지)

0214

4. 좌담회 개최후 만찬회들한식요정 향원에서 개최함.

   (가) 학계 및 법조계

성 명	소 속	전 공	비 고
1. 박관숙 (朴觀淑)	연 대	국제법	사상계 1965. 7
			경향 65. 5. 15
			" 65. 5. 22
2. 김명회 (金明會)	"	"	
3. 이한기 (李漢基)	서울법대	"	
4. 김기두 (金箕斗)	"	형법	국회보 (35호)
5. 이용희 (李用熙)	서울대 문리대,	국제법	경향 65. 1. 11
6. 박준규 (朴俊圭)	"	"	경향 65. 5. 22
7. 박재섭 (朴在灄)	고대법대	국제법	국제법 논총
8. 이윤영 (李允榮)	"	"	고대 학보
9. 민병기 (閔丙岐)	고대 문리대,	국제정치	
10. 박종성 (朴鍾聲)	중앙대	국제법	정경연구 65. 8
11. 김효영 (金孝榮)	경희대		국제법 논설집
12. 장기붕 (張基鵬)	성균관대	국제법	"
13. 박한상 (朴漢相)	인권옹호 위 회장,		국회보(35호)
14. 고재호 (高在鎬)	대한 변호사 회장		
15. 이병린 (李丙璘)	변호사		신문 논설
16. 황성수 (黃聖秀)	변호사		
17. 박원서 (朴元緒)	변호사		
18. 박승서 (朴承緖)	"		국제법 논설집 61. 12.
19. 한항진 (韓桓鎭)	"		"

   (나) 외무부 및 관계 부처

0215

1. 의무차관		외무부	11. 조약과장	외무부
2. 구미국장		"		
3. 미주과장		"		
4. 검찰국장		법무부		
5. 검찰과장		"		
6. 법무국장		"		
7. 법무과장		"		
8. 관세과장		재무부		
9. 정책과장		국방부 및 연구관 이제춘 소령임.		
10. 노정국장		노동청		

나. 초청장 내용 :

"군계

당부에서는 한.미간 주둔군 지위협정의 체결을 앞두고 동 협정 체결
에 관심을 가지고 계시는 학계 및 법조계 여러분을 모시고 그간 교섭
회의를 통하여 한.미 양국이 합의를 본 미주둔군 지위협정안을 중심으로
좌담회를 갖고저 하오니 소만 왕림하여 주시기 바랍니다.

1. 일 시 : 1965년 12월 29일 (수요일) 하오 4시.

2. 장 소 : 외무부 제 1 회의실

3. 초청자 수 : 학계 및 법조계 인사 19명.

추기 : 좌담회에 이어 만찬회가 준비되었음.

(참석 여부를 외무부 미주과 (전화 : 74-3073) 로
연락 하시기 바람.)

외무부장관 이 동 원."

외   무   부

1965. 12. 22.

"근 제"

　　당부에서는 한·미간 주둔군 지위협정의 체결을 앞두고 동 협정

체결에 관심을 가지고 계시는 학계 및 법조계 여러분을 모시고

그간 교섭 회의를 통하여 한·미 양국이 합의를 본 미주둔군

지위협정안을 중심으로 좌담회를 갖고저 하오니 소민 왕림하여

주시기 바랍니다.

　　일　　　시 : 1965년 12월 29일 (수요일) 하오 4시.

　　장　　　소 : 외무부 제 1 회의실 (초 식)

　　초청자 수 : 학계 및 법조계 인사 19명.

　　추기 : 좌담회석 석석 만찬이 준비되었음.

　　　　　(참석 여부를 외무부 미주과 (전화: 74-3073) 로 연락

　　　　 하시기 바람.)

　　　　　　　　　　외무부 장관　　　이 동 원

향원 22-3242

0217

참 석 자 명 단

성 명   성 명

朴 ⿰永結、   朴鐘聲
李 丙 璘   金 ⿰貰
韓 柏 烋   呈 一 倿
朴 元 緖.   朴 ⿰㴠㴠、
朴 觀 淑   李 攸 薰
張 恭 鵬   兪 ⿰㐥⿰
金 明 會   董 ⿰名蕎
许 亏 九   朴 俊 圭

0218

계선관 법계제 11명
관게제 8명
비무사 8명
27명

	姓名	職業	住所	電話番号
O.K.	1 朴 規 淑	延大	西大門區 北阿峴洞 1-139.	73-3519
O.K.	2 金 明 会	〃	西大門區 新村洞 131-4	73-3195
O.K.	3 李 漢 基	서울法大	城北區 敦岩洞 山81-2	92-0919
N.V	4 李 用 熙	서울文理大	鐘路區 惠化洞 15-11.	72-0692
O.K.	5 朴 俊 圭	〃	西大門區 蒼川洞 61의1.	72-8706
N.O.	6 朴 在 灝	高大法大	城北區 安岩洞 4-15	92-1966
N.V	7 李 久 学		西大門區 松月洞 13의1.	
NO.	8 閔 丙 岐	高麗大法大	城北區 安陰洞 山16-2, 住宅312舍1号	92-1952
O.K	9 朴 鋕 聲	中央大	龍山區 漢南洞 267-1.	4-3534
NO.	10 金 孝 榮	慶熙大	西大門區 本松洞 37-1.	74-5754
O.K	11 張 基 鵬	城均館大	東大門區 京墓洞 451-1号	
	12 朴 漢 相	弁護士	鐘路區 通莊洞 28의1.	
	13 高 在 鎬	〃	中區 小公洞 50(동명 빌딩5층 502호실) 高在鎬法律事務所	22-095
O.K.	14 李 丙 鎬	〃	鐘路 琮路 135. 李丙鎬法律事務所	73-5880
O.K.	15 黃 聖 秀	〃	中區 太平路 2街 88. 黃聖秀法律事務所	22-8079
	16 朴 之 緖	〃	中區 太平路 2街 330. 朴元緖法律事務所 論俉빌딩.	23-3015
	17 朴 承 緖	〃	中區 太平路 2街 69-6. (太平빌딩 501호실) 朴承緖法律事務所	22-5715
O.K	18 韓 桓 鎭	〃	鐘路區 瑞麟洞 154-24. (고려빌딩 505호실) 韓桓鎭法律事務所	72-9481
	19 金 基 斗	서울法大	龍山區 厚岩洞 283.	4-5576
不在	이 건 호		72-3883	
V	한 격 만		73-1586 종,청88, PRIS. 22-8660	

	姓名	所屬	專攻	備考
1	朴觀淑	延大	國際法	思想界 1965.7. 경향 65.5.15, 65.5.22
2	李漢基	서울法大	〃	
3	朴在灜	高大	〃	국제법논총
4	裵載湜	서울法大	〃	
5	李文永	高大	〃	경향. 65.5.22.
6	李兌榮	〃	〃	高大新報
7	秋憲樹	延大	〃	
8	河璟根	中央大	〃	
9	李用熙	서울大 (文理)	國際政治論	경향 65.1.11.
10	朴俊圭	〃 (文理)	〃	경향 65.5.22.
11	徐碩淳	延大	〃	
12	金明會	〃	〃	
13	黃山德	서울大	法學	
14	金箕斗	〃	刑法	✓국회보(35호)
15	李建鎬	高大	〃	
16	朴天植	〃	〃	
17	劉基天	서울法大	〃	
	朴鍾聲	中央大, 前敎授	國際私法博士	政經硏院 1965.8月호
18	朴漢柏	인권옹호협회 연맹 변호사		✓국회보 (35호)
19	朴元緒	변호사		조선일보(65.7.1.)
20	李丙璘	〃		
21	薛聖秀	〃		
22	高在鎬	〃		
23	林永緒	〃		

중앙 21-4251
신아 22-4175
73-0978

(나). 言論界人士名單

新聞 및 通信	編輯局長	政治部長	論說委員(外交關係)
1. 京鄉新聞	趙東建	李植俊	宋建鎬 / 閔丙岐
2. 大韓日報	金汶洙 CK	洪性源 OK	—
3. 東亞日報	千寬宇 OK	李雄熙 OK	徐碩淳 / 林極相 洪膩勉
4. 新亞日報	尹老述	鄭道亟	金鎔河
5. 서울新聞	趙庸中 ✓	李憲	孫禎植 OK
6. 中央日報	李元教	鄭光殖	申永澈
7. 朝鮮日報	金庚煥 OK	金顯昊 K 金南銶	宋興模
8. 韓國日報	張雄喜	鄭成溟	林芳鉉 / 朴東雲 OK 任洪彬
9. Korea Herald	桂光吾 K	金竜鳳 K	朱孝敏
10. Korea Times	李探現 K	張淳 K	— 14명
11. 合同通信	嚴甲稙	劉承範	
12. 東洋通信	金圭煥	金興昊 K	
13. 同和通信	李思雨 ✓	金伊九 K	
	13명	13명	

關係部處 關係局

1. 외무차관	외무부	9. 법무과장	법무부
2. 주미국장	〃	10. 정책과장	국방부
3. 미주과장	〃	11. 노정과장	노동청
4. 조약과장	〃	11명	
5. 방원과	〃		
6. 김기조	〃		
7. 이군석	〃		
8. 점찰과장	법무부		

0221

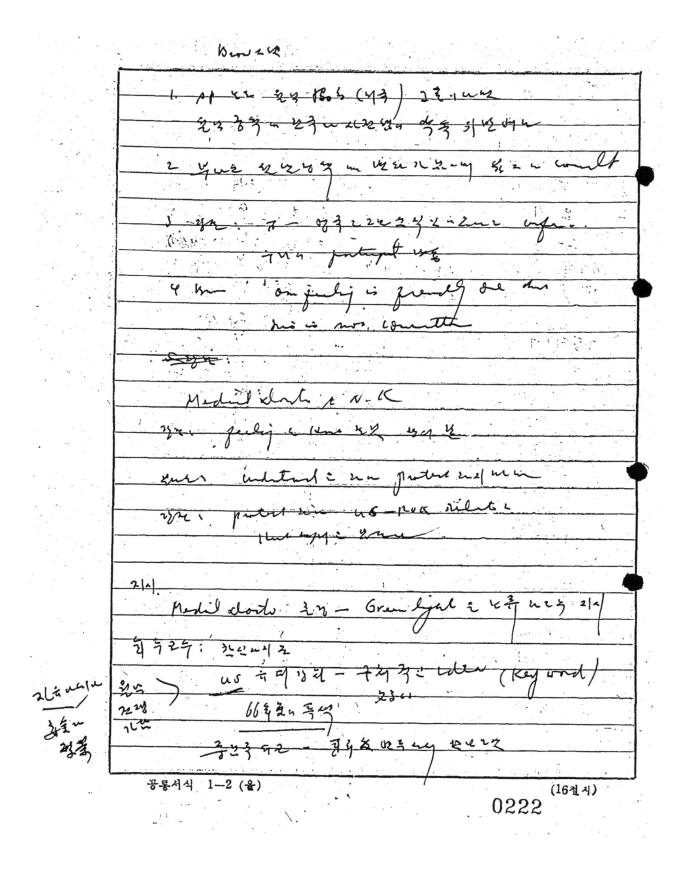

외 무 부 기 자 단

정치부장

매체	기자
✓ 경향신문	李極儉
✓ 대한일보	洪陸杓
✓ 동아일보	李雄熙
✓ 신아일보	鄭孝鄭釬
✓ 서울신문	
✓ (중앙일보)	
✓ 조선일보	金郁
✓ 한국일보	
~~산업경제~~	
서울경제	
(현대경제)	
경제통신	
무역통신	
(서사통신)	
합동통신	列承範 金洪壽
동양통신	
동화통신	金仲九
동아방송	
문화방송	
중앙라디오	
(중앙방송)	
중앙테레비	金童國 柱光基 菜鶴
코리아 헤랄드	洪喜一 (간사)
코리아 타임스	宋挑現

2반정치2층
逵
逵東蓮 金汶龍 于寅宇 尹生速 趙端圭 元敏 金庚煥 洪錐善
吳憲趙吳現 道慈常寅成

嚴甲門臨庚 金壽癀
(강사) 李懇麗

13명

정조조강배고이희박김김박배구김김김김종천삼벙 남길하섭기욱고호실전권면진경희일승문위재석출집화영엽필 성규인창흥태 태진대명자영영안천승순인영

15명

男)吉河
性)圭仁昶興太
泰鎮大俞滋英棠岸天承達仁英鎮天三
宋建鎬,南丙岐
嚴喜燮
徐硕浮,朴权相 沈承勉
鄭连賢 金鑵河
孫禳桓
申永微
金尚鎔 吳兴斗
柿芳鉉,朴唐雲
朱孝敵
郑(趙蕾姜白高崔朴金朴洪張韓金尹吳趙)
)燎練姬一松文儀在錫迷鎮和榮悦弼
)炳珊

15명

0223 0222

座談会參席者名單

姓名	所屬機關
邊永权	東亞日報社
李揆現	코리아 타임스
洪埻一	〃
鄭達賢	新亞日報社
朴지용	同和通信社
李慈蘭	서울신문
金竜國	The KOREA HERALD
金用璟	코리아 헤랄드
張星攝	法務部法務辯護
崔性源	大韓日報社
朴東雪	한국일보
申永澈	中央日報
鄭宗植	〃
孫禧楚	서울신문
金南銖	朝鮮日報
金寅昊	〃
嚴甲龍	合同通信

0224

姓 名	所屬 機關
劉承範	合同通信
金洪喆	東洋通信

0225

한 · 미간 주둔군지위협정 체결 작업 계획(잠정)

안 지.   작 업   1965. 12. 28.

12 월 29 일(수): 학계 및 법조계 인사 초청 좌담회(하오 4시)

　　　1. 협정안중 형사재판권, 민사청구권, 노무등 3 개
　　　　조항에 대한 부리핑 및 정부측 요망.

　　　2. 좌담회 후 만찬회 개최

1966 년

1 월 7 일(금) : 주요 신문사, 통신사 편집국장, 논설위원 초대 좌담회
1 월 18 일(화): 공화당 당무회의 부리핑.　　(非 公式)
1 월 19 일(수): 국회 외무위원회 부리핑.

1 월 21 일((금): 제 82 차 회의 개최(하오 3 시 부터)

　　　1. 미합의 사항에 대한 최종적인 공식 합의.

　　　2. 회의 후 한·미 공동 성명서 발표.

1 월 24 일(월): 국무회의 상정 (國務會議通過 可決)

1 월 27 일(목): 언론계 부리핑 ✓

1 월 28 일(금): 조인

　　　1. 외무부장관 및 주한미국대사가 서울에서 조인.

(추 기) 국회법 제 6 조에 의하여 임시휘의기한은 30 일 이내로 되어

있으므로 1 월 17 일 소집 예정인 임시회의 회기는 2 월

15 일 종료될 것인바 대통령 동남아 순방으로 말미아마

국회의 실질적인 심의는 3 월 초 부터 시작될 것으로 판단됨.

3/1

0226

기 안 지

<table>
<tr><td rowspan="2">기 안 자</td><td>미 주 과
이 근 팔</td><td>전 화
번 호</td><td colspan="2">공 보</td><td>필 요</td><td>불필요</td></tr>
<tr><td colspan="2">과 장　　국 장　　차 관　　장 관</td><td colspan="3"></td></tr>
</table>

<table>
<tr><td>협 조
성 명</td><td>자 인</td><td colspan="3"></td><td>보 존
년 한</td><td colspan="2"></td></tr>
<tr><td>기 안
년 월 일</td><td colspan="2">1965. 12. 30.</td><td>시 행
년월일</td><td>통
제
관</td><td></td><td colspan="2">정 서　기 장</td></tr>
<tr><td>분 류 기 호
문 서 번 호</td><td colspan="3">외구미 722.2</td><td></td><td colspan="3"></td></tr>
<tr><td>경 유
수 신
참 조</td><td colspan="3">건　　의</td><td colspan="2">발 신</td><td colspan="2"></td></tr>
</table>

제　목　주둔군 지위협정 체결에 관한 언론계 인사 초청 좌담회 개최

한·미간 주둔군 지위협정의 체결을 앞두고 국민의 여론을 선도

하기 위하여 주요 신문사 및 통신사 관계 언론인들을 초청하여 지금

까지 한·미간 교섭회의에서 원칙적인 합의를 본 협정안을 중심으로

다음과 같이 좌담회를 개최코저 하오니 재가하여 주시기 바랍니다.

가. 좌담회 개최:

1. 일 시 : 1966년 1월 7일 (금요일) 하오 4시

2. 장 소 : 외무부 제 1 회의실　　　　　編輯局長,

3. 초청자의 범위 : 주요 신문사 및 통신사의 ∧정치부장 및 논설위원

(명단 별첨)

4. 만찬회 :

좌담회 종료후 ~~참석자등 장관~~ 개최함.

나. 초청장 내용 :

" 근 계

공통서식　1-2 (갑)　　　　　　　　　　　　　　　　(16절지)

0227

당부에서는 한·미간 주둔군 지위협정의 체결을 앞두고 동 협정 체결에 관심을 가지고 계시는 언론계 여러분을 모시고 그간 교섭회의를 통하여 한·미 양국이 원칙적인 합의를 본 주둔군 지위협정안을 중심으로 다음과 같이 좌담회를 갖고저 하오니 소만 왕림하여 주시기 바랍니다.

1. 일 시 : 1966년 1월 7일 (금요일) 하오 4시.

2. 장 소 : 외무부 제 1 회의실 (413호실)

3. 초청자 범위 : 주요 신문사 및 통신사의 편집국장, 정치부장 및 논설위원.

4. 만찬회 개최 :

   좌담회에 이어 소찬이 준비되어 있음.

추기 : 참석 여부를 외무부 미주과 (전화 74-3073) 로 미리 연락
       하여 주시기 바랍.

                    외무부 장관   이 동 원 "

0228

외 　 무 　 부

1965. 12. 30.

근 계

　　당부에서는 한·미간 주둔군 지위협정의 체결을 앞두고 동
협정 체결에 관심을 가지고 게시는 언론계 여러분을 모시고 그간
교섭회의를 통하여 한·미 양국이 원칙적인 합의를 본 주둔군
지위협정안을 중심으로 다음과 같이 좌담회를 갖고저 하오니 소만
왕림하여 주시기 바랍니다.

1. 일 　 시 : 1966년 1월 7일 (금요일) 하오 4시.

2. 장 　 소 : 외무부 제 1 회의실 (413호실)

3. 초청자 범위 : 주요 신문사 및 통신사의 편집국장, 정치부장
　　　　　　　　　　　　 및 논설위원

4. 만찬회 개최 : 좌담회에 이어 소천이 준비되어 있음.

추기: 참석 여부를 외무부 미주과 (전화:74-3073) 로 미리연락
　　　하여 주시기 바림.

외무부장관　　　　　　　이　동　원

0229

기 안 지

기 안 자	미주과 이근팔	전화 번호		공 보	필 요	불필요

과 장	국 장	기획관리실장	차 관	장 관

협 조 성 명	자 명 협 안	조약과장 방교국장		보 존 년 한	
기안 년 월 일	1965. 12. 31.	시 행 년월일	통 제 관	정 서 기 장	
분류기호 문서번호	외구미 722.2-				
경 수 참 조	유신조	건 의	발 신		

제 목   주둔군 지위협정 체결 작업 계획

　　　　1962년 9월 20일 제 1 차 한.미간 실무자 교섭회의를 개최한

이래 한.미간에 진행되어오던 주둔군 지위협정 체결교섭이 최종적 단계

에 도달하였음에 감하여 당부에서는 언론계, 공화당, 국회 외무위원회

에 대한 부리핑을 비롯하여 제 82차 회의 개최, 국무회의 상정, 조인,

및 국회 비준동의 요청등 협정 체결 전후를 기한 일련의 작업일정을

다음과 같이 결정 진행코저 하오니 재가하여 주시기 바랍니다.

　　　　　　　　　　다 음

일 시　　　　　　　작 업 계 획

1966년도 :

1월 7일 (금요일) 하오 4시 : 언론계 인사 초청 좌담회 개최

　　　　　　　　　초청자 범위 :

　　　　　　　　　주요 신문사, 통신사의 편집국장, 정치부장

　　　　　　　　　및 논설위원 40명이며 부리핑 종료후

공통서식 1-2 (갑)　　　　0230　　　　　　　　　(16절지)

만찬회를 개최함.

1월 18일 (화요일):   공화당 당무위원회 부리핑 (비공식)

1월 19일 (수요일):   국회 외무위원회 부리핑 (비공식)
    17 (월요일)

1월 21일 (금요일) 하오 3시: 제 82차 한.미간 실무자 교섭 회의 개최

                    1. 협정안에 대한 최종적 공식 합의

                    2. 회의후 교섭 종결에 즈음 한.미 공동
                       성명서 발표

1월 24일 (월요일):   국무회의 상정

1월 27일 (목요일):   외무부 출입기자단에 대한 부리핑.

1월 28일 (금요일):   협정 조인.

                    외무부 장관 및 주한 미국 대사가 서울에서

                    조인.

3월 초순경: 국회 비준동의 요청.

추기: 1. 1966년도 국회 임시회의가 (제4회) 1월 17일 개최됨으로 공화당 및
          국회 외무위원회에 대한 부리핑을 국회 개회 직후에

          하는 것으로 하였으며,

     2. 국회의 비준동의 요청시기는 대통령 동남아 순방 일정관계와

          협정 조인후 국민의 여론선도를 위하여 약 1개월간의 여유
          를 둔후 3월 초순경으로 결정함.   끝.

          보통문서로 재분류 (발동시   )

0231

외교문서 비밀해제: 주한미군지위협정(SOFA) 13
주한미군지위협정(SOFA) 서명 및 발효 13

초판인쇄 2024년 03월 15일
초판발행 2024년 03월 15일

지은이 한국학술정보(주)
펴낸이 채종준
펴낸곳 한국학술정보(주)
주 소 경기도 파주시 회동길 230(문발동)
전 화 031-908-3181(대표)
팩 스 031-908-3189
홈페이지 http://ebook.kstudy.com
E-mail 출판사업부 publish@kstudy.com
등 록 제일산-115호(2000. 6. 19)

ISBN 979-11-7217-024-0 94340
      979-11-7217-011-0 94340 (set)